GENDER IN HI

C000020009

Series editors:
Pam Sharpe, Patricia Skinner and Penny Summerfield

The expansion of research into the history of women and gender since the 1970s has changed the face of history. Using the insights of feminist theory and of historians of women, gender historians have explored the configuration in the past of gender identities and relations between the sexes. They have also investigated the history of sexuality and family relations, and analysed ideas and ideals of masculinity and femininity. Yet gender history has not abandoned the original, inspirational project of women's history: to recover and reveal the lived experience of women in the past and the present.

The series Gender in History provides a forum for these developments. Its historical coverage extends from the medieval to the modern periods, and its geographical scope encompasses not only Europe and North America but all corners of the globe. The series aims to investigate the social and cultural constructions of gender in historical sources, as well as the gendering of historical discourse itself. It embraces both detailed case studies of specific regions or periods, and broader treatments of major themes. Gender in History titles are designed to meet the needs of both scholars and students working in this dynamic area of historical research.

'The truest form of patriotism'

MANCHESTER
UNIVERSITY PRESS

'THE TRUEST FORM OF PATRIOTISM'
PACIFIST FEMINISM IN BRITAIN, 1870–1902

Heloise Brown

Manchester University Press

Manchester and New York

distributed exclusively in the USA by Palgrave

Published by Manchester University Press
Oxford Road, Manchester M13 9NR, UK
and Room 400, 175 Fifth Avenue, New York, NY 10010, USA
www.manchesteruniversitypress.co.uk

Distributed exclusively in the USA by Palgrave
175 Fifth Avenue, New York, NY 10010, USA

Distributed exclusively in Canada by UBC Press
University of British Columbia, 2029 West Mall,
Vancouver, BC, Canada V6T 1Z2

British Library Cataloguing-in-Publication Data
A catalogue record for this book is available from the British Library

Library of Congress Cataloging-in-Publication Data applied for

ISBN 0 7190 6530 5 hardback
      0 7190 6531 3 paperback

First published 2003

11 10 09 08 07 06 05 04 03   10 9 8 7 6 5 4 3 2 1

Typeset in Minion with Scala Sans display
by Graphicraft Limited, Hong Kong
Printed in Great Britain
by Bell & Bain Ltd, Glasgow

Contents

Acknowledgements

This work owes a great deal to the feminist environment of the Centre for Women's Studies at the University of York. I would particularly like to thank Jane Rendall for her careful supervision of the D. Phil. thesis in which this book has its origins. Mary Maynard, Treva Broughton and Ruth Symes were immensely supportive in the early stages of my research, and Karen Hunt of Manchester Metropolitan University and Joanna de Groot of the University of York examined the completed thesis and gave valuable feedback and encouragement, as well as advice on how to go about turning it into a book.

I am grateful to the British Academy for the scholarship that enabled me to complete my D. Phil., and to the Royal Historical Society for funding a visit to Geneva to consult the International Peace Bureau archives. My thanks also to the following people, who have advised me and granted permissions: the Rev. Clive Dunnico for access to the Peace Society Archives at Fellowship House; Christina Swaine and the National Trust for access to Peckover House, Wisbech; and in particular, Ursula Maria Ruser and the staff of the League of Nations Archive Room at the United Nations Library in Geneva. I am grateful to the National Council of Women of Great Britain for allowing me to make copies of their first minute book, and for the assistance provided by numerous libraries and archives, including: Manchester Central Library, the Fawcett Library at London Guildhall University, Friends' House Library in Friends' House, London, the British Library, London, the archives of the British Library of Political and Economic Science at the London School of Economics, London Metropolitan Archives, Wisbech Public Library and Wisbech Museum, Wisbech, Cambridgeshire.

Finally, I would like to express my immense gratitude to my friends and family for their love and support over the years. In particular, my thanks and love to Julie Magill, Madi Gilkes, Deborah Wilson, Ann Kaloski and my parents Christine and Alan Brown, for their emotional and intellectual support, as well as undertaking the tedious task of actually reading and commenting on the manuscript. Last but by no means least, much love and thanks to Sam Riches, Catherine Elliott, Penny Vivian, Hilary Doran, Simon Clarke and Vicki Harding, Hanneke Hazeveld, Colin Moran, Amanda Hayler, Kate Moody and Nuala McGale for being such good friends.

Belfast, Co. Antrim

List of abbreviations

BWTA	British Women's Temperance Association
CCNSWS	Central Committee of the National Society for Women's Suffrage
CD Acts	Contagious Diseases Acts
CNSWS	Central National Society for Women's Suffrage
IAPA	International Arbitration and Peace Association
ICW	International Council of Women
ILP	Independent Labour Party
ILPL	International League of Peace and Liberty
IPB	International Peace Bureau
LBWPAS	Liverpool and Birkenhead Women's Peace and Arbitration Society
LPA	Local Peace Association
MRU	Moral Reform Union
MWPA	Manchester Women's Peace Association
NCW	National Council of Women
NCWGBI	National Council of Women of Great Britain and Ireland
NUWW	National Union of Women Workers
NWSA	National Woman Suffrage Association
P&G	*Peace and Goodwill: A Sequel to the Olive Leaf*
SACC	South Africa Conciliation Committee
WIPA	Women's International Peace Association
WIPU	Women's International Peace Union
WLA	Women's Liberal Association
WLF	Women's Liberal Federation
WLPA	Wisbech Local Peace Association
WPA	Workmen's Peace Association
WPAA	Women's Peace and Arbitration Association
WPAAPS	Women's Peace and Arbitration Auxiliary of the Peace Society
WPP	*Women's Penny Paper*
WSJ	*Women's Suffrage Journal*

Introduction

Pacifism and feminism in Victorian Britain

War is an essentially masculine pursuit. Women do not as a rule seek to quench their differences in blood. Fighting is not natural to them. (Lydia Becker)[1]

It is the truest form of patriotism to do our utmost to save our country from the crime and shame of an unjust war. (Priscilla Peckover)[2]

I N 1870, the outbreak of war between France and Prussia prompted many of the women active in the emergent feminist movement to consider their position on the use of physical force. In doing so, some, such as Lydia Becker in the first quotation above, drew upon essentialist arguments of sexual difference. Many reinforced their construction of women as moral agents who relied upon debate rather than physical force in both individual and collective relations. Some, including Priscilla Peckover, also quoted above, began to re-evaluate concepts of peace to argue that it meant more than simply the absence of war, and to redefine patriotism as a force that was primarily moral, rather than national, in its points of reference. These arguments were founded upon analyses that made pacifist ideas fundamentally useful for feminism. Because both theories could be based upon arguments about the (mis)use of power and the importance of morality, and both could accommodate a wide range of political perspectives, many feminists during the early phase of the movement were attracted to pacifist rhetoric and principles.

As a prominent, but hitherto neglected, aspect of the Victorian women's movement, it is important to understand why many feminists employed peace arguments, often relying upon the construction of femininity as passive and even pacifist, and representing these women/peace connections as located in women's reproductive role. The use of these ideas has significant implications for arguments of sexual difference, individualism versus relationalism, and maternalism in nineteenth-century feminism.[3] It can also demonstrate how feminism, in using such ideas of what was 'natural' to women, purported to speak for *all* women. It is therefore vital to illustrate the ways in which different feminist movements have utilised representations of the relationship between 'women' and 'peace'. Much work has been done on women pacifists during the First World War, and in relation to women's resistance to the presence of nuclear weapons in Britain, particularly regarding the Greenham Common missile base, in the 1980s. Yet, in its early years, organised feminism in Britain also demonstrated a concern with pacifism and the issue of women's (imagined) relationship to peace. This book charts the development of these debates within the Victorian feminist movement to illustrate the centrality of such ideas to many strands of late Victorian feminism.

In many of the arguments considered here, essentialist ideological connections are made between 'women' and 'peace' as constructed categories. As indicated by the quotations opening this chapter, a basic gendered dichotomy is often established which, while aiming to destabilise assumptions about war, instead serves to reinforce ideas of male aggression and female passivity. One central theme in this book is therefore the issue of how, with regard to questions of peace and war, some feminists worked to 'historically, [and] discursively' construct 'women' and womanhood as peaceful and moralistic.[4] Berenice Carroll has observed that there is a historical connection between the constructions 'women' and 'peace', but that this 'is a connection imposed upon women along with their subordination, their disarmed condition, and their stereotyped roles. Out of this imposed connection arises also a widespread stereotypic association between *femininity* and *passivity*.' She notes that these must be distinguished from the concepts 'feminism' and 'pacifism', both of which, she argues, are 'deliberate, conscious choice[s] of principles and policies'.[5]

In a discussion of the late nineteenth century, the use of both terms means that they must be applied anachronistically. There has inevitably been much debate on the desirability of this practice and the reasons why it might be undertaken. Nancy Cott, in particular, has argued that the changes that gave rise to the coining of the term 'feminism' mean that it should only be applied to those who have lived and worked since its introduction into the English language. In response, Barbara Caine has argued that most political terms are used retrospectively to apply to individuals or ideas 'which have some recognised or assumed similarity with those for which the term was originally coined'.[6] Philippa Levine has suggested that the refusal to adopt the term 'feminist' can itself

be dangerous: it separates issues that should be connected, and intro-
duces a hierarchy in our understanding of feminism which places the
traditionally public and political above the intentional subversion of the
concepts 'public' and 'private'.[7] Failing to recognise 'feminism' before
the term itself existed runs the risk of further alienating the feminist
movement from its origins and history.

Thus, although the term 'feminism' was not in general use in Britain
until the early 1900s, it is used here in relation to the nineteenth-century
women's movement.[8] Following Levine, the definition used is deliberately
broad: feminism involved a 'sustained critique of the gendered order
of society', but also a connection by those who practised it between the
public political questions they addressed, and 'the impact of gender on
issues of traditional private or individual concern'.[9] It was this transformation of personal or private issues into public discussions, organisations
and campaigns that gave nineteenth-century feminism its commonalities
with the twentieth-century movement that bears the name.

Like 'feminism', the term 'pacifism' is of late nineteenth/early
twentieth-century origin and its meaning has been the subject of much
debate. Émile Arnaud, president of the republican nationalist organisation, the International League of Peace and Liberty (ILPL), coined the
term in 1901 when he used it to describe the ideology of the peace party
in Europe: 'We are not passive types; we are not only peace makers;
we are not just pacifiers. We are all those but something more – we
are pacifists . . . and our ideology is pacifism.'[10] The term rapidly passed
into common use and was initially applied to all advocates of peace,
although during the First World War its usage was frequently narrowed
to apply to those advocates of peace who opposed all war, including
defensive combat. Particularly within the United States, pacifism came
to mean this particular form of 'absolute pacifism', while in Europe the
term has retained some ambiguity.[11] The campaigns for an immediate
and absolute rejection of all war, and for the eventual abolition of war
through a strengthened international system, overlapped significantly
in the British peace movement, particularly in their relations with the
feminist movement.[12] For simplicity, the term 'pacifism' is used here
in its original broad meaning, to encompass 'the renunciation of war
by the individual, at least implicitly', and the willingness to challenge
'military approaches' and to develop 'alternatives such as negotiation,
. . . nonviolent action, and international organization'.[13] 'Pacifism' is used
interchangeably with 'peace advocacy' and 'peace work'; thus it includes
absolute pacifists within its scope, although these are also referred to
specifically where relevant.

The term which is perhaps most important in this work is 'pacifist feminism'. An examination of the secondary literature shows that the earliest application of the terms 'feminist pacifism' or 'pacifist feminism' to feminist thought is in relation to the First World War. Existing accounts assume that feminists only became interested in 'peace' on any significant scale during this period. Jill Liddington's *The Long Road to Greenham*, for example, which examines women's pacifism from 1820 to the 1980s, begins to use these terms only when the chronological account reaches the 1914 to 1918 period.[14] None of the (albeit limited) material on women's earlier peace work makes use of these terms in relation to the nineteenth century. Yet although the term 'pacifist feminism' is doubly anachronistic, political perspectives developed during the late nineteenth century that combined substantial characteristics of both of these ideologies. Pacifist analyses of power relations between nations and the effects of military force were combined with feminist understandings of the ways in which women were oppressed. Ideas evolved which encompassed both the claim that women had the right to define their own place in society, and also the desire to renounce war and establish alternative models of conflict resolution. As a result, specifically 'pacifist feminist' standpoints can be identified which denote a politics where the two modes of analysis are applied together to an understanding of the social and political order.

Liberalism as it developed during the nineteenth century was all-important in the growth of these ideas. Most influential in the mid-century period was Richard Cobden, whose support for free trade between nations was based on a belief that commercial relations between nations would make them interdependent on one another, and thus make war contrary to their interests. Cobden pressed for a formal policy of non-intervention and international arbitration, and while he collaborated with absolute pacifists, he made his case on economic and financial, rather than religious, grounds. He explicitly viewed peace and free trade as one and the same cause, and his influence on the mid-nineteenth-century peace movement was more practical in its effects than that of any other single individual. Cobden put forward tactical arguments for arbitration, disarmament and non-intervention, rather than ambitious, but less easily attainable, objectives such as the creation of a Congress of Nations.[15] Forms of liberalism that aimed to establish 'the rule of law, moral and economic, in international and domestic affairs' became dominant in the 1850s and 1860s, and the Liberal party gradually became more susceptible to Cobdenite arguments for non-intervention and international arbitration. There remained some sympathy for protectionism, however, and many Radicals argued for intervention in European conflicts.[16] The party and parliamentary struggles over imperial warfare which took place during the 1870s and 1880s showed that Liberalism could not be assumed to be inherently pacifist, and that the ideals of Cobden could not necessarily be applied in practice to Liberal foreign policy.

However, Cobden's legacy of the argument for a fundamental connection between free trade and peace between nations strengthened the peace movement and provided it with the political and economic ideas that were necessary to reach a wider audience. John Stuart Mill's *Principles of Political Economy* expanded upon Cobden's thinking with regard to free trade, although Mill's particular version of liberalism was not, of itself, wholly compatible with these ideas. His commitment to *laissez-faire* economics was based upon a particular conceptualisation of the relationship between state and individual. To Mill, free trade was preferable because it was efficient, it protected against state bureaucracy, and, most importantly, it stimulated individual morality.[17]

Perhaps the strongest aid to the peace movement during the nineteenth century, and undoubtedly the factor which assisted the transferral of pacifism from a primarily religious cause to a more political one, was the idea of arbitration. If nothing else, it was an appropriately liberal solution to the problem of war. Richard Cobden, along with Henry Richard (who served as secretary to the Peace Society from 1848 to 1885) and his successors in the late nineteenth-century peace movement, argued that it was a fairer, more reasonable way to settle a dispute than resorting to arms. In support of this point, they claimed that a 'trained' body of men would be better qualified to settle disputes than a single individual, such as a monarch. Arbitration would protect weaker states, and using legal procedures in the settling of disputes would be self-advertising because once non-participants could see that it worked, they too would agree to the use of arbitration.

Despite this interest in arbitration and international co-operation, there were significant differences between British and European liberalisms, particularly with regard to war and international relations. David Nicholls has argued that the contradictions between the British liberal belief in peace through free trade and non-intervention, and the European liberal position that nationalism and wars of liberation were a prerequisite for peace, meant that the establishment of a permanent international peace movement was impossible.[18] Differing attitudes to war, social unrest and the social conditions which give rise to different kinds of wars meant that the British and European perspectives on peace and international relations were incompatible for most of the Victorian era. In consequence, British pacifists and free traders were often regarded with distrust by European pacifists.[19]

The evolution of British pacifism, and the influence of Radicals such as Cobden upon pacifist ideas, inevitably affected pacifist feminism as it began to emerge in the 1870s and 1880s. In this study, at least four distinct strands of pacifist feminism can be identified: free trade radicalism; Evangelical feminism; moderate internationalism; and international citizenship. The earliest of these, free trade radicalism, focused on Cobdenite ideas that peace would be achieved through free trade, and featured in the politics of women such as Caroline Ashurst Biggs and Lydia Becker. Free trade radicalism developed simultaneously with Evangelical feminist ideologies, which argued that the acceptance of Christian principles would result in universal peace and the elevation of women's position. Such arguments were employed by Evangelicals such as Laura Ormiston Chant and, to a lesser extent, Priscilla Peckover. In the 1880s, moderate ideas of imperialism and internationalism emerged that focused upon maintaining the existing empire while opposing its expansion, and developing international connections between feminists. This thinking influenced, to varying degrees, the arguments of Ellen Robinson, Isabella Tod and the International Council of Women. The latest strand to develop was the feminist conception of international citizenship, as envisaged by Florence Fenwick Miller and Henrietta Müller, who both used ideas of sisterhood to gloss over the power differentials inherent in international relations.

These liberal ideas can be contrasted with, on the one hand, socialist internationalism, and on the other, more jingoistic forms of imperialism. Towards the end of the period of study it is possible to identify socialist women such as Isabella Ford and Emmeline Pankhurst as taking an interest in anti-militarist arguments, although they typically maintained an ambivalent relationship to the peace ideas outlined above. While socialists such as Ford were active in the campaign against the second Anglo-Boer war, and Pankhurst and her husband were involved in some of the arbitration associations discussed in this book, there was limited engagement by socialist feminists in pacifism before the Edwardian period.[20] In contrast to both socialist and pacifist feminist arguments, there were also feminists who resisted the ideological connections between 'women' and 'peace', and rejected anti-expansionist models of imperialism. Millicent Garrett Fawcett was a prominent supporter of British rule in Ireland and South Africa, and sanctioned the use of force in both contexts. She offered a striking contrast to pacifist feminist conceptions of women as peace-loving and supposedly defensive by nature.

Another prominent feminist, Josephine Butler, emphasised in her work the importance of the fair and humane treatment of native populations, yet also supported the expansion of the British empire and the Christianisation of 'native races'.

Discourses of nationalism, imperialism and patriotism competed with one another in feminist language of this period. For the most part, feminist argument concerned itself with the importance of women and their relationship to the imperial nation. From this starting point, some feminists began to problematise the empire and to criticise the ways in which it was managed or maintained, making explicit their reservations about claiming a role in a nation that was reliant on the use of force for its maintenance as an imperial power. They developed a range of arguments that called for an end to imperial expansion and support for existing colonies so that they could, in time, become self-governing. Such women began to recognise an international community and to redefine patriotism to mean loyalty to an imagined ideal of Britishness, or a means by which the nation could serve humanity as a whole. The truest interests of the nation were seen to be bound up with the interests of 'civilisation' and humanity, and therefore could function as a means by which to rise above national differences. Pacifist feminists' conceptions of their role in the nation could from this perspective be based upon ideas of improving Britain in the eyes of the world, a national burden that loosely corresponds to Antoinette Burton's concept of the imperial burden.[21] Thus, the language of patriotism was appropriated to apply to a more ethical imperialism, or, in some cases, to pacifism.

The term 'patriotism' is of course much older than those defined above, and more than most political concepts has been mutable and subject to constant reinvention. In addition to conventional definitions of the term as meaning 'love or devotion to one's country', alternative uses developed during the eighteenth century that employed ideas of restoring the state to an imagined former purity.[22] These discourses survived throughout the nineteenth century in the radical patriotism that has been described by Margot Finn and Hugh Cunningham, among others.[23] Yet while radical patriotism served both as a tool of opposition and as a means by which marginalised groups could claim ownership of the past, by the 1870s both the Liberal and Conservative parties had appropriated its discourses. As the century drew to a close, patriotism as an ideology became increasingly dominated by the political right, and was employed to support both imperial and national concerns.

Although patriotism was claimed as a Conservative discourse during the late nineteenth century, alternative forms also developed which drew on both feminist thought and the tradition of radical patriotism associated with the peace and internationalist movements. Patriotism by this latter definition was constructed as loyalty to a higher cause than the nation, and indeed in many contexts it was represented as nothing less than devotion to humanity itself. A range of discourses contributed to the development of this alternative patriotic ideology, including Evangelicalism, Radicalism, pacifism and feminism.[24] Out of these discourses there emerged within the feminist movement, particularly where it overlapped with the peace movement, a concern with redefining patriotism and its meanings. Although feminists rarely opposed the abstract idea of working for peace, it was often the case that in practical terms during international conflicts there was disagreement over the best course of action to take. The issue of patriotism, and the various ways in which the term was used, was crucial here. In Conservative ideology, patriots were expected to support their country in times of crisis. During the period 1870 to 1902, the peace movement and some branches of the feminist movement began to re-evaluate this argument, to suggest that patriotism was best expressed by loyalty to what was morally best for one's country, rather than by supporting the 'nation' whatever its international behaviour. In exploring the diverse range of positions taken by feminist and pacifist women in the late nineteenth century, some distinctly pacifist feminist strands can be identified.

The starting point for this study is the feminist movement that was established by the end of the 1860s, after the first petition for women's suffrage had been presented to Parliament and the *English Woman's Journal* had encouraged a number of related societies to work for women's rights. By this time there existed 'both a public awareness of the question of women's rights and women's future role and . . . some sense of the emergence of an international movement among feminists themselves'.[25] Suffragists began to concern themselves with the matter of the physical force objection to women's suffrage, or the argument that because women were unable to fight, they should not be permitted to vote. A number of journals were founded including the *Englishwoman's Review* in 1866, the *Women's Suffrage Journal* in 1870, the *Women's Penny Paper* in 1888 and the *Woman's Signal* in 1895, which debated not only the physical force objection, but also feminist responses to international and imperial conflicts. During the 1880s there were a number of attempts to found an international women's organisation, at first based on the suffrage campaign, and later, in the form of the International Council of Women (ICW), based on social issues such as philanthropy and women's employment. The first major International Congress of the ICW took place in London in 1899, at which its first standing committee was established on the subject of peace and arbitration.

By 1902, the feminist movement had grown in strength and stature, winning repeal of the Contagious Diseases (CD) Acts, the right of married women to own property, and increased political representation for women on School Boards, Poor Law administration and local government. Women had still not been granted the parliamentary franchise, however, and it was this factor that was the key influence on the development of the movement between 1905 and 1918. Neither could women join political parties, though from the 1880s they could join the Primrose League, the Women's Liberal Federation or the Women's Liberal Unionist Association if they wished to support (respectively) the Conservatives, Liberals or Liberal Unionists.[26] This study ends with a discussion of responses to the Anglo-Boer war of 1899–1902, because this was a crucial phase for the feminist movement. With the Anglo-Boer war, women became more prominent in public and political life: Millicent Garrett Fawcett led the first all-female government inspectorate into conditions in the British concentration camps in South Africa, while the British government deported Emily Hobhouse from the Transvaal for her attempts to publicise atrocities in the camps. Women's attitudes to war thus became an increasingly public question at this time, not least because of Fawcett's prominent role in the suffrage movement. The feminist movement underwent a significant transformation in the Edwardian period, although the women's peace campaigns of the First World War confirmed that pacifism continued to be a strong influence on much of feminist politics.[27]

The period under consideration saw a rapid, and on occasion confusing, growth in peace and arbitration organisations. Only one – the Society for the Promotion of Universal Peace, otherwise known as the Peace Society – significantly predates the period this book is concerned with. Founded in 1816 and dominated by nonconformists, it demonstrated an early radicalism but by the 1870s was the most cautious and circumspect peace organisation in Britain. It upheld the principle of absolute pacifism, or the idea that all war, including defensive war, was unlawful, and while it held firm to this principle throughout the century, in practice many of its arguments involved compromises with non-absolutists (who were also eligible for membership of the Society, though not its Executive Committee). A closer examination of the peace movement for the later half of the century also shows that many of its supposedly absolutist members could strategically shift between the absolutist 'peace at any price' argument and the non-absolutist point of view. There was less tolerance, however, of feminist politics: the Peace Society's women's auxiliary was founded in 1874 and its activities were subjected to strict control in an attempt by the Peace Society's Executive Committee to distance it from any connection with the feminist movement.

A number of radical peace movements were formed in continental Europe in 1868, and the Franco-Prussian war of 1870–71 stimulated the work of these organisations. Radical continental pacifists tended to be not only non-absolutists, but what Martin Ceadel has called 'crusaders': they believed that the use of military force was justified if it created the conditions for a lasting peace.[28] This activity in Europe gradually led British pacifists to seek changes closer to home. In 1880 a non-absolutist British peace organisation was founded, the International Arbitration and Peace Association (IAPA). The IAPA was more receptive to feminism, but again, its women's auxiliaries went through a number of incarnations during the period of study, from a splinter group of the Peace Society's Women's Peace and Arbitration Auxiliary in 1881, to a much smaller Women's Committee in 1887. Just as an international women's organisation developed in the 1890s, so did an international peace association, the International Peace Bureau (IPB). This was a European network of pacifists, which worked with varying levels of success with the men and women active in the British peace societies.

Two of the most influential women within the peace movement in this period were Priscilla Peckover and Ellen Robinson, both Quaker ministers who held absolute pacifist beliefs but made concerted efforts to work closely with non-absolutists such as the IAPA and the IPB. Peckover epitomised the self-effacing and Evangelical woman who appealed to the men who ran the Peace Society, while Ellen Robinson represented the more politicised and feminist woman whom the IAPA targeted. Importantly, however, both women worked together and across all of the organisations discussed here. In contrast to the male-dominated movement, they consistently aimed to promote cross-organisational co-operation, and therefore provide a useful contrast to the somewhat troubled male movement of this period.

The conclusion of the Anglo-Boer war was a significant moment for the peace movement, as it found itself in an increasingly untenable position. It had become clear during the war that public agitation for peace was a futile strategy, as pacifists' best efforts made no headway in tempering the national enthusiasm and government support for the war. By 1902, many British pacifists were convinced that campaigns for the prevention of war needed to be aimed at changing government policy rather than popular opinion, and it was this strategy that dominated, with little success, the Edwardian period.

The emphasis in this book is upon identifying the diverse strands of feminist thought that began, by the turn of the century, to make use of pacifist discourses. Through an understanding of the relationship between pacifism and feminism, feminist perspectives on questions of nationalism, patriotism and imperialism can be better understood. The starting point in this project is the feminist movement itself, and an examination of the routes by which many Victorian feminists came to consider questions of peace and war.

Notes

1 *Women's Suffrage Journal (WSJ)* (1 September 1870), p. 70.

2 *Peace and Goodwill: A Sequel to the Olive Leaf* (16 October 1899), p. 97.

3 Ideas of 'relationalism' have been applied to both nineteenth- and twentieth-century feminisms. See for example: Carol Gilligan, *In a Different Voice* (Cambridge, Mass.: Harvard University Press, 1982); Karen Offen, 'Liberty, equality and justice for women: the theory and practice of feminism in nineteenth-century Europe', in Renate Bridenthal, Claudia Koonz and Susan Stuard (eds), *Becoming Visible: Women in European History* (Boston: Houghton Mifflin Company, 1987).

4 Denise Riley, *Am I That Name? Feminism and the Category of 'Women' in History* (Basingstoke: Macmillan, 1988), pp. 1–2.

5 Berenice Carroll, 'Feminism and pacifism: historical and theoretical connections', in Ruth Roach Pierson (ed.), *Women and Peace: Theoretical, Historical and Practical Perspectives* (London: Croom Helm, 1987), pp. 15–16. Emphasis in original.

6 Barbara Caine, *Victorian Feminists* (Oxford: Oxford University Press, 1993), p. 6; Nancy Cott, *The Grounding of Modern Feminism* (New Haven, Conn.: Yale University Press, 1987), p. 3.

7 Philippa Levine, *Feminist Lives in Victorian England: Private Roles and Public Commitment* (Oxford: Basil Blackwell, 1990), p. 3.

8 Offen notes that the term 'féminisme' was first used in French in 1872, and in English in 1894, although it did not pass immediately into general use. Offen, 'The theory and practice of feminism', p. 362.

9 Levine, *Feminist Lives*, p. 2.

10 *L'indépendance belge* (August 1901), cited in Sandi E. Cooper, *Patriotic Pacifism: Waging War on War in Europe, 1815–1914* (Oxford: Oxford University Press, 1991), p. 60; *The Oxford English Dictionary*, prepared by J. A. Simpson and E. S. C. Weiner, 2nd edn., vol. 9 (Oxford: Clarendon Press, 1989), p. 38.

11 Charles Chatfield and Peter van den Dungen, 'Introduction', in Charles Chatfield and Peter van den Dungen (eds), *Peace Movements and Political Cultures* (Knoxville: University of Tennessee Press, 1988), p. xiv.

12 See Martin Ceadel, *Semi-detached Idealists: The British Peace Movement and International Relations, 1854–1945* (Oxford: Oxford University Press, 2000); Paul Laity, *The British Peace Movement, 1870–1914* (Oxford: Oxford University Press, 2001).

13 Peter Brock, *Freedom from War: Nonsectarian Pacifism, 1814–1914* (London: University of Toronto Press, 1991), p. vii; Chatfield and van den Dungen, 'Introduction', p. xiv.

14 Jill Liddington, *The Long Road to Greenham: Feminism and Anti-Militarism in Britain since 1820* (London: Virago, 1989), pp. 59, 73.

15 David Nicholls, 'Richard Cobden and the International Peace Congress Movement, 1848–1853', *Journal of British Studies*, 30 (October 1991), pp. 351–76; Alan Sykes, *The Rise and Fall of British Liberalism, 1776–1988* (London: Longman, 1997), ch. 2.

16 Sykes, *British Liberalism*, p. 65.

17 John Stuart Mill, *Principles of Political Economy* (London: John W. Parker, 1848); Richard Bellamy, *Liberalism and Modern Society: An Historical Argument* (Cambridge: Polity Press, 1992), pp. 29–30.

18 Nicholls, 'Richard Cobden', p. 360.

19 *Ibid.*, pp. 360–1.

20 June Hannam and Karen Hunt, *Socialist Women: Britain, 1880s to 1920s* (London: Routledge, 2002), p. 181.

21 Antoinette Burton, *Burdens of History: British Feminists, Indian Women and Imperial Culture, 1865–1915* (London: University of North Carolina Press, 1994).

22 *Oxford English Dictionary* (1989), pp. 349–50; *Oxford Dictionary of English Etymology*, ed. C. T. Onions (Oxford: Clarendon Press, 1966), p. 658. The *OED* notes the use of 'patriotess' to refer to female patriots during the nineteenth century, by Thomas Carlyle as early as 1837, and the *Daily News* in 1894.

23 Margot Finn, ' "A Vent which has Conveyed our Principles": English radical patriotism in the aftermath of 1848', *Journal of Modern History*, 64 (December 1992), pp. 637–59; Hugh Cunningham, 'The language of patriotism, 1750–1914', *History Workshop Journal*, 12 (1981), p. 9.

24 See Linda Colley, *Britons: Forging the Nation 1707–1837* (London: Yale University Press, 1992).

25 Jane Rendall, *The Origins of Modern Feminism: Women in Britain, France and the United States, 1780–1860* (Basingstoke: Macmillan, 1985), p. 2.

26 While most of the women discussed in this book had a broad attachment to liberal ideas of individual liberty and political and social reform, they also tended to support a wide range of causes which were not championed by the Liberal party itself. Their interests did not necessarily fit into the political spectrum as it is usually understood, and indeed, the patterns of their allegiances were often complex and unpredictable. For example, Patricia Hollis has noted that the Women's Liberal Federation originally aimed to 'advance the principles of liberalism, which . . . were larger than the views of Liberal men within the Liberal party'. The terms Liberal, Radical and Conservative are used in this work to refer to parliamentary politics, while their 'lower-case' equivalents – liberal, radical, conservative – refer to the wider political traditions from which these parties drew their policies. Patricia Hollis, *Ladies Elect: Women in English Local Government, 1865–1914* (Oxford: Oxford University Press, 1987), p. 57.

27 Liddington, *Long Road to Greenham*, chapter 5; Anne Wiltsher, *Most Dangerous Women: Feminist Peace Campaigners of the Great War* (London: Pandora Press, 1985).

28 Ceadel, *Semi-detached Idealists*, p. 6.

1

The physical force objection to women's suffrage

T HE SUFFRAGE MOVEMENT was a central strand in Victorian feminism, and one of its primary aims was confronting anti-suffragists' opposition to the enfranchisement of women. A principal argument for opponents of women's suffrage was the physical force objection: the principle that women were unable to take up arms to defend their country, and therefore could not qualify for the franchise. In engaging with this question, many feminists began to approach the question of why and under what circumstances they might sanction the use of physical force. This led many to develop pacifist, anti-imperialist or internationalist agendas, which in turn enabled a minority to redefine discourses of patriotism.

It is by no means a new argument to state that Victorian feminism was imbued with the aspirations and preoccupations of imperialism. But imperialism was not a homogeneous entity, and the debate about force was heavily influenced by the various feminist discourses of nationalism and imperialism that were available. The emergent perspectives on the role of force included critiques of any war entered into without prior recourse to arbitration, or any imperial war conducted against native or 'other' settler populations. These in turn were instrumental in the development of pacifist feminism during this period. If it could be argued by suffragists that moral force was preferable to and more effective than physical force, it could also be argued that many, if not all, physical conflicts were unnecessary.

This debate was taken up by some of the key thinkers on women's suffrage during the late nineteenth century. Suffragists such as John Stuart Mill and Lydia Becker argued that physical force was not a requirement for citizenship, and therefore that moral force should outweigh physical force in a civilised society. Anti-suffragists such as James Fitzjames Stephen and Goldwin Smith focused on the importance of the threat of physical force, to argue that those who could not bring it to bear could not be entrusted with the privileges of citizenship. Their arguments relied upon the popular anti-suffragist idea that women would not be fit to exercise imperial power, and indeed some of the most prominent suffragists, including Millicent Garrett Fawcett, had reservations on this issue. Their discussions of the physical force objection illustrate the various perspectives possible within liberal thinking on the uses and roles of force within both the empire and the international arena.

John Stuart Mill's *The Subjection of Women*, a text which is recognised as a 'classic statement of liberal feminism', rested on the argument that most sexual differences are likely to be social or cultural in origin.[1] Mill (1806–73) had by the time of its publication in 1869 a dominant position in Victorian intellectual debate, particularly as a result of his liberal utilitarian philosophy. *The Subjection of Women* became an important text for the early feminist movement: although Mill's arguments were not new, it was nonetheless the first time that such ideas had been publicly put forward by a respected (and male) writer. Mill's central argument in *Subjection* was that true male and female natures were unknowable, because individuals are always guided and constrained by social factors. Those who based their arguments on ideas about male or female nature therefore ignored the role that social conditioning played in guiding individual growth. Because men and women had always been raised differently and subjected to different treatment and expectations, Mill argued that it was impossible to know which, if any, gender differences were based in nature. He also specifically attacked marriage and marriage law, arguing that as it then existed, marriage kept women in subjection to men. This was not only detrimental to women, Mill argued, but it also tended to damage men's moral sensibilities, and therefore to inhibit the improvement of society as a whole.[2]

Mill pre-empted the physical force objection by arguing that 'The influence of women counts for a great deal in two of the most marked features of modern European life – its aversion to war, and its addiction to philanthropy. Excellent characteristics both.'[3] The argument that women were averse to war implied that there was a social basis behind this stance, and also served to reinforce popular notions of women's 'nature' as pacific.[4] The power imbalance between men and women, he argued, 'has no other source than the law of the strongest'. He disputed the argument that 'the rule of men over women . . . [is not] a rule of force', by citing cases when women had individually or collectively protested against male laws, and been ignored.[5]

Mill held that women were physically weaker than men, yet, as Susan Mendus has argued, he did little to relate his claims to the realities of (particularly working-class) men and women's lives. He saw in history a slow march of human progress, from the abandonment of the use of force to the acceptance of obedience to the rule of law. As a number of writers have shown, Mill's views on physical force paralleled his opinions on Ireland. He believed that if Britain could not conciliate the Irish population to British rule, then its governance of Ireland was morally unjust. His concern at this possibility was directed as much at what it would do to Britain's international standing, as it was at the inherent undesirability of rule by force.[6]

Mill's contemporary, James Fitzjames Stephen, produced the most comprehensive refutation of Mill's ideas in his 1874 volume *Liberty, Equality, Fraternity*.[7] Stephen was a barrister who supplemented his income with journalism, and eventually went on to become a High Court judge. His career and his background at Cambridge located him as much closer to the establishment than Mill, who had been educated by his father, James Mill. Stephen had been an early contributor to the *Saturday Review*, and by the 1870s epitomised a conservative liberalism that was very different in its aims and expression from Mill's progressive approach.[8] Yet the similarities between both writers were in some ways more marked than their differences: both equated equality with sameness and inequality with difference; and both assumed that the natural state for women was marriage and had little to say on the subject of single women.

Stephen's treatise on equality retraced Mill's arguments in *Subjection of Women* (a work from which Stephen 'dissent[ed] from the first sentence to the last') and concluded that Mill was in fact advocating equality 'as an end in itself'. Mill argued that if civilisation created obedience to the rule of law, then the existence and practice of the law in itself demonstrated an increase in equality. Stephen disputed both assumptions on the grounds that Western society was still reliant on force, and the replacement of physical force with legal force did not of itself mean a new egalitarianism. He argued that it was indisputable that 'men are stronger than women in every shape. They have greater muscular and nervous force, greater intellectual force [and] greater vigour of character . . . These are the facts.' Consequently, men and women 'are not equals, because men are the stronger'.[9]

Stephen's first illustration of this 'fact' used the example of compulsory military service. It cannot be argued, he wrote, that both men and women should be subject to such a measure, because anyone holding such a view 'has got into the region at which argument is useless.

But if it is admitted that this ought not to be done, . . . where are you to draw the line?' Similarly, marriage was accepted by Stephen as a contract involving 'subordination and obedience on the part of the weaker party to the stronger', a position that was in direct conflict with that of Mill.[10]

It can thus be seen that Stephen and Mill held fundamentally different views on the meaning of force. As James Colaiaco notes, they agreed that the meaning of liberty was 'the absence of restraint', but could not agree on how important a point it was in relation to the law.[11] Stephen believed in the greater value of law, viewing liberty as having only contingent value. Mill had a more 'affirmative' idea of liberty, believing it to be crucial in halting the encroachment of government and law onto individual freedom. The pair consequently differed with regard to the issue of women's suffrage. Stephen believed that democracy posed a threat to law and order, while Mill held that liberty was endangered if law played too strong a role. Correspondingly, Mill took a democratic approach to the physical force objection, arguing that it did not matter if men were stronger or more intelligent than women, because such differences should not have political consequences. Reform of the law was therefore necessary. Stephen took an approach consistent with his views on law and liberty, arguing that the fact that 'for centuries women had been in subjection furnished proof' that their inequality and disenfranchisement was 'expedient'.[12] His opposition to Mill's ideas on women's suffrage were based on a recognition of the revolutionary changes that would be necessary in order to make women equal, and a belief that the conservative force of law should prevail. Unlike Mill, Stephen saw change, rather than progress, in history. From this he drew the conclusion that 'even if the inequality between men and women is a vestige of the past, and is likely to be destroyed by the same process which has destroyed so many other things, that is no reason for helping the process on'.[13]

The disagreement between Stephen and Mill over the place of physical force in relation to women's suffrage provides an illustration of the debates that drew many feminists of this era into considerations of the nature and practical uses of force. Brian Harrison's summary of the physical force debate argues that it rested on the importance of three issues: maintaining British dominance over the empire; the precariousness of public order in Britain, particularly given the absence of a welfare state; and the constant possibility of international conflict.[14] Thus feminists found it necessary to consider questions of imperial dominance, of public order, and of peace and war when formulating arguments to support their claim for enfranchisement.

Suffragists' responses to Stephen rested on a number of mutually exclusive claims: firstly, that the entitlement to citizenship did not rest on the ability to use force; secondly, that women were equipped with the physical presence to possess and use force; and finally, that women's use of force was inherently defensive. The first of these arguments overlapped with liberal theory, which did not define individual citizenship in this manner. The latter two arguments are perhaps more specifically feminist in nature, although they were of course influenced by the feminist movement's grounding in liberal thought.

Miss Lydia Becker (1827–90) published a response to Stephen in the *Women's Suffrage Journal* (*WSJ*) in 1874, based on the first argument about the role of force in citizenship.[15] Taking Stephen's fundamental assumption that men and women were not and could not be equals, Becker stated that:

> if the personal rights of all men are equal in all things that concern their individuality as men, notwithstanding all differences of personal strength and power, logic seems to demand that the personal rights of women and men shall be equal in all that concerns their individuality as human beings, notwithstanding any difference which may exist between them in physical strength.[16]

Rights, therefore, ought to be bestowed on men and women as individuals, not as persons who meet a set of required criteria.

Becker took this further in her response to Stephen's account of the physical force objection. She wrote that 'no-one proposes to recognise a difference in the personal rights of able-bodied and infirm men, based on their liability to compulsory military service', and that in the case of a national emergency requiring conscription, women would make their own contribution to the effort:

> There are more kinds of service, even of military service, than actual bearing of arms, and more kinds of force, even in warfare, than material force . . . [T]he womanly spirit of courage, patriotism, and self-devotion . . . is of no particular age or country; and . . . in any great crisis touching the life of the nation the daughters of England, as well as her sons, would bear an equal if not a similar part in the services and sacrifices which the nation as a whole was called upon to render.[17]

Becker drew here on conceptions of sexual difference, and by arguing that women would take 'an equal if not a similar part' in serving the nation, recognised the crux of the 'equality or difference' debate, by assuming it to mean equivalence, rather than sameness or similarity.

Becker recognised the principle that women's labour contributed to any national war effort, and also made more explicit the slippage between Mill's and Stephen's perceptions of the meaning of 'force'. By drawing on the concept of women as transnational, or even transhistorical, citizens, she evoked images of women as patriotic to humanity itself, rather than any one nation. Becker also argued that this commitment to humanity, with its 'spirit of courage, patriotism and self-devotion', could be used in the service of the nation. Because women's humanitarian patriotism incorporated a willingness to sacrifice the individual to the higher good, these ideas could be applied to the national context. She went on to show that the physical force question was not limited to military and national concerns, but cut across wider debates of women's rights within marriage. 'If', Becker paraphrased Stephen's argument, 'physical force is the foundation of personal rights, the man who beats his wife establishes his right to do so by that which Mr Stephen considers the foundation of all law.'[18] Men, being capable of physical force, qualified for the franchise, and thus their use of physical force over their subordinates was by Stephen's argument enshrined in law.

With regard to the second argument, that women were equipped with the physical presence to possess and use force, suffragists drew upon the fact that women were, under certain circumstances, subject to legal contracts that rested on the premise that they could use force. For example, if women could be found guilty of murder or bodily harm, they were clearly capable of using physical force. If they could undertake citizen's arrests (and the *Women's Suffrage Journal* reported incidences when women did so) they were also capable of the use of force. Thus the feminist response included the reassertion of arguments of sexual difference and an emphasis upon the legal anomalies that derogated women by viewing their physical abilities in terms of the prevailing domestic ideology. But the suffragists' final line of argument (that women's use of force was inherently defensive) was a much more difficult route to take, given that they were also trying to emphasise that whenever a woman was charged with murder or violent crime, she was demonstrating her ability to use force.

The *Women's Suffrage Journal* never made explicit the disparity that existed between its use of arguments based on the violent crimes committed by mainly working-class women against spouses or other men (although it was careful to acknowledge that in many cases the violence was provoked by male domestic violence), and the inherently defensive stance that would, it was argued, be taken by middle-class, householding women voters in the case of war. The inference of this stance was that if working-class women could defend themselves and their families against violent men, then middle-class women would reflect this disposition towards defence at a national level.

In the same year that Becker published her response to Stephen she held a debate in the *Women's Suffrage Journal* focused on the role of the military. In addition to the wider context of Stephen's treatise, Becker extracted a debate from a military journal, the *Broad Arrow*, which had been published in the *Herald of Peace*, the official organ of the Peace Society and a journal Becker frequently extracted in the *WSJ*.

The debate arose in response to an article on 'Female suffrage' by Goldwin Smith, which had been published in *Macmillan's Magazine*. Smith had, like Mill and Stephen, been a member of the intellectual elite during the 1850s and 1860s, when he held the post of Regius Professor at Oxford. He had been a Radical and a reformist within this context, serving for example as a member of the Jamaica Committee, which supported the prosecution of Governor Eyre, in 1866. He emigrated to Canada shortly afterwards, and his arguments began to appear increasingly out of step with British politics, although he was a vocal supporter of Irish Unionism and imperialism, and remained an anti-suffragist.[19]

Smith argued in 'Female suffrage' that to date, women's 'privileges have been connected with her disabilities. If she had made war by her vote, she could not have claimed special respect as a neutral, nor will she be able to claim special respect as a neutral if she makes war by her vote hereafter.'[20] In response to his arguments, the *Broad Arrow* claimed that 'If they [women] must have a vote, are they willing also to shoulder a gun? If not, their whole position is weak and untenable, and they must relinquish it.' It went further, saying: 'A citizen, unable to bear arms in defence of the State, and yet of ripe and proper age, is an anomaly that cannot be tolerated. The State has the right to the military service of all its citizens.'[21]

The *WSJ* not only extracted this debate from the *Herald of Peace*, but it also published the replies that women had sent in to the *Herald*. These disputed that force was a qualification for citizenship, drawing on maternalist and suffragist arguments that women bore children, which was equally as dangerous as bearing arms, and that the clergy and the physically infirm were exempt from bearing arms and yet were given citizenship rights. The responses to the debate from *WSJ* readers created a great deal of interest in the question over the following months.[22]

Smith's position on men and women's capacity for the use of force was inherently contradictory, as some of his critics in the *WSJ* were anxious to show. In 'Female suffrage', he argued that 'the love of liberty

and the desire of being governed by law alone appear to be characteristically male'. He drew a distinction based on sexual difference, as
follows:

> The female need of protection, of which, so long as women remain
> physically weak, and so long as they are mothers, it will be impossible
> to get rid, is apparently accompanied by a preference for personal
> government . . . [T]here can be little doubt that in all cases, if power
> were put into the hands of the women, free government, and with it
> liberty of opinion, would fall.[23]

Those women who were not wholly in the grip of the clergy, he believed,
would vote for those candidates whom they liked, and continue to
re-elect their favourite 'till his power became personal, and perhaps
dynastic'. Smith relied upon similar arguments to Stephen in his analysis
of the use of force. Law, he continued, 'rests at bottom on the force of
the community, and the force of the community is male. No woman can
imagine that her sex can execute, or in the case of rebellion re-assert,
the law; for that they must look entirely to the men.'[24]

The *WSJ* disputed this using many examples of women detaining
thieves or other criminals until the arrival of the police. It also provided
a number of arguments against Smith's (somewhat contradictory) point
that women in public life would prove more violent than men. Smith's
argument was that women were 'more excitable . . . having, with more
warmth and generosity of temperament, less power of self-control,
. . . [they would] be not less but more violent than men'. He drew on
examples from the French Revolution and the American Civil War to
show how the women had 'rivalled the men in fury and atrocity',
and promoted the idea that 'the most effective check on war is . . . that
every one should do his own fighting. But this check cannot be applied
to women, who will be comparatively irresponsible in voting for war.'
Following the terms of the debate as set out by Mill, Smith entirely
neglected any consideration of unmarried or widowed women, and
concluded that women did not constitute a class, as 'the great mass of
them are completely identified in interest with their husbands', and the
remainder could hardly be said 'to have any common interest, other
than mere sex', which would be affected by class legislation.[25]

Mrs Millicent Garrett Fawcett (1847–1929), a mainstay of the
women's suffrage movement from 1869 until equal suffrage was achieved
in 1928, was, with Lydia Becker, one of the most prominent members
of the women's movement to publish a critique of Stephen's response
to Mill.[26] In the early 1870s she was widely known as the wife of the

Radical MP Henry Fawcett, and was respected in her own right for her skills as a political economist. In 1870, Fawcett criticised the general objection that men and women should have different political rights because they possessed differences in strength. She argued that inferiority was not a just defence for the denial of the franchise, because its logical conclusion would be the granting of more power to the physically strong and the mentally superior, and the removal of the franchise from the elderly, the weak, and those proved to be inferior in intellect, regardless of their gender.[27]

In her 1873 response to Stephen, Fawcett discussed his account of marital relations in some detail, but without relating this to the specific question of force. His points on the supremacy of the husband over the wife were met by Fawcett with the argument that this effectively gave wives legal immunity if they carried out murder on their husband's instructions, and his comparison of marriage relations with those of employment was met with the statement that wives did not have the same means to dissolve their contracts as did employees. Her response was indeed primarily philosophical, particularly when compared to Lydia Becker's arguments. Fawcett evaluated the (in)consistency of Stephen's ideas, their logical conclusions and social implications, but she did not relate them to the questions of politics or government. She did not address the grounds for entitlement to citizenship, women's capacity for the use of force, or the argument that women used force differently from men. In doing so, she began to distance herself from the physical force argument and the question of women's potential contribution to the imperial nation.[28]

Fawcett's pragmatic role in the women's movement helped to establish her as a 'major figure in public life', and even the fiercely anti-suffragist *The Times* acknowledged in 1889 that no woman was more highly qualified to speak on the suffrage question, 'and none has had greater opportunities to obtain that training in practical affairs in which women as a rule are deficient'.[29] Yet Fawcett's commitment to the maintenance of the empire, and to force as an effective and legitimate means of power, particularly in the aftermath of the Home Rule debate of 1886, served to undermine her objections to the validity of the physical force argument.[30]

In 1889 she entered into correspondence with *The Times* in reply to Goldwin Smith's arguments that 'law rests at bottom on force, and force is rule', and that this force was therefore central to the maintenance of the empire. Fawcett did not respond to Smith's ideas on the question of the use of force, but argued instead that in contrast to Smith's expectation, women would not vote 'like a flock of sheep' for the Conservatives, and that women had been voting in the Isle of Man, and in the territory of Wyoming in the US, without the collapse of the rule of law. Enfranchising women, she argued, would only bring their political status into line with their social and educational status.[31]

The Times pointed out in response that these were mere territories, not imperial powers comparable in size or influence to Britain. The editorial continued thus:

> There is nothing on the face of the earth, and nothing, so far as we know, in the history of mankind at all comparable to the transfer of Imperial authority, military, naval, and diplomatic, to the hands of women, which is now calmly contemplated as a natural extension of our Parliamentary system and a convenient counter in the great and noble game of party.[32]

Fawcett was accused of failing to understand the vast difference between 'municipal management' and 'supreme power over Imperial policy'.[33] The imperial nation was represented as consisting of two separate spheres, the public (imperial or international) and the private (internal or 'domestic'). Correspondingly, women were argued to be capable of dealing with 'domestic' affairs, but not with matters of imperial or international importance.

While she clearly was capable of understanding the difference defined in *The Times* editorial, Fawcett was unable to answer it convincingly on behalf of the suffrage movement. Her political position as an advocate of the use of force in the empire appeared to prevent her from adequately addressing the question of why or how women were qualified to exercise imperial power. The physical force question was therefore an argument that she was unable to answer satisfactorily.[34] Her views on the empire and suffrage largely contributed to the stance she took on the legitimacy of the Anglo-Boer war, as Fawcett could argue that if the voting rights of settlers in South Africa were important enough to draw the nation into war, then Britain should take the same principled stance on the enfranchisement of its own women.[35]

Questions of force went to the heart of the suffrage debate. At stake was Britain's (self-) image as an imperial power, and any challenge to this power base was therefore an indirect threat to the strength of the nation. For imperialists such as Fawcett, the case for the suffrage was a difficult one to make when the physical force objection required discussion. It was impossible, given the constraints of Victorian femininity, to introduce arguments that the presence of women would strengthen the imperial nation from a physical force perspective. As a result, Fawcett's imperialism relied upon established definitions of patriotism, which focused on the need for a strong and independent nation. In contrast, opponents of imperialism in its various guises redefined patriotism and attempted to present it as a moral or ethical ideal, or a means of serving humanity using the power of the nation. The focus was upon the moral strength of the nation, rather than its capacity for the use of physical force. There were a number of distinct strands in this revision: for example, in Mill's argument, patriotism could mean loyalty to and defence of Britain's reputation abroad, or the protection of Britain's character in the eyes of the world; while for Becker, it could signify the commitment to defensive combat as a means of protecting the integrity of the nation. Most importantly, however, all these strands could be used to argue that women were eminently capable of such patriotic loyalties. The debates over the physical force objection thus provided an important battleground for arguments over women's role in the imperial nation. They were, however, primarily reactive arguments: the effectiveness of men such as Stephen and Smith in putting forward the physical force objection is shown not only in Fawcett's and Becker's responses to their arguments, but in the fact that debates on women's suffrage before this point rarely made use of the objection, or discussed it in any depth.[36]

In the following chapter, the focus shifts to the feminist print networks of the 1870s onwards, to examine how far feminists voluntarily initiated discussions regarding women's relationship to pacifism.

Notes

1 John Gray, introduction to John Stuart Mill, *On Liberty and Other Essays*, ed. John Gray (Oxford: Oxford University Press, 1991), p. xxiv.

2 Stefan Collini, *Public Moralists: Political Thought and Intellectual Life in Britain, 1850–1930* (Oxford: Clarendon Press, 1991), p. 152.

3 John Stuart Mill, *The Subjection of Women*, in Mill, *On Liberty*, ed. Gray, p. 566.

4 See Julia Annas, 'Mill and the subjection of women', *Philosophy*, 52 (1977), p. 189, for a discussion of Mill's use of the concept of 'nature'.

5 Mill, *Subjection*, p. 484.

6 Susan Mendus, 'The marriage of true minds: the ideal of marriage in the philosophy of John Stuart Mill', in Susan Mendus and Jane Rendall (eds), *Sexuality and Subordination: Interdisciplinary Studies of Gender in the Nineteenth Century* (London: Routledge, 1989). For more on Mill and Ireland, see Collini, *Public Moralists*, chapter 4; E. D. Steele, 'J. S. Mill and the Irish question: the principles of political economy, 1848–1865', *Historical Journal*, 13:2 (1970), pp. 216–36; E. D. Steele, 'J. S. Mill and the Irish question: reform, and the integrity of the Empire, 1865–1870', *Historical Journal*,

13:3 (1970), pp. 419–50; Bruce L. Kinzer, 'J. S. Mill and Irish land: a reassessment', *Historical Journal*, 27:1 (1984), pp. 111–27.

7 James Fitzjames Stephen, *Liberty, Equality, Fraternity* (London: Smith, Elder and Co., 1874; reprint Cambridge: Cambridge University Press, 1967). Page references throughout are to reprint edition.

8 Collini, *Public Moralists*, p. 53.

9 Stephen, *Liberty, Equality, Fraternity*, pp. 188, 193.

10 *Ibid.*, pp. 194, 196.

11 James A. Colaiaco, *James Fitzjames Stephen and the Crisis of Victorian Thought* (London: Macmillan, 1983), p. 127.

12 *Ibid.*, p. 151.

13 Stephen, *Liberty, Equality, Fraternity*, p. 200.

14 Brian Harrison, *Separate Spheres: The Opposition to Women's Suffrage in Britain* (London: Croom Helm, 1978), p. 76.

15 With the first substantial discussion of a subject, their name and title is given in the preferred style of the day. Elsewhere, titles are omitted for the sake of brevity.

16 Lydia Becker, 'Liberty, Equality, Fraternity', *WSJ* (1 October 1873), pp. 141–5, reprinted in Jane Lewis (ed.), *Before the Vote was Won: Arguments for and against Women's Suffrage, 1864–1896* (London: Routledge and Kegan Paul, 1987), p. 225.

17 *Ibid.*, pp. 228–9.

18 *Ibid.*, p. 233.

19 Christopher Harvie, *The Lights of Liberalism: University Liberals and the Challenge of Democracy, 1860–1886* (London: Allen Lane, 1976).

20 Goldwin Smith, 'Female suffrage', *Macmillan's Magazine*, 30 (June 1874), pp. 139–50, reprinted in Andrew Pyle (ed.), *The Subjection of Women: Contemporary Responses to John Stuart Mill* (Bristol: Thoemmes Press, 1995), p. 275.

21 *WSJ* (1 September 1874), p. 122.

22 *Ibid.*, p. 122; (1 October 1874), p. 137; (2 November 1874), pp. 149, 151.

23 Smith, 'Female suffrage', p. 276.

24 *Ibid.*, p. 277.

25 *Ibid.*, pp. 282–3, 285.

26 For more on Fawcett, see David Rubinstein, *A Different World for Women: The life of Millicent Garrett Fawcett* (London: Harvester Wheatsheaf, 1991); Caine, *Victorian Feminists*, ch. 4.

27 Millicent Garrett Fawcett, 'The electoral disabilities of women', *Fortnightly Review* (1870), pp. 622–32, reprinted in Pyle (ed.), *Subjection of Women*, pp. 223–35.

28 Millicent Garrett Fawcett, *Mr Fitzjames Stephen on the Position of Women* (London: Macmillan and Co., 1873), in M50/2/36/10, Millicent Garrett Fawcett Letter Collection, Manchester Central Library (MCL), Manchester.

29 Caine, *Victorian Feminists*, p. 210; *The Times* editorial (4 January 1889), cuttings file of Millicent Garrett Fawcett in M/50/2/1/71–2, MCL.

30 Rubinstein, *A Different World for Women*, chap. 10.

31 Fawcett, in *The Times* (4 January 1889), cuttings file of Millicent Garrett Fawcett in M/50/2/1/71–2, MCL.

32 *The Times* (4 January 1889), cuttings file of Millicent Garrett Fawcett in M/50/2/1/71–2, MCL.

33 *Ibid.*

34 Fawcett's continuing interest in the physical force question can be seen in a cutting preserved in her files of a letter from Emily Davies to *The Times* on 'The physical force argument against women's suffrage', *The Times* (17 August 1908), M/50/2/19/6, MCL.

35 Ray Strachey, *The Cause: A Short History of the Women's Movement in Great Britain* (London: G. Bell and Sons, 1928), p. 288.

36 See, for example, Fawcett, 'The electoral disabilities of women', in Pyle (ed.), *Subjection of Women*; Helen Taylor, 'The Ladies' Petition', *Westminster Review* (January 1867), pp. 63–79, reprinted in Lewis (ed.), *Before the Vote was Won*, as 'The claim of Englishwomen to the suffrage constitutionally considered'; and Barbara Leigh Smith Bodichon, *Reasons For and Against the Enfranchisement of Women* (London: Spottiswood and Co., 1869), reprinted in Lewis (ed.), *Before the Vote was Won*.

2

'The women of the whole world form ... a unity': feminist journals and peace questions[1]

THROUGH THE DEBATES on physical force, many women active in the feminist movement were drawn to consider wider issues of military conflict and war. Such well-known feminists as Josephine Butler, Millicent Garrett Fawcett, Lydia Becker, Caroline Ashurst Biggs (editor of the *Englishwoman's Review* from 1871 to 1889) and Henrietta Müller (editor of the *Women's Penny Paper* from 1888 to 1892) intervened in debates about the role of the armed forces and the utility of warfare. These women held widely differing perspectives, and Fawcett in particular emerged as a supporter of imperialism and armed intervention. But Butler, Becker and many other feminists opposed war in principle and in practice. Rather than selecting individuals to study here, this chapter discusses the approaches which four feminist journals – the *Englishwoman's Review*, the *Women's Suffrage Journal*, the *Women's Penny Paper* and the *Woman's Signal* – took towards pacifism and internationalism. The journals provide a history of feminist debates and disagreements over the role of force in this period: debates on peace and war occurred in relation to a number of different campaigns, including for example the movement for the repeal of the Contagious Diseases Acts, and within a range of organisations, such as the Women's Liberal Federation (WLF), the British Women's Temperance Association (BWTA), the Moral Reform Union (MRU) and the International Council of Women. The journals used here provided media within which the peace question could be discussed in relation to these diverse campaigns and societies. An examination of each shows how these fragmented approaches to peace questions could come to form part of a wider analysis of the connections between women's subordination and the sanctioning of physical force.

The feminist journals discussed here catered for a variety of political perspectives and all included coverage of international issues affecting women. The *Englishwoman's Review* took a 'classic "bourgeois" constitutional feminist' position, although under the editorship of Caroline Ashurst Biggs radical liberal ideas and concerns were often introduced. Each issue contained a few long articles and a great quantity of short notices of feminist activities and events, and the journal's main function therefore tended to be as 'a current awareness bulletin'.[2] The *Women's Suffrage Journal* (*WSJ*) was the first specialised British suffrage periodical, although it also covered many other contemporary feminist issues, such as the campaign for married women's right to own property. Its most important influence was that of its editor, Lydia Becker, and throughout its lifespan the *WSJ* closely reflected her radical liberal and internationalist interests. The *Women's Penny Paper* exhibited a more '[l]ively and uncompromising feminism' than either the *Review* or the *WSJ*, and Doughan and Sanchez have characterised it as 'the most vigorous feminist paper of its time'.[3] It contained information and debates on a wide range of feminist campaigns, as well as biographical interviews with leading feminists, and constitutes an invaluable resource for the historian of the Victorian women's movement. The *Woman's Signal* was likewise concerned with a much broader range of feminist topics than the *Review* or the *WSJ*. Its editor, Florence Fenwick Miller, gave considerable space to issues such as women's suffrage, education, employment, involvement in local government, domestic violence, and new developments such as the founding of the British National Council of Women (NCW). She was a prominent voice calling for a feminist influence on any social or political question that could be argued to affect women.[4]

A comparison of these journals is unfair in some respects. The *Review* ran for much longer than the period we are concerned with here, while the *WSJ* ran for twenty years from 1870, ceasing publication on the death of Lydia Becker in 1890, only a short time after the *Women's Penny Paper* was launched. The *Penny Paper* was transformed after just three years into the *Woman's Herald*, and after a further four years, during which it declined in popularity, it was taken up by Florence Fenwick Miller as the *Woman's Signal*. The *Signal* was thus the product of a later era than the *WSJ* or the *Penny Paper*, and the discussion of its content reflects this.

The *Englishwoman's Review*, 1866–1910

The *Englishwoman's Review* developed as a successor to the first British feminist journal, the *English Woman's Journal*, and was initially edited by Jessie Boucherett. Caroline Ashurst Biggs (1840–89) took over in January

1871, editing the journal until her death. Boucherett again spent a brief spell editing the *Review*, until Helen Blackburn and Antoinette Mackenzie took over the editorship in June 1890. The background of the *Review* and its close ties with both the Langham Place Circle and the *English Woman's Journal* made it a relatively moderate publication in feminist terms, focused as it was around campaigns such as the Society for Promoting the Employment of Women, women's suffrage, improved access to education, and the reform of the married women's property laws. Its editors were influential in directing the politics and scope of the journal, and in relation to questions of peace it is easy to see the different editorial policies at work.

During the period when it was edited by Caroline Ashurst Biggs, the *Review* regularly covered not only general issues of peace and anti-militarism, but the work of women's peace organisations. Biggs came from a large family of radicals: she was the granddaughter of the Owenite Unitarian lawyer, W. H. Ashurst, and her mother, Matilda Ashurst Biggs, had been brought up to be independent, adopting her father's feminism and attending the 1840 World Anti-Slavery Convention. As Kathryn Gleadle has shown, the Ashursts formed part of a prominent network of 'radical Unitarians' who shared advanced feminist and republican views.[5] This background undoubtedly influenced Caroline Ashurst Biggs: she corresponded with the Italian revolutionary Guiseppe Mazzini at the age of seven, signed the first suffrage petition in 1866 and became one of the most active advocates of women's suffrage during the 1870s and 1880s. She was prominent in the campaign for the return of women as Poor Law guardians and the election of women onto School Boards. As editor of the *Englishwoman's Review* from 1871 to 1889, she introduced radical liberal ideas into what was, for the most part, a bourgeois feminist paper.[6]

Under Biggs's editorship the *Review* demonstrated an interest in peace that was lacking in the work of her predecessor, Jessie Boucherett, and was also notably absent from the approach of her successors. With Biggs as editor, the *Review* contained frequent articles on abstract questions of peace and war, as well as regular reports of women's peace activities. Under the guidance of Blackburn and Mackenzie, a more jingoistic approach was adopted, in which lip service was paid to the importance of questions of international peace and the prevention of war, but outspoken support was given to imperialist expansion, notably in the case of the second Anglo-Boer war. The *Review* reported The Hague Peace Conference of 1899 in positive tones, but on the outbreak of war later in the year placed its support firmly behind the Government, and denounced 'pro-Boers'.[7]

The pacifist arguments drawn upon during Caroline Ashurst Biggs's editorship were piecemeal and often divergent in their politics. They were broadly focused around representations of women as inherently peace-loving, and assumed a higher moral nature for women that supported the feminist argument for their greater involvement in public life. In April 1871, an extract from the *Examiner* was published in the *Review*, which argued, in terms reminiscent of Mill, that as the main object of society shifted from being based on war to being based on industry, women 'would necessarily become equal with men in social importance'.[8] 'Woman' had greater scope in industry than in war. The *Examiner* argued that:

> By emancipating women we should liberate a great peace-loving power, and enormously strengthen the pacific tendency of commerce. If, in addition, women obtained the political influence given to wealth or labour, the security of peace would be increased. In war, they have everything to lose, nothing to gain.[9]

Women, it was argued, were inclined towards peace not only in international political relations, but also in international (free) trade, as their emancipation would 'strengthen the pacific tendency of commerce'.[10]

Arguments of sexual difference were developed when a review of *Conversations on War and General Culture* noted that the author, Sir Arthur Helps, advanced the view that there were 'souls masculine and souls feminine'.[11] Biggs used the review to clarify her position on sexual difference, noting 'the feminine souls are not always women nor the masculine souls men'.[12] She argued that femininity and masculinity could be attached to individual souls, and therefore sexual difference might be moral or psychical in nature. In her contention that imagined sexual differences do not necessarily assign the feminine qualities to women and the masculine ones to men, she implied that these differences were not biological in basis. Yet arguments of essential sexual difference were still in common use. In a report of a meeting of the Women's Peace and Arbitration Auxiliary of the Peace Society (discussed in chapter 4), Biggs reintroduced these ideas by commenting: 'We believe that one great effect of the recognition of the right of women to co-operate with men in political life will be that the horrors of war will in a great measure be averted, and its sufferings alleviated.'[13] The presence of women in public life was thus argued to morally improve the policies that would be pursued, to the benefit of not only the nation, but also the international community.

In May 1878, the *Review* carried an anonymous article on 'The Peace-makers'. Making similar assumptions to Biggs about female nature, it argued that women's 'direct' interest in the maintenance of peace and their exclusion from the franchise served 'to weaken proportionately the hands of the Peace party in England'. The article discussed a recent pamphlet issued by Maria Tayler, a member of the Women's Peace and Arbitration Auxiliary. Tayler focused upon the economic effects of war on both working- and middle-class women, and concluded that 'Women are injured morally and physically by the vice and immorality which is found [to be] inseparable from the military system in time of peace as well as war.' The *Review*'s article took issue with those who disagreed that 'women are almost unanimously against war', and concluded with the suffragist argument that 'the Peace party in the country would have received a larger augmentation of force if women had equally with men possessed the authority of citizens to elect their governor'.[14] Such ideas were characteristic of Caroline Ashurst Biggs, not least in the implicit connection that was drawn between the Liberals in the 1870s as the party of 'Peace, Retrenchment and Reform' and women as political reformers.

Among these arguments that sexual difference affected individual politics – a case which was put by both pro- and anti-suffragists – were gendered ideas regarding what was biological in basis. Women were viewed as less susceptible to moral corruption and therefore somehow more pacific, and men were seen as possessing greater intellect and physical strength. However, the boundaries of what was assumed to be biological, moral or intellectual were always hazy. Despite efforts by Mill and many others to show that gender differences were more likely to be social or cultural in basis than biological, discourses of sexual difference were so prominent during this period that the women's movement increasingly relied upon and developed arguments of this nature in order to deal effectively with its critics.

The death of Caroline Ashurst Biggs in 1889 effectively ended the coverage of peace issues in the *Review*. After this date, discussions of peace were rare and conducted in relation to specific wars, in particular the Anglo-Boer war of 1899 to 1902. Blackburn and Mackenzie, as editors, reproduced in the *Review* similar imperialist attitudes to those put forward by Millicent Fawcett, denying that British forces in South Africa were guilty of any wrongdoing in their management of the concentration camps, and labelling all those who protested against the war 'pro-Boers'. In a series of articles by Maude A. Biggs, Caroline's younger sister, it was argued: 'Even those who disapprove of the war, as war, can hardly disapprove of the efforts made to soften its horrors and sufferings.' A philanthropic approach to the war was emphasised to the exclusion of all other perspectives, clearly illustrated by Biggs's argument that

'South Africa, like the poor, is always with us'.[15] Britain's involvement in the war was justified on the grounds that its 'democratic' influence was required in the South African republics, and that its charity was the only means by which the Afrikaners could become a 'civilised' society. This argument also served to justify the involvement of middle-class British women in the war effort, as they could reproduce patriotic, imperialist ideas of their own unique 'moral burden', just as they did in undertaking philanthropic reforms at home.

The content of the *Englishwoman's Review* over the 1870–1902 period showed just how closely editorial policy depended on individual politics. These women drew their principles from established traditions such as liberalism and radicalism, yet each editor drew upon different elements of these, and this was reflected in the content of the journal. Biggs's radical liberal feminism was prominent in her issues of the *Review*, particularly when contrasted with Blackburn and Mackenzie's jingoistic imperialism. The matter of editorial policy is an important factor to bear in mind given that the other journals in question here were continuously produced by single individuals, and therefore the effects of editorial differences are not visible.

The *Women's Suffrage Journal*, 1870–90

The influence of a prominent and active editor can perhaps be seen most clearly in the example of the *Women's Suffrage Journal*. Lydia Becker founded and edited the paper from 1870 until her death in 1890, and although a number of other feminists regularly contributed to the journal – including Biggs and Blackburn – on Becker's death it was decided that no one was able to take up the task of continuing it. The *WSJ* was primarily concerned with the campaign for women's suffrage, although it did reflect Becker's interests in its coverage of other feminist issues, such as the work of the Married Women's Property Committee, campaigns for women's education, issues of crime and the law, and the international progress of the women's movement. Its content demonstrated Becker's commitment to international co-operation and her Cobdenite radicalism, particularly with regard to free trade and European liberation movements. These issues dominated her approach to questions of peace, and in addition to the theoretical debates about the physical force objection discussed above, the *WSJ* contained many anti-war arguments in relation to specific conflicts. Becker's responses to the Franco-Prussian war of 1870–71, the Bosnian conflict of 1876, and the Anglo-Boer war of 1878 were particularly strongly expressed.

Becker took the Franco-Prussian war as an example of the fate of nations when governed by dynastic, undemocratic forces. The war occurred within months of the launch of the *WSJ*, and the editorial response to it was one of detailed and wholehearted condemnation. Implicit in much of Becker's criticism was the argument that Prussia was exploiting its own people, and that a more representative government was required in order to end oppression within the state, as well as to put a stop to war with other nations. Becker was more detailed in her arguments than was Biggs in the *Review*, as she explicitly supported national liberation movements and refused to condemn war as a means of conflict resolution. 'War', she wrote, 'should be the last resort after negotiation and arbitration have failed.' She criticised not only the 'dynastic' forces which were causing working men to die on behalf of a quarrel that was between governments, but also the treatment of women in war:

> if our sympathies are aroused on behalf of the masses of Frenchmen plunged into war . . . what must they be for the nations of French and German women on whom the burden and the misery of war falls in an equal or even greater measure than on men, and who are denied the right to a voice in deciding whether it shall or shall not be laid upon them . . . [L]et the feminine *plébiscite* be appealed to as having a right to be heard, and who can doubt that the unanimous vote . . . from princess to peasant, would be given for peace between peoples and reunion in homes.[16]

In arguing that women would not vote for war, Becker used ideas of sexual difference – and to some extent, of class interest – to support her main argument about the importance of individual rights.

These sexual difference debates echo the discussions in the *Englishwoman's Review*, although Becker framed her arguments in terms of contemporary notions of 'race' and social Darwinism, which illustrated even more clearly the idea that women's 'innate' love of peace could attach itself to artificially constructed bodies such as nations:

> We believe that the combative instinct, that which fights for fighting's sake, or from mere love of conquest, is much more strongly developed in the male than in the female sex. We also believe that the instinct which fights for that which it holds dear is more strongly developed in the female sex than in the male . . . We believe that in the face of a foreign foe the women of a nation would be inspired with the most determined and self-devoted spirit.[17]

Becker argued that women had a place within the imperial nation, and presented them as having a 'natural', 'instinctive' role as patriotic defenders of the nation. Implicitly, she drew a contrast between men's supposed love of an abstract concept ('conquest'), and women's emphasis upon their relationships with others, to indicate that it was relationalism that could be of greatest service to the nation.

Becker presented the sexual difference debate in more overtly political terms than Biggs, although her arguments still rested on familial and biological imagery. Women, Becker argued, have a 'self-devoted' spirit that is concerned with protection and defence, rather than aggression. In this, she allied herself with non-absolutist peace activists who had been arguing throughout the nineteenth century that they considered defensive wars to be justifiable. Her contention that women's wars, if there were such things, would be defensive was one way of arguing that women would be more peaceable in international conflict than men.

In claiming that women, by virtue of their instincts and their social conditioning, would alter the conduct of war, Becker concluded that ultimately 'The women's vote would put an end to offensive war.' Again using assumptions of biologically-based sexual difference, she argued that: 'War is an essentially masculine pursuit. Women do not as a rule seek to quench their differences in blood. *Fighting is not natural to them.* The male sex is the combative sex throughout the animate world.' Becker's ideas of sexual difference did not extend to Biggs's claim that women could be 'a great peace-loving power', but they were based on similar principles, in that the foundation of both arguments was that women's vote would put an end to war. Women's 'self-devotion', as Becker termed it, was the crucial factor in their fighting instinct.[18] They were by 'nature' defensive, and it was only as exceptions to the rule that they would seek out combat.

As her response to other conflicts showed, Becker was careful to keep closely to the argument that the suffrage was essential for women. In her ideas about women's political representation, she brought her concern with logic and rationality to bear on their exclusion from political power where questions of life and death were concerned. In response to fighting in Bosnia-Herzegovina in 1876, she stated that:

> We claim for our sex a share in the moral responsibility for the action of our country ... [The British government's policy] is to be determined by the mind and heart of the nation at large, on broad principles of justice and humanity which can be understood [*sic*] of the people, and in this judgement women have a right and duty to bear their part, which they cannot abdicate nor men deny.[19]

In applying concepts of justice, humanity and morality to an international stage, Becker argued that women's absence from national and international politics did not mean that they were not culpable for the actions of their governments.

When peace or war hung in the balance in South Africa in 1878, Becker wrote that: 'An unnecessary war is a national crime. Shall women be dragged into this crime against their consent? A war involves heavy and grinding taxation . . . A war means bereavement and misery.'[20] There was an even greater need to obtain the suffrage for women if Britain was to be drawn into a state of war. She argued that military conflicts could in many cases be prevented by means of negotiation and arbitration, that the extension of the franchise furthered democracy, and that democracies would be more peaceable and just than nations with a limited franchise.

Becker's radicalism blended liberal feminism with Cobdenite ideas of free trade and the European democratic pacifism which supported wars of national liberation. This strand of pacifism had developed during the mid-nineteenth century and from 1867 was represented by the republican nationalist peace organisation, the International League of Peace and Liberty, which was based in Switzerland and linked to the Workmen's Peace Association (WPA) in Britain and, from 1880, the IAPA. However, Becker maintained a distance from these organisations, developing her ideas in the exclusively feminist context of the *WSJ*. Although this journal was intended to function as a single-issue paper, it did of course include discussions of wider debates within the feminist movement. In contrast, Henrietta Müller's *Women's Penny Paper* was founded in order to provide an open forum for feminist debate which was distanced from specific campaigns, including the peace movement.

The *Women's Penny Paper*, 1888–90

The *Women's Penny Paper* (*WPP*) ran for just over two years, from October 1888 to January 1891, when its title changed to the *Woman's Herald*. It was edited by Miss Henrietta Müller (*c.* 1851–1906) under the pseudonym Helena Temple, until April 1892, at which point it was handed over to the Women's Liberal Federation. It was explicitly feminist in its politics and featured an immense variety of feminist concerns, including temperance, the suffrage campaign, Liberal politics, the sexual double standard, the employment of children, rescue work and the bastardy laws. Every issue included a long biographical interview with a well-known woman, and during the two years for which the *Penny Paper* ran, it featured such diverse personalities as Priscilla Bright McLaren, Annie Besant, Pandita Ramabai and Emmeline Pankhurst, among many others.

Henrietta Müller was a member of the younger breed of women whom Judith Walkowitz has termed a 'transitional generation', which was already enjoying the benefits won by the women's movement of the 1860s and 1870s, but was also committed to working for more concrete gains. Müller, the daughter of a German businessman and sister of Eva Müller (who married Walter McLaren), perhaps epitomised the image of the 'Glorified Spinster', the woman possessing an independent income who chose not to marry. She studied at Girton under Emily Davies, and was the first woman to be elected onto the London School Board. She was active in a wide range of feminist campaigns: the National Society for Women's Suffrage, the Personal Rights Association, the National Vigilance Association, and the Society for the Return of Women as Poor Law Guardians. After handing the *Woman's Herald* over to the WLF in 1892, she travelled to India to pursue her interest in theosophy.[21]

Müller was motivated to found the *Women's Penny Paper* after her resignation from the Men and Women's Club, where she had felt frustrated at the intellectual intimidation of women members by the more educated and experienced men members.[22] Initially intending to found a women-only discussion group, she instead produced the *Penny Paper*. Her rationale for starting a newspaper rather than a discussion group was largely based on her dissatisfaction with the *Women's Suffrage Journal*, which she dismissed as 'a little monthly leaflet, not worthy the name of a newspaper'. She intended the *Penny Paper* to be as independent as possible, giving women 'a newspaper of their own through which to voice their thoughts', and ultimately aiming to 'further the emancipation of women in every direction and in every land'.[23]

Although the *Penny Paper* did not pursue an explicitly pacifist policy, most of its issues carried items on peace and the women's peace movement. There were often editorial comments, arguing that 'It is time that peace-lovers should speak out boldly and loud enough to be heard.' One of Müller's early *WPP* editorials emphatically opposed the military action in the Sudan. She acknowledged that there could be 'righteous' wars, but that this was not one of them, because 'the great authorities on the Soudan [*sic*] . . . maintain that not only is peace possible, but that it is the only right and reasonable course'.[24] Henrietta Müller's personal politics clearly encompassed pacifism, and not from the British perspective alone. She was keen to include the communications and work of European pacifist women, particularly Marie Deraismes and Virginie Griess-Traut, and supported the efforts for peace by working men in Italy.[25] In an early paper to the Men and Women's Club, she had drawn attention to the importance of reorganising society around criteria of 'moral strength' rather than physical power and force.[26] She was instrumental in a trans-organisational peace meeting in early 1889, at which Walter McLaren acknowledged that their interests lay in proving that 'the vast majority of wars can be avoided'. McLaren's focus was on the principle of non-intervention and the need for a court of arbitration. He concluded that: 'The time is coming when the Parliamentary Franchise will be given to women. They will have a crime on their shoulders if they do not try to check the war spirit.'[27]

The pacifist arguments that emerged within the pages of the *Penny Paper* were distinct from the resolutely Christian work of the Peace Society, and independent of the International Arbitration and Peace Association, an organisation to which Müller's editorial approach, like that of Becker, was perhaps closer in terms of politics. The *Penny Paper* outlined a vision of peace that was based upon moral righteousness and transnational justice, a liberal feminism that recognised the need for balance in, and a degree of regulation of, international affairs. Yet the *Penny Paper* also rested on fundamental arguments of moral and intellectual sexual difference, particularly the principle that women's contribution to government, if they were enfranchised, would vastly improve political life on both a national and an international scale. In a report on the 1889 peace congress in Paris, Müller wrote: 'If provocation [to war] come at all ... it can only arise in those countries where true progress has scarcely begun, and womanly influence has never permeated political life.' This approach echoes the arguments of Ellen Robinson, although Robinson was careful never to make women's suffrage an issue in pacifist circles. The *Penny Paper* gave frequent reports of Robinson's work for peace, often including extracts from her lectures.[28]

In November 1889, the *Penny Paper* included a critique of a newly-established peace society, the 'Christian Union for promoting International Concord'. Twenty-nine men, Müller informed readers, constituted the Union's Executive Committee, and yet, she remarked, 'How a Society can style itself a Christian *Union*, (?) [*sic*] or hope to succeed as such, when it deliberately ignores one half of Christendom, passes comprehension. No section of the community is more interested in the maintenance of peace than are women.' Müller astutely concluded: 'We must strongly urge women to withhold pecuniary support from any society which excludes them, but not their purses, from the management.'[29] The issue of women being expected to help fund societies that accorded them no executive power is one that recurs in the late nineteenth-century feminist movement. At this stage, the Peace

Society had been calling for and accepting donations from women for over seventy years, and yet, as Müller was probably aware, it refused to accord them any official role or recognition.

The tensions between the peace movement and early forms of pacifist feminism were put squarely before the readers of the *Women's Penny Paper*. The London Universal Peace Congress of 1890 was criticised by Henrietta Müller for its neglect of the pacific power of women. She wrote: 'One looked in vain among the large attendance of delegates from various Peace Societies for the faces of women . . . [T]he Congress should this week pass a resolution in favour of more women delegates and more women speakers.' In response, the *Penny Paper* received a letter the following week from Louisa Bigg, a suffragist and secretary of the Luton branch of the IAPA, pointing out that there were 'at least 50 or 60 of us [women], of various nationalities, and speeches were delivered by [a number of women]'.[30] Müller's point is nonetheless important in emphasising the paradox into which women working for peace fell during this period. The peace movement, undervalued and overlooked as it was, desperately needed supporters in influential political positions, which inevitably meant *men*. The need to court prestigious supporters far outweighed the desire to hold the moral high ground by obtaining the support of women, and indeed, giving women a high profile even risked increasing the ridicule with which many peace societies were met. They were already dismissed as utopian, unrealistic and impractical. The inclusion of numbers of the new 'platform women' in their meetings could only diminish the movement in the eyes of its critics.

In 1891, the *Women's Penny Paper* changed its name to the *Woman's Herald*. A year later, Müller transferred the journal to the ownership of the Women's Liberal Federation, and in 1893, it became jointly owned by the Women's Liberal Federation and the World Women's Christian Temperance Union (WWCTU). Müller's term as editor had seen the *Women's Penny Paper* report the work of British women's peace associations in a feminist context, and disseminate information about 'crusading' European women's peace movements. In addition, the principle of arbitration was repeatedly promoted. However, in pursuing this course, Müller's *Penny Paper* served to emphasise the shortcomings in feminist thought where questions of peace were concerned. On the one hand, Müller put forward the feminist argument that women had a significant role to play in the peace movement. On the other, she had to acknowledge that the peace movement was male-dominated for very practical reasons. Müller could write about the 'pacific power of women', but she rarely moved beyond the rhetoric to ask what women could actually do to promote peace on national and international levels. We can see how these debates developed during the 1890s through a study of the content of the *Woman's Signal*.

The *Woman's Signal*, 1895–99

In January 1894, the WWCTU and its president, Lady Henry Somerset, re-launched the *Woman's Herald* as the *Woman's Signal*. It failed to attract subscriptions, however, and within less than two years was running at a loss. It was taken over in September 1895 by the established feminist journalist Florence Fenwick Miller, who made an agreement with Lady Henry Somerset to include in the *Signal* any WWCTU news she submitted. Fenwick Miller's project to make the *Signal* into a financially independent paper was soon realised, as it became the voice of *fin de siècle* feminism.

Florence Fenwick Miller (1854–1935) was another member of the 'transitional generation'. She had become involved in the women's movement at the age of eighteen, trained in medicine at the University of Edinburgh only two years after Sophia Jex-Blake had forced this institution to accept women as students, and was elected onto the London School Board at the age of twenty-two. On her marriage she changed her title from 'Miss' to 'Mrs', but refused to change her name, a choice that caused some controversy on the School Board, as Patricia Hollis has noted.[31] Fenwick Miller stood down from the Board in 1885 as financial pressures forced her to turn to full-time lecturing and journalism. She was a 'platform woman', highly skilled in public debating and lecturing, and by 1895 had built up a considerable reputation as a journalist and public speaker. One London journalist noted how 'I have seen men grow visibly paler as she dissected – or rather vivisected – their halting arguments with her pitiless logic; she would leave nothing but shreds behind'.[32]

Barbara Caine has contrasted Fenwick Miller's *Signal* with the contemporary *Shafts*, arguing that in the context of the 1890s the *Signal* was relatively unfashionable, perhaps even outdated. It did indeed struggle with the concept of the 'New Woman' during the late 1890s, as Caine has discussed, and maintained strong links with mid-Victorian feminism. It dealt with new issues, such as rational dress and cycling clubs, but it is arguable whether, as Caine suggests, it really 'could not take on board with any ease any wholesale recasting of feminine behaviour or morals'.[33] Fenwick Miller focused upon change through legal and political channels rather than through social behaviour, but she had also been instrumental in modifying accepted feminine behaviour through her refusal to take her husband's name. Fenwick Miller's feminism was strongly influenced by the mid-Victorian phase of the movement, but she was nonetheless forward thinking in her politics. She was committed to neo-Malthusianism as a result of her medical training, declared herself an agnostic, and ran the *Signal* with astute business sense. She was, for her generation, a radical and independent thinker.

The anti-militarist feminism that emerges from the pages of the *Signal* shows a sympathy with the pragmatic pacifism of the IAPA, but also some arguments against war which can be identified as distinctively feminist. Fenwick Miller paid regular tribute to the work of Hodgson Pratt of the IAPA and William Randal Cremer, the anti-suffragist leader of the Workmen's Peace Association (renamed the International Arbitration League in 1888). She published in the *Signal* news of the Universal Peace Congresses and pacifist articles from diverse sources, including *War or Brotherhood?*, the peace journal of the Society of Friends.[34] The progress of the Anglo-American Arbitration treaty of 1898 received detailed coverage in the *Signal*, as did the work of the International Council of Women (ICW) and the embryonic National Council of Women. Yet Fenwick Miller as editor avoided outspokenly pacifist arguments, instead condemning militarism and blending her critiques of war with feminist ideas.

Ideas of progress were connected to arguments for arbitration. For example, in a report on the arbitration treaty between Britain and the USA, Fenwick Miller argued that progress was inherent in partnership, as 'combined, we serve to show the more backward nations in which militarism still holds a primary place, that women can advance not only without disadvantage but with benefit to the community'. These ideas led to the development of arguments about sisterhood, with Fenwick Miller arguing that its emergence was due to women overcoming the 'backwardness' of military societies. As civilisation progressed, the 'sense of a sisterhood of women must make for peace and for union throughout the world'. The idea that women the world over had common interests, and that their influence would be pacific, suggests that Fenwick Miller conceptualised feminism in international terms. In response to the progress of the ICW, she wrote that 'there is more international feeling between the women of the world at present than between any section of men. The women of the whole world form, in a way, a unity.'[35] Unsurprisingly, these ideas of international sisterhood tended towards essentialism. Statements such as 'We all rejoice in any onward step made by the women of any part of the world!' reflected the optimism of the ICW, but glossed over the difficulties and divisions encountered when trying to make it work in a practical sense.[36] Characteristically for feminist arguments of this period, Fenwick Miller assumed that women's interests were homogeneous, that their interests would not conflict with one another, and that advancement meant the same things for different women.

Fenwick Miller began to develop an anti-militarist, almost pacifist line of argument based on broadly humanitarian beliefs that physical force was not necessary, and combined this with a feminism based on ideas that women's common oppression could be overcome by their social, political and economic advancement. For example, in an editorial on the conquest by the British at Khartoum in 1898, Fenwick Miller argued that there was 'little reason for any great glorification' of such a victory. The numbers killed and wounded were far greater on the side of the native people, which showed 'that the conquest was preposterously unequal, and [should] justly [prevent] . . . any display of national vanity.'[37] Her broad critiques of imperialism and sympathy for wars of national liberation brought her much closer to the IAPA's pacifism than the absolutism of the Peace Society. Fenwick Miller also forged links with women working for peace, though less with the work of Ellen Robinson than with the feminist campaign that was being carried out on a smaller scale by the Manchester Women's Peace Association (MWPA). The MWPA had its origins in the suffragist movement of 1870s Manchester, and for the most part operated separately from the peace movement. Fenwick Miller's interest in its work emphasised her commitment to specifically feminist rather than pacifist politics.[38]

Fenwick Miller decided to discontinue the *Signal* months before the outbreak of the second Anglo-Boer war, but her editorials up to this date clearly demonstrated an interest in gendered peace arguments. The explicit connection she made between the moral character of the nation and its treatment of women formed part of a trend that can be identified throughout the Victorian women's movement.

The language and arguments used in the four journals discussed here can be seen to develop over the thirty-year period of study, with Biggs's and Becker's radical liberal politics giving way to what we would today recognise as a more feminist discourse. Biggs and the *Review* drew on a wide range of ideas, including that of Cobdenite free trade, but it was Becker's *Women's Suffrage Journal* that was clearly closest to Cobden's radicalism. Neither journal developed critiques of empire as such, although both opposed imperial wars, for example, the Franco-Prussian war and the Anglo-Boer conflict of 1878. Predominantly, however, the discourses employed were those of nationalism and internationalism, which were compatible with Cobdenite ideas of free trade but could not accommodate the possibility of power differentials between nations.

Müller's *Women's Penny Paper* and Fenwick Miller's *Woman's Signal* infused these earlier Cobdenite ideas with a heightened awareness of the consequences of power and the use of force, and evaluated their importance for the feminist movement. Ideas of justice and moral righteousness began to be applied to the imperial and international arenas, as Müller and Fenwick Miller became critical of the use of physical force between combatants who were unequal in strength. As a result, Fenwick Miller in particular argued that women's moral righteousness, which was intended to counterbalance men's use of physical force, made all women into an equal, unified sisterhood. Thus, to some extent she politicised the internationalist ideas and simultaneously exaggerated the sexual difference arguments that had developed during the 1860s and 1870s.

An analysis of these journals shows that peace questions frequently appeared in feminist arguments and campaigns, although on the surface they may have appeared only tangentially relevant. Issues such as women's employment, a major strand of the feminist movement of the 1860s and 1870s, were linked with peace by Biggs in the *Review*, to show that women's involvement in industry would incline them towards free trade. Peace was linked with the Liberal party and the Women's Liberal Associations by Biggs and Müller, and of course with the suffrage movement through debates on the physical force objection. Becker in particular linked the suffrage and peace questions to wider issues of the importance of democracy and national representation.

In all four journals, issues of pacifism, nationalism, imperialism and internationalism were hotly debated. Campaigns such as women's suffrage were linked to wider arguments on the importance of national representation and influence for women, and how this intersected with their potential role in the empire and the nation. There was limited consensus over whether nationalism could be compatible with feminism, and where there was potential conflict – for example in Fenwick Miller's arguments on internationalism – the national interest was redefined to coincide with the feminist interest in the imagined international arena. Women's emancipation was only possible in a 'civilised' society, and 'civilisation' was only to be achieved through peace and justice. The connections between anti-militarism, peace and feminism were therefore easy for many Victorian feminists to make.

Notes

1   *Woman's Signal* (21 January 1897), p. 40.
2   David Doughan and Denise Sanchez, *Feminist Periodicals, 1855–1984: An Annotated Critical Bibliography of British, Irish, Commonwealth and International Titles* (Brighton: Harvester, 1987), p. 3.
3   *Ibid.*, p. 13.
4   *Ibid.*, p. 17.
5   Kathryn Gleadle, *The Early Feminists: Radical Unitarians and the Emergence of the Women's Rights Movement, 1831–51* (New York: St. Martin's Press, 1995), pp. 40–1.
6   E. F. Richards (ed.), *Mazzini's Letters: To an English Family, 1844–54*, vol. 1 (London: John Lane, The Bodley Head, 1920), p. 72; *Englishwoman's Review of Social and Industrial Questions (Review)* (14 September 1889), pp. 386–7; Eugene L. Rasor, 'Matilda Ashurst Biggs', in Joseph O. Baylen and Norbert J. Gossman (eds) *Biographical Dictionary of Modern British Radicals (BDMBR)*, vol. 2 (London: Harvester Wheatsheaf, 1988), p. 60.
7   *Review* (15 July 1899), p. 169.
8   *Ibid.* (April 1871), p. 110.
9   The *Examiner*, quoted in *ibid.*
10 *Ibid.*
11 Arthur Helps, *Conversations on War and General Culture* (London: Smith, Elder and Co., 1871), p. 72.
12 *Review* (July 1871), p. 191.
13 *Ibid.* (15 June 1876), p. 272; (15 September 1876), p. 411.
14 *Ibid.* (15 May 1878), pp. 207, 211.
15 *Ibid.* (15 October 1900), p. 228; (15 July 1901), p. 155.
16 *WSJ* (1 September 1870), p. 69. Emphasis in original.
17 *Ibid.*
18 *Ibid.*, p. 70. Emphasis added.
19 *Ibid.* (1 August 1876), p. 112.
20 *Ibid.* (1 February 1878), p. 22.
21 Judith R. Walkowitz, *City of Dreadful Delight: Narratives of Sexual Danger in Late-Victorian London* (London: Virago, 1994), p. 141; Hollis, *Ladies Elect*, p. 100; Lucy Bland, *Banishing the Beast: English Feminism and Sexual Morality, 1885–1914* (London: Penguin, 1995), pp. 27–31, 40–6; Doughan and Sanchez, *Feminist Periodicals*, p. 13.
22 Bland, *Banishing the Beast*, pp. 27–31, 40–6.
23 *Women's Penny Paper (WPP)* (28 November 1891), p. 916.
24 *Ibid.* (29 December 1888), p. 4.
25 *Ibid.* (26 January 1889), p. 4; (5 January 1889), p. 3. For more on Marie Deraismes and Virginie Griess-Traut, see Patrick Kay Bidelman, 'Marie Desraismes', in Harold Josephson (ed.-in-chief) *Biographical Dictionary of Modern Peace Leaders (BDMPL)* (London: Greenwood Press, 1985), p. 208;. Stephen C. Hause with Anne R. Kenney, *Women's Suffrage and Social Politics in the French Third Republic* (Princeton: Princeton University Press, 1984), p. 8; Claire Goldberg Moses, *French Feminism in the Nineteenth Century* (Albany: University of New York Press, 1984), pp. 179–85, 273.
26 Walkowitz, *City of Dreadful Delight*, pp. 151–2.

27 *WPP* (2 March 1889), p. 6.

28 *Ibid.* (29 June 1889), p. 6; (2 November 1889), p. 18; (10 May 1890), p. 338.

29 *Ibid.* (2 November 1889), p. 21. Emphasis in original.

30 *Ibid.* (19 July 1890), p. 462; (26 July 1890), p. 476. For more on Bigg, see Lewis (ed.), *Before the Vote was Won*, pp. 366–9.

31 Hollis, *Ladies Elect*, p. 91; see also Catriona Blake, *The Charge of the Parasols: Women's Entry to the Medical Profession* (London: The Women's Press, 1990), part 3; Rosemary T. VanArdsel, 'Florence Fenwick Miller, feminism and the *Woman's Signal*, 1895–1899' (Tacoma, Wash.: University of Puget Sound, 1979), unpublished paper, Fawcett Library, London, p. 6; Rosemary T. VanArdsel, 'Victorian periodicals yield their secrets: Florence Fenwick Miller's three campaigns for the London School Board' (Tacoma, Wash.: University of Puget Sound, 1980–85?), unpublished paper, Fawcett Library, London.

32 Hollis, *Ladies Elect*, p. 91.

33 Barbara Caine, *English Feminism, 1780–1980* (Oxford: Oxford University Press, 1997), p. 140.

34 *Woman's Signal* (2 September 1897), p. 149; (7 October 1897), p. 229; (21 April 1898), p. 246; (22 September 1898), p. 183.

35 *Ibid.* (21 January 1897), p. 40.

36 *Ibid.* (14 July 1898), p. 441.

37 *Ibid.* (22 September 1898), p. 184.

38 *Ibid.* (27 October 1898), p. 271. For a discussion of the formation of the MWPA, see Heloise Brown, ' "The gentle process of womanly sympathies"? The founding of the Manchester Women's Peace Association', *Women's History Notebooks*, 8:1 (Summer 2001), pp. 21–30.

3

'Conspicuous' philanthropists:[1] nonconformist religion in nineteenth-century pacifism

T HE ROLE of nonconformist religion in the early feminist movement has been widely acknowledged. From the Unitarian Caroline Ashurst Biggs, to the Quaker Priestman and Bright family networks, feminist politics developed in significant part within the context of nonconformity. It was much the same for the peace movement. Two issues were key to religious perspectives on peace in the nineteenth century: one was Quaker theology and the commitment to testimony against war; the other, the influence of Evangelicalism. This chapter considers the importance of Evangelical religion in nonconformist pacifism, particularly the Peace Society, and the impact that theological developments within the Society of Friends had upon the peace movement.

David Bebbington has argued that Evangelicalism was based upon four key elements: conversion, in which an individual experienced a crisis which changed their personal faith; activism, or a commitment to spreading the word about the importance of conversion; biblicism, or love of the Bible; and crucicentrism, a focus on the atoning sacrifice made by Christ on the cross. A number of feminists in this period (Josephine Butler being a prominent example) identified conversion experiences that turned them towards religious and philanthropic work.[2] Women's religious 'mission' was borne out by activism, not only in the sense of spreading the gospel but also, throughout the mid- to late nineteenth century, through social work and philanthropy. The two were, for Victorian society, closely intertwined. Women did much of the district visiting, fundraising and social concern work that was required by Evangelical churches.[3] Biblicism was also a prominent aspect of Evangelicalism, and many absolute pacifists and social purity feminists relied heavily on biblical quotes in their arguments. Priscilla Peckover, for example, often referred to 'our Bible-reading Christian land', and built the following quotations into the declaration of her Local Peace Association: 'We are bound "to love our neighbour as ourselves;" "to render to no man evil for evil;" "to overcome evil with good".[4]

Concepts of sacrifice were common in the women's movement, but crucicentrism, or the idea of atonement, was not a common motif within the peace movement. The notion of sacrifice on the Cross carried undertones of death and struggle that were too close to military ideals to make them safely adaptable to the peace cause. Instead, peace arguments focused more upon the birth of Christ. For example, a leaflet issued to juvenile members of the Local Peace Associations in the 1890s referred to 'the beautiful banner of Peace on Earth and Goodwill to Men, brought down from heaven by the angels on the first Christmas Day, as they sang for joy at the birth of the Prince of Peace'. It also included a quote from the Old Testament: 'Behold to obey is better than sacrifice.'[5]

Although pacifists drew selectively on those aspects of their faith that suited their cause, it is unarguable that Evangelicalism was a key factor in the birth and growth of the nineteenth-century peace movement. This can be seen in the development of Britain's oldest pacifist organisation, the Society for the Promotion of Permanent and Universal Peace (usually known as the Peace Society or the London Peace Society), which was founded on 14 June 1816. It dominated the British peace movement until the late 1860s and 1870s, when the politics and methods of those involved began to diversify. The Peace Society arose in response to the Napoleonic wars of the early nineteenth century, as a result of Quaker pacifist sentiments which at this time began to gain support among non-Quakers, particularly dissenters, and some clergy and lay persons of the established church.[6] While the Evangelical urge to reform society was an important factor in its foundation, alongside these religious motives against war were the secular influences of liberalism and humanitarianism, which stemmed from the Enlightenment of the eighteenth century. Such arguments held that conflicts between states should be resolved without resorting to war, and that reason could replace violence.

Although the original idea for such a society came from a non-Quaker dissenting minister, Dr David Bogue, the men who actually founded the Peace Society were Quakers: William Allen and Joseph Tregelles Price. However, a number of non-Quakers rallied to support the Society, including Bogue and Anglicans Thomas and John Clarkson (who had, like the founders of the society, been active in the anti-slavery agitation and other reform causes). The founders thus combined their religious arguments with liberal and humanitarian ideas to argue that all wars were unchristian and immoral. This starting point remained the ideological basis of the Society until well into the twentieth century, by which time its influence and significance had considerably declined.[7]

As Alan D. Gilbert has shown, the rise of popular dissenting Protestantism during the early nineteenth century began to rival the strength of the Church of England, as Congregationalists (or Independents), Baptists, Wesleyans and Primitive Methodists all gained firm bases of support.[8] Despite the fact that Quakers were a tiny religious grouping when compared to Anglicans or Congregationalists, their lack of numbers was offset by their members' wealth and influence. In 1800 there were approximately 19,800 Friends in England and Wales, most of whom were middle class. They declined in number during the early to mid-nineteenth century, largely as a result of the exclusive and excluding nature of the Society of Friends. While Evangelical dissenters such as the Congregationalists and Methodists aimed to 'win converts from the world' and yet still maintain their gathered subculture of believers, Quakers were more likely to try to preserve their exclusivity and in the process they maintained policies which worked against recruitment, such as disownment on marriage to a non-member. As a result they declined in number during this period, from a high of almost twenty thousand in 1800 to an estimated low of fourteen thousand in 1861, although after the disownment policy was abandoned in the 1860s membership numbers again began to increase.[9] Despite the fluctuations in membership, the influence of Quakers in the area of social reform was maintained throughout the century. They gained greater representation in this period among the upper middle classes, as the wealth and influence of Quaker merchants and manufacturers increased.

The centrality of the peace testimony to Quaker doctrine meant that numerically and financially, Quakers dominated the peace movement. Their long history of radical resistance to the demands of the state, notably through their refusal to bear arms, placed them within a historical tradition from which it was possible to critique state power and oppose or defy established religion. Organised opposition to the state's authority to declare war was therefore a short but significant step to make.[10] Throughout the nineteenth century, Quakers formed the majority of supporters and members of the Peace Society. However, among all Quakers only around ten per cent actively supported the peace movement or joined the Peace Society, and likewise, it was not the case that Quakers ever wholly dominated the Society itself on an executive level. If anything, the opposite was the case, particularly in the second half of the century when both Quaker and non-Quaker Executive Committee members sought to publicly downplay the influence of the Friends in order to avoid giving the impression that the Society was dominated by this relatively small and traditionally radical sect. By 1830 the Peace Society had built up a core membership of 1,500 people, of whom at least half were Quakers, who provided the Society with a steady source of income.[11] But despite the loyalty of this core membership and the importance of their donations, the Society of Friends' influence on the Peace Society in the second half of the nineteenth century was over-shadowed by that of the two secretaries to the Peace Society from 1848 to 1918, Henry Richard and William Evans Darby, both of whom were Congregationalists.

An all-Quaker membership was never the intention of the men who formed the Peace Society, although the Society embraced those who wished to work for peace using Quaker principles of 'absolute pacifism'. It pledged itself to be against *all* wars, including those that were supposedly defensive, and it was written into the Society's rules in 1821 that no one would be eligible for membership of the Executive Committee if their principles were not in strict accordance with the absolute pacifism of the Society. However, this rule effectively offered a compromise between absolutism and pragmatism, because it meant that members who were not absolute pacifists could involve themselves in other aspects of the Society's work, particularly in regional branches where they were eligible for committee positions.[12]

Of non-Quaker Peace Society members, most were Congregation-alists, Baptists or Unitarians. The Congregationalists had a significant influence upon the peace movement, supporting the Peace Society in large numbers and comparable in strength to the Baptist influence on the Society, but not of course to that of the Quakers.[13] The structure of Congregationalism had been developed primarily by Evangelicals since the formation of the Congregational Union in 1832, and like other non-conformists, particularly Primitive Methodists, the occupational structure of its membership was heavily biased towards skilled labourers.[14] During this period it was more of an academic and intellectual movement than other Evangelical Churches, but it also demonstrated a long-standing concern with social reform. Although it asserted a thoughtful, intellectual theology, it did not adhere to rationalism or address the conflicts between intellect and personal faith. Its members' tendency to reject war was therefore a means of reaffirming their faith in the face of a society dedicated to material and financial accumulation.[15] Congregationalists were ultimately set apart by this intellectual framework, much as Quakers were set apart through their history of defiance of the state.

Over the nineteenth century, a struggle developed within Quakerism between older radical currents and the Evangelical arguments that began to dominate Victorian religion during this period. This was to have a considerable impact upon the Quaker role in the peace movement. In particular, conflicts in American Quakerism influenced the British Society of Friends. In 1827 Elias Hicks withdrew from the Evangelical American Society of Friends, on the grounds that he believed in the importance of the 'Inner Light' to the exclusion of all other sources of spiritual knowledge. Hicks became something of a 'spiritual bogey-man' to Evangelical Friends, who mistrusted his attempts to substitute personal faith for biblical authority.[16] These divisions also affected Quakerism in Britain, where Evangelical Friends also took the content of the Scripture as central and effectively rejected any independent spirituality. The Hicksite split therefore had the effect of motivating British Evangelical Friends to make their theological commitment more precise. This in turn further alienated the Quietists, who maintained the original Quaker beliefs in a form of Inner Light and independent spirituality in human beings, in addition to that contained within the Bible.[17]

Quietist Friends remained dominant in Yearly Meetings in Britain until mid-century, but the increasing divisions can be seen in the establishment of two Quaker periodicals in 1843: *The Friend*, which was to cater for the Evangelical wing; and *The British Friend*, for the Quietist wing. As Martin Ceadel notes, the *British Friend* eschewed support for the Peace Society and was indeed more likely to publicise the Society's rivals, confirming that Quietist Friends were increasingly hostile to Evangelicalism.[18] The centrality of the Bible as the source of knowledge of God within Evangelicalism meant the abandonment by these Friends of the traditional core Quaker doctrine of the Inner Light. Unsurprisingly, this abandonment caused the alienation, resignation or disownment of many Quietist Friends who continued to uphold what had been Quakerism's core doctrine. After these struggles in the 1830s to 1850s, although a number of Quietists continued to be vocal and influential within the Society of Friends, the Evangelicals established a dominance within the Society which lasted until the mid-1880s.[19]

The Evangelical phase of Quakerism witnessed further splits within the Society in the 1860s and 1870s. During the 1860s, as a result of divisions caused by William Hodgson in the US between what he viewed as 'pure' (traditional) and 'tainted' (reforming) Quakers, a number of British Quietists separated themselves from the established, Evangelical-dominated meetings.[20] The committee that was appointed to restore unity to the Friends was of strictly Evangelical orthodoxy and thus it seemed this wing had finally achieved absolute dominance within Quakerism, both in Yearly Meetings and in the British Society of Friends as a whole during the 1870s.[21] However, this dominance was disrupted by the gradual inroads made by liberal theology and intellectualism into Quakerism. Concurrent with the 1860s and 1870s splits there appeared a third strand, a minority of liberal Friends. These were a younger breed of mostly university-educated men who, from the 1870s onwards (and through their establishment in 1867 of the journal *Friends' Quarterly Examiner*), rejected the relatively new dominance of Evangelicalism within Quakerism and argued instead for a more liberal, 'progressive' theology that ultimately allowed modern thought to expand within twentieth-century Quakerism.[22]

These inroads by liberal theology came about because one of the achievements of Evangelical Quakerism was to help destroy the concept of Friends as 'Peculiar People'. During the 1850s, Evangelicals had successfully campaigned for the abolition of the signifiers which separated Friends from other Christians – particularly Quaker dress and peculiarities of speech – with the consequence that, as Isichei argues, Evangelical Friends could feel closer to non-Quaker Evangelicals than to Quietist Friends.[23] Evangelicalism had the effect of making Friends more ready to work with non-Quakers in philanthropic or social reform causes although, like the anti-slavery movement, the Peace Society with its interdenominational co-operation predated the period when Evangelicalism took off within the Society of Friends. Evangelicalism was nonetheless a vehicle for some Quakers to reject the traditional eschewal of worldly activity and instead participate in reform, philanthropic and political causes.

The anti-Evangelical liberal movement within Quakerism, which gained ground in the 1880s, drew its inspiration from Quietist teachings. As a result of the Darwinian theory of evolution and the popularisation of biblical criticism, liberal Quakers regarded the Bible as fallible and therefore had no certain source of theological knowledge. Thus a new emphasis developed on religious experience as the foundation for faith, and the concept of the Inner Light was successfully revived as a core doctrine. However, the new liberal Quakerism also conflicted with some of the Quietists' central tenets, particularly the rejection of the study of religion and of organised social action. Anti-intellectualism had been a persistent characteristic of Quietism and one of its enduring strands of difference from Evangelical Quakerism, although Evangelical Friends were to be charged with the same trait by liberals, who accused them of a blindness to intellectual thought and the theological issues of the moment.[24]

Although the liberal strand rejected Quietism *per se*, including the doctrines of Original Sin and the Atonement, many liberal Quakers nonetheless had sympathy for the Quietists, seeing Evangelicalism as their common enemy. The liberal Friends had their origins in meetings held with Unitarians in Manchester in the late 1860s, where the liberal theology that was to become dominant had been pioneered. By the 1880s, many of the exponents of liberal views were Quakers who exercised a significant degree of influence over Quaker thought. Two of these men, William Pollard and John Wilhelm Rowntree, were members of the Executive Committee of the Peace Society. Pollard was co-author of the first Quaker statement of liberal theology, *A Reasonable Faith*, published in 1884, and with his co-authors became involved in the publication of the Quietist *British Friend* in 1891, implying that the differences between Quietist and liberal theologies were gradually being overcome. In contrast, John Wilhelm Rowntree came from a well-known Evangelical background but was referred to after his death as the 'prophet of the [liberal Friends'] movement'.[25]

The new Quaker theology spread with incredible rapidity. In 1885, the authors of *A Reasonable Faith* were only 'daring pioneers', but by 1895, a conference was held in Manchester to discuss the relationship of the Society of Friends to modern thought. The Friends had at this time less than 16,500 members, including children, yet the predominantly Quaker attendance at the conference ranged from 1,000 to 1,300 people and four out of five addresses on theology were given by well-known liberals. Two years later, a Summer School to bring Friends into contact with modern thought was benignly reported by the Evangelical *Friend*, and thus liberal theology quietly became orthodoxy within Quakerism.[26] This liberal trend was pioneered, at least in part, by men who were also active within the peace movement.

However, these changes in Quakerism were largely overshadowed within the Peace Society by its Evangelical Congregational secretaries, Henry Richard and William Evans Darby, who between them dominated the Society throughout the second half of the nineteenth century. Richard (1812–88) served as secretary of the Peace Society from 1848 to 1885 (after which he was made permanent chairman of the Society), and was also a Member of Parliament for Merthyr Tydfil from 1868. He was Welsh, a Congregationalist minister and a political Radical. His greatest achievement for the peace movement was that he managed to unite peace advocates regardless of whether they accepted the Peace Society's principle of absolute pacifism. His arguments stressed that war was economically wasteful, destructive of human lives, a threat to liberty, incapable of determining which side was right, and incompatible with Christianity. Under his leadership, the Peace Society was transformed from a solidly Christian body that exerted little practical influence in politics, to one that could make some impact, however modest, on governing circles. Richard's strength was in tailoring his arguments to his audience, but his ability to unify advocates of peace did not mean that his own principles were not firmly and seriously upheld. While he did make the Peace Society more influential and accessible to the outside world, he preserved its aims and principles within the Society so effectively as to almost embody it himself. From an internal perspective, he upheld rather than diluted its message, and his skill in doing so meant that under his leadership its reputation as an absolute pacifists' society was reinforced.[27]

From mid-century onwards, Richard was instrumental in furthering the spread of arbitration principles. Support for arbitration developed significantly during the course of the nineteenth century, and it was used as a means of resolving national disputes twenty-three times between 1794 and 1840. From the 1840s onwards, the concept of arbitration grew faster in popularity than any comparable alternative to war, such as disarmament, neutralisation or the establishment of a court of nations. In 1849 the first motion in the House of Commons in favour of a system of arbitration was put forward by Richard Cobden.[28] Although the motion failed, it was the first time that a serious discussion had taken place on the uses of arbitration, and its influence was felt not only in the increased impetus given to the peace movement, but also in the fact that the number and importance of cases submitted for arbitration began to increase. Similar motions were put forward in other legislatures in Europe, and reports in favour of its use were made in the Senate of the United States. It was Henry Richard who, in 1873, successfully carried a motion for arbitration in the House of Commons, and in the following two years this move was echoed by the legislatures of Italy, the United States, Sweden, the Netherlands and Belgium.[29]

In addition to arguments for arbitration, the Peace Society attempted to popularise other pacifist ideas, including for example non-intervention. Although non-intervention was a less popular strategy in the late nineteenth century than arbitration between nations, the Peace Society's uncompromising perspective on non-intervention meant that it clashed with the republican nationalists who dominated the Continental peace movement. The Peace Society's perspective originated with Henry Richard's views on non-intervention. As a Welshman, Richard strongly supported the idea that cultural rights would result from the establishment of civil rights and liberties. However, his cultural nationalist devotion to Welshness stopped short of any desire for political autonomy or independence, and indeed, he was fiercely critical of the idea of nationalism, seeing it as damaging to the peace process. Richard sympathised with republican nationalists on the continent who supported the use of force as a means of overcoming domestic oppression, but could not advocate it himself as he believed that the use of force corrupted men to the extent of making them unfit for citizenship. Constitutional government in oppressed states was only to be won, Richard argued, by nurturing moral ideas in the 'hearts of the people'.[30] It was this policy that became synonymous with the Peace Society's aims, and which it advocated despite the distance thereby created between itself and the Continental peace movements.

The Reverend William Evans Darby became Peace Society secretary in 1888 when William Jones, Richard's short-lived successor, resigned. Like Richard, he was a Congregationalist, a proponent of arbitration, and committed to absolute pacifism, but in contrast, he lacked public influence. Outside the Peace Society, Darby's power was limited: Richard had enjoyed a public platform as an MP, and by the time of Darby's appointment both his main rivals in the peace movement, William Randal Cremer and Hodgson Pratt, had established their reputations in Britain and on the continent. Under Darby the Society became increasingly insular, concerned with retaining its existing membership and ensuring its own survival, but doing little to reach out to new members or develop new policies. Internally, however, Darby made a number of welcome changes, and significantly, he widened the roles available to women in the Society. Most notably, he invited Priscilla Peckover to join the Executive Committee (she declined, and the committee remained all male until the early twentieth century) and he recruited four female vice-presidents, also a first for the Society. Thus, although it became increasingly distant from any new sources of support, Darby's term of office nonetheless ensured that the Society offered its members more scope for involvement than had been the case under Richard's secretaryship.

The social background of the women members of the Peace Society between 1816 and 1870 was similar to that of the men so involved. The Society's annual membership fee was five pounds and five shillings, which ensured that members were almost exclusively middle class. At the time of its first subscription list in 1817, women made up ten per cent of the Peace Society's 190 Committee members and subscribers. By 1822, when the Society had already greatly expanded, this figure rose to 11.2 per cent, a figure roughly comparable to the level of female participation in other philanthropic societies at this time.[31]

For the most part, women were invisible within the Peace Society in its early years. From 1819 the Society produced an official journal, the *Herald of Peace* (from 1883 the *Herald of Peace and International Arbitration*), which, in the first years of publication, functioned mainly as a discussion forum for male members of the Society.[32] During its first two decades the Peace Society also printed thirteen tracts, which expounded its basic doctrines. These were published in one volume in 1840, and included works by Thomas Clarkson, David Bogue, Jonathan Dymond (a Quaker author who became a committee member of the Society in 1824), Joseph John Gurney, and two tracts by an author going under the pseudonym of 'A Lady'. These were *An Examination of the Principles which are Considered to Support the Practice of War* (1825) and *Historical Illustrations of the Origin and Consequences of War* (1831). The 'lady' was Mary Roberts who, although 'born and educated a Quaker', had left the Friends on the death of her father. Mary Roberts was also the author of a duodecimo series of tracts published by the Peace Society in 1831–32.[33] However, Roberts was the exception among the Society's women members. It was not until the 1850s that significant numbers of women began to become actively involved in peace work, in the context of the Olive Leaf Circles. These were promoted by an American non-absolutist, Elihu Burritt, and consisted of groups of middle-class women who met regularly in one another's houses. Their activities included the exchange of 'Friendly Addresses' between France and England, holding discussion groups and fundraising meetings, corresponding with other Olive Leaf Circles and writing pacifist stories for children. The peace movement at the time largely ignored the existence of the Circles, however, and the *Herald of Peace* for this era made no mention of the work of women, noting their peace work only within the confines of the donations and subscriptions column.[34]

Religious motivations may explain why many women joined the Peace Society in its early decades, although Stephen Conway and Eric Sager have debated the role of social and economic uncertainty in the Society's membership levels. Sager has argued that the Peace Society was 'a response by the non-industrial middle class to the problem of their own ambiguous social status and their sense of political exclusion'.[35] Perhaps more than men, middle-class women may have felt acutely aware of their political exclusion and unsure of their social status, and this perhaps explains why a number of them joined the Peace Society in its early days. Such 'conspicuous philanthropy', as Conway terms it, may have been motivated by the desire for greater social acceptance.[36] But Conway rejects Sager's argument on the grounds that a number of 'conspicuously philanthropic' men were in a position to be so precisely because they were already highly successful in their own areas of business. Measuring philanthropic motivation by levels of financial success is of course less relevant in understanding the motivations of middle-class women, because their attitudes to their social position and their feelings of social (in)security are much harder to determine. Socio-economic explanations must form only part of the picture, as religion and the role pacifism played within it were also highly important elements in the motivations of those who worked for peace.

The Peace Society's second wave of popularity in the late 1840s led to a renewed interest from women, and it was at this time that the Olive Leaf Circles were founded. Almost mythical in their status during the late nineteenth century, the Circles have frequently been mentioned in twentieth-century literature, although almost invariably in disparaging tones. According to Eric Sager, the Circles were for 'small town pacifist[s]', dominated by 'aggressively respectable and intensely status-conscious women' who supported 'a bewildering array' of humanitarian causes.[37] Their founder Elihu Burritt's purpose in promoting the Circles was, Sager argues, to create a form of feel-good pacifism, where local rifts and class differences were healed while the reform message – practical steps to promote peace – was very much secondary. For Sager, Burritt's concept of brotherhood was 'applied explicitly to the envy, the petty animosities, and the tensions bred by such [status] distinctions'.[38]

Alex Tyrrell's account of the Olive Leaf Circles is rather more enlightening. He notes that the modes of women's participation in philanthropy changed throughout the nineteenth century, and that ideas of 'woman's mission' could be adapted to interest middle-class women in causes that they would otherwise have ignored. He shows that while the definition of a separate 'woman's sphere' conferred respectability, it also justified greater degrees of inflexibility and extremism because movements undertaken as moral or religious 'missions' could accept no compromises.[39] However, he suggests that the Circles did benefit women members to a significant degree. The role of women in contributing to public opinion at a time when it was increasingly accepted as relevant to national policy-making meant that women began to carve out a niche within which they could successfully attempt to influence public opinion themselves. Thus, although the focus of the Olive Leaf Circles was firmly upon the values of home, family and religion, they nonetheless offered their members the chance to extend their imagined 'woman's sphere' to the male-dominated arena of international relations.[40]

The role of the Olive Leaf Circles confirms that the Peace Society only countenanced women's involvement in the peace movement when they did not appear to challenge prevailing norms of feminine behaviour. As Alex Tyrrell, F. K. Prochaska and Kathryn Gleadle have shown, there were many motivations for women's philanthropy other than religious inspiration during this period.[41] Tyrrell's argument that women were drawn into male-dominated movements as a source of low-skilled labour, useful mainly for fundraising purposes, matches the tone of the Peace Society's appeals to women not only during the 1850s and 1860s, but well into the 1870s and 1880s, as shown in the following chapter. In the period leading up to 1870, women occupied only a minor role within the Peace Society, although there were continued appeals for the support and involvement of women in the work. When, in the 1870s, the Peace Society issued a renewed call for organised peace work by women, it still expected them to function predominantly as a source of financial support.

Throughout the century, women struggled for recognition within not only the Peace Society, but also the Society of Friends. Women had always been largely excluded from the administrative work of the Society of Friends, but after the rise of Evangelicalism they were also excluded from theological debates. Liberal theology's reliance upon the younger generation of male Friends who had been educated at university meant that, initially at least, women's contributions to these debates were limited. However, liberal Quakerism developed simultaneously with an increasing openness to women at administrative levels within the Society, so that towards the end of the century women were able to participate in both theological and administrative matters to a greater degree than previously, although their influence was still very much auxiliary to that of the men.

Although Quakers adhered to the principle of women's spiritual equality with men, until the early twentieth century this equality was theoretical rather than practical, as it did not extend to organisational or political equality within the Society. Neither did Quakerism lend its support to the movement for women's rights. Although a number of Quaker women became active feminists in the late nineteenth century, it does not follow from this that the Society of Friends itself supported the principle of women's rights at this time.[42] In the 1870s and 1880s, debates on the role of women Quakers increased among those active within the Society of Friends and the feminist movement, particularly the Priestman and Bright networks. Yet Quaker resistance to formal equality can be seen in the fact that it was not until 1896 that the Yearly Meeting agreed that women Friends should be recognised as 'forming a constituent part of our Meetings . . . equally with their brethren'.[43] There was some debate among Quaker women regarding whether the Meetings should amalgamate (which they did in 1907), and while the majority of feminists supported unification, this was not the case across the board. Many women argued that they had greater opportunities to develop skills in separate Meetings. However, the problem remained that the Women's Meeting generally took a pastoral role in the Society, whereas the Men's Yearly Meeting was concerned with the central issues of policy, administration and organisation.[44]

It has been widely noted that many Quaker women were at the forefront of the women's movement from the 1870s to 1890s. Margaret Hope Bacon argues that these women were influenced by personal responsibility, which was in turn fuelled by their notion of spiritual equality. She concludes that this ultimately led to the embodiment of many Quaker values within the ideology and practice of feminism. These values included the use of non-violence within protests, the insistence on the equality of women of all classes and races, the preference for democratic consensus rather than hierarchical decision-making, and the ties between the women's movement and the peace movement.[45] However, it is also possible to argue that Quaker women were drawn to the feminist movement precisely because its concern with manifestations of power resonated with their own views on women's spiritual or moral authority and their opposition to the use of force.[46]

Evangelicals dominated the nonconformist peace movement for much of the nineteenth century, although the movement accommodated with apparent ease the rise of the new liberal Quaker theology in the 1880s and 1890s. Women were largely excluded from both this theology and the organised peace movement, although they were present and often active in supporting roles. By the end of the century the influence of Quakers, and nonconformists in general, upon the British peace movement was clearly in decline. Dissent from within gradually became less significant than the emerging range of secular campaigns and, despite the overrepresentation of nonconformist women in the feminist movement, it was to the secular organisations – rather than the nonconformist Peace Society – that many of these women were drawn. The following chapter explores why this was the case.

Notes

1 Eric W. Sager, 'The social origins of Victorian pacifism', *Victorian Studies* 23:2 (Winter 1980), p. 220.
2 Caine, *Victorian Feminists*, pp. 12–13, 162–3.
3 David Bebbington, *Evangelicalism in Modern Britain: A History from the 1730s to the 1980s* (London: Unwin Hyman, 1989); Deborah Valenze, *Prophetic Sons and Daughters: Female Preaching and Popular Religion in Industrial England* (Princeton, NJ: Princeton University Press, 1985).
4 *Peace and Goodwill* (*P&G*) (April 1882), p. 3; (14 July 1883), p. 74.
5 Enclosed in letter from Priscilla Peckover to Élie Ducommun, 27 December 1895, Box 162, Document 12, IPB 1892–1914, International Peace Movement, League of Nations Archives, United Nations Library, Geneva, Switzerland.
6 For a discussion of the 1793 to 1815 period, which contextualises the origins of the Peace Society, see J. E. Cookson, *The Friends of Peace: Anti-war Liberalism in England, 1793–1815* (Cambridge: Cambridge University Press, 1982).
7 Brock, *Nonsectarian Pacifism*, pp. 21–3; W. H. van der Linden, *The International Peace Movement, 1815–1874* (Amsterdam: Tilleul Publications, 1987), pp. 4, 7–8.
8 Alan D. Gilbert, *Religion and Society in Industrial England: Church, Chapel and Social Change, 1740–1914* (London: Longman, 1976), pp. 34, 37–9, 63, 205. See also David Hempton, 'Religious life in industrial Britain', in Sheridan Gilley and W. J. Shiels (eds), *A History of Religion in Britain: Practice and Belief from Pre-Roman Times to the Present* (Oxford: Basil Blackwell, 1994), p. 311; Leonore Davidoff and Catherine Hall, *Family Fortunes: Men and Women of the English Middle Class, 1780–1850* (London: Hutchinson, 1987), pp. 74–8; Edward Norman, 'Church and State since 1800', in Gilley and Shiels (eds), *History of Religion in Britain*, pp. 278–86; Sheridan Gilley, 'The Church of England in the nineteenth century', in Gilley and Shiels (eds), *History of Religion in Britain*, pp. 293–304; Gail Malmgreen, *Religion in the Lives of English Women, 1760–1930* (London: Croom Helm, 1986), pp. 3–4, 7.
9 Membership levels returned to just under twenty thousand by 1914. Gilbert, *Religion and Society*, p. 40; Elizabeth Isichei, *Victorian Quakers* (Oxford: Oxford University Press, 1970), p. 111; Edward H. Milligan, ' "The ancient way" ': The conservative tradition in nineteenth century British Quakerism', *Journal of the Friends' Historical Society*, 57:1 (1994), p. 96.
10 Gilbert, *Religion and Society*, pp. 87–8.
11 Stephen Conway, 'The politicization of the nineteenth-century Peace Society', *Historical Research: Bulletin of the Institute of Historical Research*, 66:161 (1993), p. 273.
12 Brock, *Nonsectarian Pacifism*, pp. 23–4.
13 Sager, 'Social origins of Victorian pacifism', p. 213; Conway, 'The nineteenth-century Peace Society', p. 273. For more on the role of Baptists in the Peace Society, see Paul R. Dekar, 'Baptist peace-makers in nineteenth-century peace societies', *Baptist Quarterly*, 34 (1991), pp. 3–13.
14 Gilbert, *Religion and Society*, p. 63.
15 Sager, 'Social origins of Victorian pacifism', pp. 213–14.
16 Thomas C. Kennedy, 'Heresy-hunting among Victorian Quakers: the Manchester difficulty, 1861–73', *Victorian Studies*, 34:2 (Winter 1991), p. 228.
17 Milligan, ' "The ancient way" ', p. 75.

18 Ceadel, *Semi-detached Idealists*, p. 113.

19 Milligan, 'The ancient way', p. 80; Isichei, *Victorian Quakers*, ch. 1.

20 Milligan notes that three groups can be identified among Quietist (or conservative) Friends: purists, preservationists and conservationists. See Milligan, '"The ancient way"', p. 96.

21 Milligan, '"The ancient way"', pp. 80–91.

22 *Ibid.*; Thomas C. Kennedy, 'An angry God or a reasonable faith: the British Society of Friends, 1873–1888', *Journal of the Friends' Historical Society*, 57:2 (1995), pp. 183–98.

23 Isichei, *Victorian Quakers*, pp. 10–11, 23.

24 *Ibid.*, p. 19.

25 *Ibid.*, p. 33.

26 *Ibid.*, pp. 40–1.

27 Brock, *Nonsectarian Pacifism*, pp. 34–5, 173–5, 184; van der Linden, *International Peace Movement*, p. 195.

28 Nicholls, 'Richard Cobden', *passim*.

29 Christina Phelps, *The Anglo-American Peace Movement in the Mid-Nineteenth Century (1835–1854)* (London: P. S. King and Son Ltd., 1930), pp. 152, 158; *Herald* (1 August 1873): *passim*.

30 Anon. [Henry Richard], 'Liberty not to be advanced by the sword', *Herald* (February 1851), pp. 90–1, and (March 1851) pp. 102–3, in Brock, *Nonsectarian Pacifism*, pp. 181–3.

31 Conway, 'The nineteenth-century Peace Society', pp. 267–8.

32 Brock, *Nonsectarian Pacifism*, pp. 24–5; van der Linden, *International Peace Movement*, pp. 5–6.

33 Both van der Linden and the British Library catalogue give Mary Roberts as the author of the Peace Society tracts, though Liddington, quoting Posthumus-van der Goot, attributes them to Elizabeth Clarke of Lymington. Van der Linden, *International Peace Movement*, pp. 12–13; Posthumus-van der Goot, *Vrouwen Vochten Voor de Vrede* (Arnhem: Van Loghum Slaterus, 1961), pp. 15–16, in Liddington, *Long Road to Greenham*, p. 289.

34 Brock, *Nonsectarian Pacifism*, pp. 100–9; Liddington, *Long Road to Greenham*, p. 15; Alex Tyrrell, '"Woman's mission" and pressure group politics in Britain (1825–1860)', *Bulletin of the John Rylands Library*, 63 (1980–81), pp. 218–19.

35 Sager, 'Social origins of Victorian pacifism', p. 222.

36 Conway, 'The nineteenth-century Peace Society', p. 272.

37 Sager, 'Social origins of Victorian pacifism', pp. 220–1.

38 *Ibid.*, p. 222.

39 Alex Tyrrell, '"Woman's mission"', pp. 218–19.

40 *Ibid.*, p. 219; Liddington, *Long Road to Greenham*, pp. 14–15.

41 Tyrrell, '"Woman's mission"'; F. K. Prochaska, *Women and Philanthropy in Nineteenth-Century England* (Oxford: Oxford University Press, 1980); Gleadle, *Early Feminists*.

42 Sandra Stanley Holton and Margaret Allen, 'Offices and services: women's pursuit of sexual equality within the Society of Friends, 1873–1907', *Quaker Studies*, 2 (1997), pp. 1–29; Margaret Hope Bacon, *Mothers of Feminism: The Story of Quaker Women in America* (San Francisco: Harper and Row, 1986); Margaret Hope Bacon, 'The establishment of London Women's Yearly Meeting; a transatlantic concern', *Journal of the Friends' Historical Society*, 57:2 (1995), pp. 151–65.

43 Bacon, 'Women's Yearly Meeting', pp. 161–2.
44 A full account of this process can be found in Holton and Allen, 'Offices and services'.
45 Bacon, *Mothers of Feminism*, introduction and p. 137.
46 Despite the number of Unitarian women active in the early feminist movement, it seems that, with a few exceptions, they did not tend to become drawn into the peace movement to the same degree as Quaker and Congregationalist feminists. Levine, *Feminist Lives in Victorian England*, pp. 32–3.

4

'The antagonism of sex': the Peace Society and women[1]

URING THE SECOND half of the century there was a declining emphasis upon the importance of Christianity within the peace movement. The Peace Society had developed by the 1870s into a political and pragmatic movement that employed, albeit on a limited basis, liberal and non-absolutist arguments against war. However, it simultaneously sought to control the contributions of women, and to restrict the role of feminism within the movement. This is particularly noteworthy given that the Evangelical wing of the peace movement was dominated by Quakers, a sect from which many feminists of this era originated. One consequence of this was that feminists were drawn instead into the International Arbitration and Peace Association (IAPA) as the radical (and feminist-friendly) wing of the peace movement, rather than the Evangelical and absolutist Peace Society. By 1902, pacifism and feminism were far more alike in their aims, ideals and priorities than they had been in the 1870s, but the Peace Society did little to encourage this convergence: the women who continued to work within it were typically Quakers, absolutists and non-feminists.

Throughout the century, women's role in the Peace Society's work was at best minor, and was heavily subject to the Society's control. The early 1870s saw the first independently organised efforts for peace by women, and this chapter describes the process by which the Peace Society resisted this work, refused to collaborate with women who were not under its control, and established its own organisation for women interested in promoting peace. These women frequently employed the language and ideology of Evangelical Christianity in order to make their arguments respectable to the Society. The women's Auxiliary to the Peace Society split in 1882, and after this date the Auxiliary became more provincial, lacking a central leadership or even a clear relationship to the Society. In the 1890s, William Evans Darby attempted to include women more directly in the Society's work, but he succeeded only in drawing in high-profile individuals, rather than strengthening the women's Auxiliary to generate a mass movement of women for peace.

The 1870s saw the increased diversification of the peace movement, particularly from an international perspective. In 1867–68, the radical International League of Peace and Liberty (ILPL) and the International Association of Women were founded in Geneva, and in 1870, William Randal Cremer's Workmen's Peace Association (WPA) was founded in Britain. The ILPL consisted of a network of European radicals, republicans and revolutionaries who held that permanent peace could only be achieved through democratic liberty. For peace on both individual and national levels, the liberation of the nation was required. The central figure of the League was Charles Lemonnier, a Saint-Simonian. Lemonnier approached Henry Richard and asked him to co-operate with the ILPL, but he refused even to attend the 1867 Congress at which the ILPL was formed, identifying it as overtly political.[2] The League found few supporters in Britain, despite translating only its 'tamest' messages into English.[3] On its foundation a female ILPL member, Marie Goegg, requested that women be able to take an equal part in the League. In 1868 she was appointed its secretary and founded the International Association of Women as a semi-auxiliary. The aim of this women's association was to assist men in promoting 'liberty, education, welfare, and fraternal union', and to work for the 'intellectual and social improvement of woman'. It claimed that women should be granted 'an equal share in all the rights which men enjoy in the State and Society', and quickly established a network of contacts and officers across Europe and the US.[4]

William Randal Cremer's Workmen's Peace Association was founded in July 1870, and renamed the International Arbitration League in 1888. Cremer (1828–1908) had been present at the Geneva Congress when the ILPL was formed, and as a Radical and labour leader was more sympathetic than the Peace Society to the Continental perception of peace as achieved through individual liberty and democracy. Cremer had been a leading figure in the First International, but in the 1860s his attention increasingly began to turn towards peace.[5] The WPA's condemnation of war included demands for 'the rights of citizenship' for working men, and its rhetoric was heavily reliant on Chartist aims and ideology. Needless to say, this distinguished it from the middle-class Peace Society, yet the Society affiliated the WPA as one of its auxiliaries and spent considerable sums on supporting it financially throughout the 1870s and 1880s. It gained considerable popular appeal and in 1872, even excluding the Peace Society's contribution, its income was double that of the Trades Union Congress.[6] Its aims and principles – which qualified it for the Peace Society's support – included arbitration or a supreme international court, the rejection of standing armies, and partial, and ultimately total, mutual disarmament. The First International held that workers' political and social emancipation was the prerequisite to universal peace, yet the Workmen's Peace Association argued that peace was an essential precondition of liberty and social justice. This reversal effectively depoliticised socialist internationalist ideology, even while it made use of much of its rhetoric.

Despite these transformations in the peace movement, the Peace Society remained relatively static in its approach during the 1870s and 1880s. It was concerned to prescribe certain roles for women within the movement, typically focused around their responsibility to educate the young and their suitability for meetings such as drawing room discussion circles. These fora of course kept women strictly within the domestic context and upheld ideas of respectable middle-class femininity. There was even one Olive Leaf Circle still in existence in 1870.[7] In the early 1870s, the *Herald* continued to print the Olive Leaves (short tracts on peace issues) issued by Elihu Burritt, while also indirectly advancing the cause of some feminists (such as Josephine Butler) by opposing the Contagious Diseases (CD) Acts as part of its opposition to standing armies. By 1873, however, it began to reduce its coverage of the campaign against the Acts, arguing that repeal would make no difference to the effects of the Acts as long as standing armies – 'their root and source' – continued to exist.[8]

Thus by the 1870s, the Peace Society was maintaining an inward conservatism even while its work was becoming increasingly acceptable to the outside world. This conservatism was based upon the desire to maintain the Christian focus of the Society and its neutrality towards issues of party politics. It was clearly interested in drawing supporters from the substantial numbers of middle-class women involved in philanthropic and social reform causes in the 1870s, but it was careful to distance itself from any aspect of this work which might be viewed as feminist. The women's movement, which drew many of its supporters from similar backgrounds to those involved in social reform and in the peace movement, was viewed as a dangerous ally by the Peace Society, which had reservations about the respectability and legitimacy of the feminist movement and consequently, about how far the two causes should publicly associate with one another. While the

Society was trying to promote its message among certain groups of women, it also maintained a level of suspicion when women came forward to offer their help.

This can be seen in the Executive Committee's reaction to a proposal in 1871 to ask 'some ladies to speak in public on the Peace Question'. It was decided that whilst the Committee 'considered that it was of great importance to take every available opportunity of enlisting the sympathies of women in this direction', it was 'not prepared at present to take any definitive step in this direction'.[9] Six months later, there was a further illustration of this ambivalence when Julia Ward Howe, who was on a lecture tour of Britain holding meetings on peace, applied to speak to the Peace Society's annual meeting. The Committee responded that it:

> felt a cordial sympathy with the object proposed by that lady [but] they were also of [the] opinion that the greatest care is requisite on the part of this Society in relation to any formal support of efforts in no way under its control. Hence, inasmuch as Mrs. Howe's printed programme of operations includes a variety of subjects as, for example, 'the antagonism of sex,' the Committee were not prepared to take any direct action in uniting with her meetings or lectures.[10]

In order to affiliate with women during this period, it was essential for the Peace Society that such women were 'under its control'. It was not necessarily the case that greater sexual equality existed among Quakers than within wider society and therefore it cannot be assumed that the Quakers on the Peace Society's Committee, however forward-thinking they might have been in respect to other issues, would have been open to the principle of women's equality in any area other than spiritual matters.

As a feminist and a suffragist, Mrs Julia Ward Howe (1819–1910) was to have a crucial role in the divisions that occurred within the Peace Society over the following decade. In September 1870, in response to the Franco-Prussian war Howe issued an 'Appeal to Womanhood throughout the World', calling for universal action by women in favour of peace. This led to the founding of the US-based Women's International Peace Association (WIPA) in spring 1871, with Howe as its president.[11] Despite being refused an audience by the Peace Society, Howe undertook a speaking tour of Britain and Europe in 1872, assisted by the Anti-CD Act campaigner, Josephine Butler. Two branches of her Women's Peace Association were founded in 1872, by Mrs E. M. King in London and Maria Atkinson in Manchester. However, the London branch was short-lived due to the fact that the Peace Society established its own London-based women's auxiliary soon afterwards. Howe's 'Appeal to Womanhood' failed to inspire an international campaign, but Howe did find a niche within the American Peace Society and the women's movement.

The Peace Society's 1873 Annual Report recognised the work of Mrs E. M. King (b. 1829/1830).[12] King was active in the Ladies' National Association for the Repeal of the Contagious Diseases Acts, and had spoken on the formation of a Women's International Peace Association at the Social Science Congress at Plymouth in September 1872. She called for an association of men and women that was concerned with 'ensuring to women the right to be heard or represented' in any future settlement of international disputes. She listed the aims of the association as being the establishment of a permanent court of arbitration, gradual general disarmament, and the instruction of the working classes in international law and the evils of war – all issues for which the Peace Society had sympathy. Her interest had been kindled by her campaign against the Contagious Diseases Acts, as she argued that one of the evils of war was the necessity of standing armies, and the 'special laws or regulations' by which military systems were maintained. Like Josephine Butler, King linked the Anti-CD Act cause to a more general critique of the military system, and in this respect differed from the Peace Society in that she argued for the reform of the military rather than its abolition: for example, she held that permitting marriage in the army would reduce 'moral and physical' disease.[13]

A month after the publication of the 1873 Annual Report, the *Herald* advertised an essay competition on its front cover. The prize was offered by the Women's Peace Association, whose secretaries were given as E. M. King in London and Miss Maria Atkinson in Manchester.[14] Although Henry Richard had voted in support of the 1870 and 1883 women's suffrage bills, the Peace Society as a whole was explicitly opposed to suffragism and feminism, and it moved fast to establish its own women's auxiliary, to ensure that a society was founded that was wholly under its control and in accordance with its principles. The Peace Society journal, the *Herald of Peace*, was the leading pacifist journal during this period and the Society used its columns to advertise its new women's auxiliary and ensure that it dominated public accounts.

The Executive Committee's minute books clearly support this. In March 1874, Henry Richard received several communications from a Friend, Mrs E. M. Southey, and from other women regarding the possibility of initiating a women's peace association. Richard wrote to Southey to approve the formation of a ladies' auxiliary peace society, and stated 'the party represented by Mrs King' might be 'better apart from us as it seems to contain some elements that might not very comfortably amalgamate with us'.[15] Southey was an Evangelical Quaker who espoused social purity feminism, and she was therefore an ally for the Peace Society against the Anti-CD Act campaigners, such as King and Butler, who insisted on publicly addressing such unladylike issues as prostitution. A rift had developed in the early 1870s between the Peace Society and Anti-CD Act campaigners as a result of disagreements over the role of standing armies, and the Peace Society withdrew all support from the campaign to repeal the Acts. Not only had King been a member of the repeal organisation, the Ladies' National Association, but she had also been involved in a direct public protest against the Acts: she was arrested in Plymouth in 1870 for obstructing the police while they escorted a woman to a lock hospital, and this made her particularly undesirable from the Peace Society's point of view. Her libertarian political views, rather than any religious or Evangelical beliefs, informed her feminist work, which included 'antimedical and antimilitary' campaigns.[16]

Richard was keen to recruit women with religious and absolutist sentiments on peace, rather than non-absolutists who were portrayed as more explicitly 'political'. In his letter to Southey, he went on to suggest Priscilla Bright McLaren, Margaret Bright Lucas, Mrs Pennington (aunt of Priscilla, Margaret, Jacob and John Bright), or 'ladies of the Society of Friends' who would 'with yourself make excellent leaders in the cause'.[17] All the women concerned – King, Howe, Southey, McLaren, Lucas and Pennington – were suffragists (as was Henry Richard), but King in particular employed political rather than religious arguments in support of peace. In her paper to the Social Science Congress in 1872 she rejected religious arguments against war, and the Peace Society were reluctant to publicly associate with a woman who, although similar to them in her use of non-absolutist arguments, could be viewed as 'unwomanly' in her rejection of religious authority.[18]

The 'provisional secretary' of the new Auxiliary was announced as E. M. Southey, and from the outset it was stated that 'Christian women, of every denomination' were invited to join. The *Herald* reported the formation of the Auxiliary in detail, arguing that because of their 'power over the young' and 'their general strength of sympathy and persuasion', women were expected to occupy themselves with enlisting religious ministers and young children to the peace cause.[19] The final section of the *Herald*'s report stated that the work of the Auxiliary would be all the more 'efficient' and 'successful' because:

> it adheres to ... that fundamental principle which the recently-organised Committee of Ladies has cordially and decidedly elected to take its stand upon – the spirit of Christianity. There may be, and indeed are, worthy persons, whether Jews or others, who are ready to co-operate in the cause whilst not accepting such a principle; yet it is only Christianity, in its scriptural form and historic actuality, which can supply the strongest motives for effort and perseverance in this direction ... [I]t is one of the most hopeful and promising features of the new movement among the English ladies that ... they have so decidedly and emphatically expressed their resolve to take this powerful and supreme principle as the distinctly Christian basis of their operations.[20]

This emphasis upon 'scriptural form' and activism indicates that the women who influenced the Committee were Evangelicals, probably mainly Evangelical Quakers. Although the Peace Society was by the mid-1870s beginning to feel the tension between public persuasiveness (which meant non-absolutism) and Christian orthodoxy (which meant opposition to all war), and made use of politically-based arguments for practical steps such as arbitration, it clearly expected its women's auxiliary to focus solely on religious arguments and the education of the young.

This expectation can be seen in the *Herald*'s report of the inaugural meeting of the Auxiliary. Southey argued that in the formation of the Women's Peace and Arbitration Auxiliary of the Peace Society (WPAAPS) it was important, firstly that a Christian basis was agreed upon, and secondly that it was agreed to co-operate with the Peace Society.[21] When it was proposed to constitute the Auxiliary on the same Christian basis as the Peace Society, one woman present objected to the term 'Christian', arguing that it excluded Jews. She was told that while 'the co-operation of such persons would always be welcomed and courteously met, ... it was desirable that a body distinctly auxiliary to the Peace Society should, so far as possible, adopt the same fundamental principles'. A 'unanimous' decision followed this exchange, in which it was agreed to accept the term 'Christian'.[22]

For the Peace Society, the meeting was a success, as the Auxiliary was established upon the desired lines. In the aftermath of the Franco-Prussian war, and in the midst of the movement against the Contagious Diseases Acts, it appears that the time was right for some form of women's peace society. Rather than face a loss of women's membership

to the feminist movement, the Peace Society quickly facilitated the formation of an official female auxiliary that observed the same principles as
the parent society.

The character of the Auxiliary can best be seen in its annual meetings. Its members did not tend to be 'platform women', and therefore
finding female speakers meant approaching those who did not accept the
cultural taboos on women speaking in public – that is, women who were
already involved in the feminist movement. At the first annual meeting, the only women speakers were Lydia Becker and Maria Atkinson,
both of whom originated from the 'Manchester School' rather than the
Evangelical religious background that was more common to the WPAAPS
membership. Neither was a member of the Auxiliary, and Becker was
outspoken in disagreeing with the principles expressed by the Peace
Society's male speakers, arguing that women had 'a responsibility as to
the exercise of their capabilities for public influence', and should not seek
to confine themselves to the 'obscurities of their homes'. Maria Atkinson,
representing the Manchester Women's Peace Association, read a letter
from Julia Ward Howe and reported on the progress of her association,
which was linked to Howe's Women's International Peace Association rather than the WPAAPS. (Although King's London branch of
the Women's Peace Association was incorporated into the Auxiliary to
the Peace Society, Atkinson's Manchester Association lasted for several
decades.) The *Herald* supported the presence of women speakers, noting
that 'Miss Becker . . . evinced a power and liveliness of oratory which very
pleasantly affected and animated the meeting, and induced wishes that,
another year, the Ladies Society may exercise a little more independence
of gentlemen speakers, at least on an occasion peculiarly their own.'[23]
Yet despite this conclusion, only one female speaker (Mrs Sarah Sheldon
Amos, also a suffragist) was invited to the second annual meeting, alongside seven men.[24]

Although again chaired by a popular figure in the peace movement,
Leone Levi, and addressed by male Peace Society members, the 1877
meeting was also addressed by five very prominent women, two of whom
– Lydia Becker and Julia Ward Howe – were potentially controversial.
The other three, Clara Lucas Balfour, Margaret Bright Lucas and Margaret
Parker of Dundee, were active within the temperance movement, a
cause that overlapped but was by no means synonymous with peace. In
1876, Parker and Bright Lucas had been instrumental in founding the
British Women's Temperance Association (BWTA), of which Parker
was appointed president in 1876, Bright Lucas in 1877 and Lucas Balfour
in 1878.[25] The BWTA connection between these three women suggests

that they were chosen to speak as a result of their work in the temperance movement. But what of Julia Ward Howe and Lydia Becker?

Howe's speech was uncontroversial. She was, she said, 'glad that the ... [WPAAPS] was an "auxiliary" to that of the men', and she focused on the importance of motherhood as work for women, emphasising that mothers had a duty to educate their sons to respect moral rather than physical force. These comments were unremarkable for the Peace Society and indeed upheld some of its more traditional ideas. Howe's feminism was undoubtedly problematic in this context, but as the WPAAPS meeting included other suffragists such as Margaret Bright Lucas, it is unlikely that Howe appeared particularly controversial. Lydia Becker gave a more provocative speech. She 'spoke of the importance of women rightly informing themselves as to the extent of their own influence. She would have [women] study public questions also, not to read their Bibles less, but their newspapers more.' This emphasis on women's role in the public sphere was extreme from the perspective of the Peace Society, though perhaps less so by this time for the WPAAPS. She went on to argue that 'every shilling [women] earn, every cup of tea they drink, is taxed or mulcted for war expenditure', a point that highlighted the economic connections between supposedly separate public and private lives.[26] Becker's pacifism was based on Cobdenite free trade arguments, and sympathy for republican nationalism. She was a 'rationalist' rather than a religious woman, so her invitation to speak to a specifically Christian body of women indicates the internal tensions within the WPAAPS that were to lead to its split in 1882. Becker was politically closer to the secular IAPA, and in 1884, allowed them to use her *Women's Suffrage Journal* to put their message across to women.[27]

The *Herald* acknowledged that the success of the WPAAPS was largely owed to Southey.[28] The Auxiliary's membership rose to over 350 women in 1878, and the broad support forthcoming from the feminist movement can be seen in the fact that a memorial to the Queen calling for a congress of European powers was signed by thirteen thousand women, including leading lights of the feminist movement such as Maria Grey, Emily Shirreff, Elizabeth Garrett Anderson, Anna Swanwick, Isa Knox and Frances Buss. In addition, the 1879 Annual Meeting included addresses from Josephine Butler and Eliza Sturge.[29] However, the Auxiliary increasingly suffered from a lack of funds. The Peace Society regularly contributed to the Auxiliary, usually in the realm of £20 per year in response to requests by Southey, yet the WPAAPS constantly experienced difficulty in covering its expenses. This can be contrasted with the sums paid each year to Cremer's Workmen's Peace Association, which although it had markedly different aims to the Peace Society received between £100 and £400 per year until it separated from the Society in 1888. In addition, fifty or sixty pounds was paid each year to the Peace Society's local auxiliary in Liverpool.[30] The fact that the women's association was not supported to the same degree as other auxiliaries indicates that the Peace Society viewed women's involvement in its work as of only limited relevance and importance.

The Peace Society resisted feminist efforts to work for peace, and by establishing its own women's auxiliary weakened other (rival) women's peace societies and forced them to disband or become marginal to the work of the Society. King's branch of the Women's Peace Association lost support with the establishment of the WPAAPS, though Maria Atkinson's Manchester Women's Peace Association was tolerated by the Peace Society and treated almost as an auxiliary member by the WPAAPS, probably because it was a smaller organisation and provincial in its location. Furthermore, the Peace Society typically only promoted the work of the WPAAPS when religious language and imagery was employed in its arguments. This was seen as a more respectable approach than Lydia Becker's opinion that women should be brought out of the domestic sphere. Yet the events of the early 1880s proved that a substantial number of WPAAPS members were not comfortable with the control that the Peace Society exerted over its women's Auxiliary, and while not dissenting from its religious focus, nonetheless wanted to apply their own social and moral purity views more fully within the movement.

The Peace Society's reluctance to associate itself with feminists created tensions for its women's Auxiliary between those who preferred a feminist approach and those who held more religious views. Not surprisingly, permanent divisions developed. In the early 1880s, an Evangelical Quaker named Priscilla Peckover became drawn into the peace movement and revitalised the WPAAPS's membership. This occurred simultaneously with the founding of a new, radical peace association, the International Arbitration and Peace Association. The feminist members of the WPAAPS broke away to affiliate to the new Association, while the more steadfast members such as Peckover and Mrs Henry Richard formed a new auxiliary to the Peace Society. The work of Priscilla Peckover in Wisbech is described in some detail in chapter 5. Here, it is enough to say that after one year of work, from 1879 to 1880, her Local Peace Associations had amassed nearly 900 members in Cambridgeshire alone, in comparison to the WPAAPS's national total of 442 members.[31]

The split within the peace movement caused problems for the Peace Society, and in the long term can be seen as a signal of its declining influence. The peace movement as a whole was beginning to require greater pluralism both in terms of the politics and policies of individual associations, and in its methods of bringing the peace question before Parliament and the public. Despite Henry Richard's ability to tailor his arguments to his audience, under his leadership the Peace Society gained the reputation of being an absolute pacifist organisation. It was often difficult to distinguish between what the Society advocated as religious ethics, and what were its practical policies.[32] Unlike its effects, the cause of the split was relatively trivial. The Executive Committee discovered that its subscription agent, Lewis Appleton, had been collecting sub-scriptions and donations and failing to pass them all on to the Society. He was dismissed and immediately began to organise a 'rival' society that he tried to build up using his Peace Society contacts. This was not difficult as the scandal was kept private and subscribers had no know-ledge that Appleton, who had been well known as the Society's agent, was suddenly not to be trusted. 'Unpleasant correspondence' continued throughout 1881 as a result of the way the new society was operating. To add fuel to the fire, the Peace Society's Committee discovered that Southey was issuing public approvals of the new society using the name of the WPAAPS. There was 'some correspondence' with Southey over this, although the reason for distancing the old from the new society was not explained to her.[33]

Within a matter of months, the Committee realised that a split in the women's auxiliary was unavoidable, and Henry Richard wrote to Priscilla Peckover as a representative of one of the WPAAPS's branch associations. He informed her that 'you should be aware that Mrs Southey is trying ... to separate the Women's Peace Auxiliary from the Old Peace Society to which it was an auxiliary' in order to affiliate it to Appleton's new IAPA. Again, Richard would not explain the details of the scandal, but instead remarked that the Committee 'felt them-selves obliged to part with [Appleton] and on his dismissal from our service he started a new and *what we cannot but regard as a rival Society* founded on the exclusion of the Christian principle from its constitution'. The IAPA, he said, 'only proposes to do precisely the same work in the *way of practical measures* which we are doing already'. He went on to say that he was only informing her of this situation 'in case any communication is made to you', so that Peckover would know how things stood.[34]

Henry Richard wrote on the same day to Mr J. W. Harvey, who was the husband of an active member of the women's peace move-ment in Leeds. Again, Richard assumed 'some sort of relation' between

Mrs Harvey's branch and the WPAAPS, and informed Mr Harvey in confidence of the financial discrepancies in Appleton's accounts, telling him that 'in revenge for his dismissal' Appleton had started a society that was causing the Peace Society 'great trouble'. He gave his reason for contacting Harvey as being that Southey had, 'without consulting us . . . [sent] to the papers a resolution of their committee though probably representing three or four persons only[,] expressing their cordial approval of the new society'. Richard was aware that Southey intended to separate the Auxiliary from the Peace Society and transfer its affiliation to the IAPA. He made it clear that he did not think that 'other ladies who have been acting with her' would approve of this step, and he therefore 'mention[ed] it to [Mr Harvey] . . . to place them on their guard'.[35] Faced with the possibility of losing some or all of their official women's auxiliary, the Peace Society attempted to muster support amongst the regional women's branches, perceiving the central WPAAPS as having only distant relations with the branches, who might be unlikely to transfer their affiliation to the IAPA. Neither Peckover nor Harvey were personally known to Henry Richard at this time, but he presumably felt confident of being able to rely on their support.

The Peace Society then instructed the WPAAPS to call a meeting to decide which society they wished to affiliate with, and asked to be allowed to send a deputation of Peace Society representatives to this meeting 'to make verbal explanations'. At the meeting it was reported in the Peace Society's minutes that the ladies had 'expressed their desire for continued and harmonious connection' with the Society. But less than two weeks later, it was discovered that the WPAAPS had continued its communications with the IAPA. A new minute was substituted for the one previously passed, detailing that while the Peace Society was very glad to maintain its connections with the WPAAPS, it could only do so 'by the Auxiliary conducting its operations in harmony with those of the Peace Society and entirely apart from any other organisation'.[36]

Why did Southey and a number of women in the Auxiliary embrace the prospect of separating from the Peace Society and amalgamating with the IAPA? The IAPA's principal differences from the Peace Society were that it was secular and it did not require its members to adhere to Christian absolute pacifism, or the renunciation of all war. It did, however, employ Christian principles in its arguments, including the idea that war was at variance with the principles of Christianity. But the majority of women who were dissatisfied with the affiliation to the Peace Society were in fact Friends, so it seems unlikely that their motivation to affiliate with the IAPA was driven by the desire for a more secular association that was not founded on the Christian (or Quaker) principle.[37] Instead, it seems that the deciding factor was that of women's activism. The Peace Society offered only a circumscribed role for women, while the IAPA was open to a more feminist approach and women were eligible to sit on its Executive Committee. Although a number of women elected to stay affiliated to the Peace Society, a substantial proportion of the WPAAPS's Executive Committee decided to leave. The 1881 annual meeting, which took place just before the final split, featured Margaret Bright Lucas and Helen Taylor as speakers, and both women remained active in the WPAAPS after it split from the Peace Society and joined the IAPA.[38] The more supportive attitude of the IAPA towards women's work for peace was an important factor in their decision, and indeed, it seems that the members who left took with them most of the expertise on arranging meetings with well-known speakers, devising methods of campaign, and providing a central body for the women's peace movement as a whole. Even if they did not take the membership of the WPAAPS with them, it seems they took most of the organisational experience.

Following the communications with the Executive Committee, Southey wrote to the Peace Society in late April 1882 explaining that the WPAAPS had now decided to constitute itself on an independent basis (renaming itself the Women's Peace and Arbitration Association, or WPAA), and the *Herald* reported that she had 'resigned'.[39] The Ladies' Peace Auxiliary in its new form was officially inaugurated on 12 July 1882, with Priscilla Peckover as treasurer and Mrs Henry Richard as president. From this point, the Auxiliary began to become more provincial in its membership and methods, lacking a strong leadership in London. However, it retained a formidable campaigner in Priscilla Peckover, and it was she who became the dominant figure in the women's peace movement. Peckover dominated the Auxiliary with her work at Wisbech, until a fellow Quaker, Ellen Robinson from Liverpool, took over the Auxiliary in 1896. Peckover distanced the Auxiliary from political questions and strengthened its links with Sunday Schools, religious ministers and provincial women. While Peckover's own Local Peace Association (LPA) movement expanded greatly, the Peace Society's Auxiliary did not experience any significant growth in its popularity. It sank from 350 members in 1878 to just over one hundred members in 1885, by which time Peckover's Local Peace Associations had attracted over nine thousand members across Britain, most of whom were women, and nearly half of whom belonged to her Wisbech branch.[40]

During the 1880s, changes occurred within the Peace Society itself, which helped to draw women more into its own work and reduced the need for a women's auxiliary. In March 1885, Henry Richard resigned as secretary; by August 1888, he was dead. He had become the 'embodiment' of the Society over his forty years of involvement in its affairs, and a short period of crisis followed his death that was exacerbated by the simultaneous resignation (for unrelated reasons) of William Jones, his successor as secretary.[41] The end of 1888 thus saw the appointment of a relatively new face within the Executive Committee of the Society, the Reverend William Evans Darby (1844–1922), who came highly recommended by none other than Priscilla Peckover.[42]

Darby continued Richard's methods of working with pacifists of many persuasions, while keeping the Society as a Christian, absolutist body that restricted its executive positions to those who held such views. Perhaps because Darby had only a short history of work in the peace movement and had not previously been involved in the Peace Society's Executive Committee, he had a harder task than Richard in maintaining the Society's aims. Darby's term of office, which lasted from 1888 to 1915, initially heralded a number of changes and brought the methods of the Society more up to date for the late 1880s and 1890s. Women in particular became more publicly involved in the work of the Society after Darby assumed the secretaryship. Yet although in the short term Darby modernised the Society to some degree, and perhaps managed to prolong its influence by a number of years, his long term of office was ultimately to witness the decline of the Society's influence within the British peace movement.[43]

Within three months of Darby's appointment, the first woman (Priscilla Peckover) was invited to join the Executive Committee. Although Peckover was highly respected within the Peace Society, it was a significant step that it was willing to accept the input of a woman on its decision-making body. Priscilla Peckover, however, felt that such an appointment would be too public a role for her to take and she declined the offer. At the same time, the first women were invited to act as vice-presidents of the Society. They were Sarah Pease, Priscilla Peckover, Mrs Henry Richard and Laura Ormiston Chant. Chant and Peckover were also suggested as possible speakers for the annual meeting. Margaret Bright Lucas was appointed a vice-president within a matter of months, as was Priscilla Bright McLaren, after Lucas's death in early 1890.[44] It was also in 1890 – at Darby's second annual meeting as secretary – that a woman, Ellen Robinson, first addressed the assembly.

The Peace Society's choice of vice-presidents was significant. Mrs Henry Richard was an obvious choice for appointment after the death of her husband, and she was also president of the women's Auxiliary. Similarly, Priscilla Peckover was a natural choice after she refused the post on the Executive Committee. She was perhaps the best representation of Evangelical Quakerism among the four women, yet she had also shown, through her journal Peace and Goodwill, an awareness of how to work with other pacifist bodies. Miss Sarah Pease (1828–1929) was a member of the Quaker Pease family of Darlington, which had been heavily involved with the Peace Society since its foundation. Joseph Pease (1799–1872) had been its president from 1859 to 1872, his brother Henry (1807–81) succeeded him on his death and Joseph's son Joseph Whitwell Pease (1828–1903) succeeded his uncle. Joseph Whitwell Pease was also the father of Sarah, and cousin to Elizabeth Pease Nichol (1807–97), who was appointed a vice-president of the Peace Society in 1891.[45] Sarah Pease was not actively involved in the work of the Peace Society, and was most likely appointed because of the prominence of the Peases in the history of the Peace Society's presidency, and the family's willingness to donate funds.

The appointment of Laura Ormiston Chant (1848–1923) is another matter. Unlike Pease, Peckover and Richard, she was a nondenominational preacher and writer and does not appear to have had family connections which would have recommended her for such a post. She was reported to be an excellent public speaker, and yet the Peace Society did not avail itself of her skills in this area until 1895. The Society was, it seems, influenced by Chant's politics: she was an Evangelical feminist whose interests were mainly focused around Liberal politics and social purity issues. With Millicent Garrett Fawcett she had been the subject of controversy in feminist circles in 1889 as a result of her involvement in the National Vigilance Association's closing of brothels. Unlike E. M. King and Josephine Butler, who publicly opposed the CD Acts, social purity feminists such as Chant were concerned with eradicating 'vice' rather than working with prostitutes to get them into paid jobs with better working conditions. Social reformers such as Butler argued that by eliminating prostitution without making alternative work available, Chant and Fawcett were taking a repressive approach that forced working-class women further into poverty.[46] Chant also relied heavily on maternalist rhetoric, utilising concepts of 'natural' femininity that represented all women as bound by middle-class concerns with respectability, passivity and nurturance. She assumed that motherhood was a universal experience for women, and one that took place within the confines of the middle-class home.[47]

As a Liberal, an Evangelical and a social purity feminist, Chant was a 'respectable' choice for the Peace Society, which perhaps felt that it needed to include an active feminist on a list of women who, it must be said, were not known primarily for their political activities. However, the two women later appointed as vice-presidents, Margaret Bright Lucas and Priscilla Bright McLaren, had for some time been highly active in feminist campaigns. As prominent, well-connected Quakers, they had enjoyed the support of the Peace Society since the 1870s when Henry Richard had suggested that they would make 'excellent leaders' of the WPAAPS. Although Lucas had been made president of Southey's IAPA-affiliated WPAA in the 1880s, the decline in antagonism between the Peace Society and the IAPA over the following decade may have led the Society to formalise its relationship with the figurehead of the WPAA by appointing her to the Society.[48]

The Peace Society was also at this time experiencing a new struggle with regard to peace movements in Europe. The 1892 Peace Congress in Rome had voted for the creation of an International Peace Bureau (IPB) as a permanent body to provide information on peace movements in different nations, and to unite these movements if such action was called for. This call originated with the republican ILPL, and the Peace Society was initially concerned that the international body would be dominated by the republicans. The ILPL, it argued, was 'of an avowedly political character and of *advanced* political views', and the Society therefore, 'while wishing it well', was 'unable to place itself unreservedly at the mercy of "united action" in Continental politics, in which it would have but a minor voice, and of which it might not approve'.[49] Its hostility to the new IPB seems to have been based as much on the desire to maintain international control over the movement as on the worry that the Peace Society would be lost among the European organisations. It argued against the formation of the IPB on the grounds that the Peace Society and the American Peace Society were already performing the functions of such a Bureau. The IPB made many attempts to reassure the Peace Society that it intended to work simply as an international source of information and support, but Darby was never wholly convinced and the relationship between him and Élie Ducommun, the secretary of the IPB and an ILPL member, was always tense.[50]

This hostility to the Continental movement seems more a product of Darby's approach than that of Richard. Richard was first drawn into the peace movement in the late 1840s when some of the largest Peace Congresses were being held on the Continent. He argued in 1885 that in his four decades of experience, 'we have found no practical difficulty whatever in working with all sorts and conditions of men at home and abroad'.[51] Yet as European pacifisms began to influence the British peace movement, and the strength of radical organisations such as the IAPA increased, Darby's Peace Society found international co-operation increasingly difficult.

Over the last decades of the nineteenth century, there was a gradual increase in the levels of co-operation and collaboration between feminists and absolute pacifists. Organised women's pacifism in the 1870s was dominated by Evangelicalism, as a result of the Peace Society's manip-ulation of the women's peace movement. By the 1880s its women's Auxiliary had split, with Evangelical feminists opting for an organisation that allowed them some political independence, while the remaining members chose to continue working with the Peace Society in a specific-ally auxiliary context. During the 1890s, the Peace Society began to accept the possibility that women could be both public speakers and active members of the Society. As a result of the work undertaken by Peckover and Robinson, the Auxiliary became more forward-looking and truly international than the Peace Society could ever have envisaged.

Notes

1 Peace Society Minute Book, 3 July 1872, Peace Society Archives, Fellowship House, London (hereafter PSA).

2 Van der Linden, *International Peace Movement*, pp. 724–5, 925–6.

3 *Ibid.*, p. 724.

4 First two quotations in *ibid.*, p. 815; third from *Women's Suffrage Journal* (1 Septem-ber 1870), pp. 70–1. See also *Englishwoman's Review* (July 1870), p. 233.

5 Claire Hirschfield, 'William Randal Cremer', in Josephson (ed.) *BDMPL*, pp. 181–2.

6 E. W. Sager, 'The working-class peace movement in Victorian England', *Social History*, 12 (1979), p. 122.

7 *Herald* (1 March 1870), p. 3 (inside back cover).

8 *Ibid.* (1 September 1873), p. 305.

9 Peace Society Minute Book, 4 December 1871, PSA.

10 *Ibid.*, 3 July 1872.

11 Van der Linden, *International Peace Movement*, pp. 930–1. See also Paul S. Boyer, 'Julia Ward Howe', in Edward T. James (ed.), *Notable American Women, 1607–1950: A Biographical Dictionary* (Massachusetts: Harvard University Press, 1971), pp. 225–9; Ellen Carol DuBois, *Feminism and Suffrage: The Emergence of an Independent Women's Movement in America, 1848–1869* (Ithaca: Cornell University Press, 1978), ch. 5.

12 *Herald* (2 June 1873), p. 252; (2 June 1879), p. 264.

13   *WSJ* (1 October 1872), p. 137 and *Herald* (1 October 1872), p. 135. See also Judith R. Walkowitz, *Prostitution and Victorian Society: Women, Class and the State* (Cambridge: Cambridge University Press, 1980), pp. 170–3; *The Shield: The Anti-Contagious Diseases Acts Associations' weekly circular*, 40 (10 December 1870), p. 326.

14   *Herald* (1 July 1873) front cover; also August and September 1873, front covers.

15   Henry Richard to Mrs Southey, 5 March 1874, Executive Committee of the Peace Society Letter Book, PSA.

16   Walkowitz, *Prostitution and Victorian Society*, pp. 171–3.

17   Peace Society Minute Book, 4 March 1874, PSA; Henry Richard to Mrs Southey, 5 March 1874, Letter Book, PSA.

18   *WSJ* (1 January 1872), p. 2.

19   *Ibid.* (1 April 1874), p. 59; (1 May 1874), p. 61.

20   *Ibid.*

21   This is the name later settled upon (June 1874) and used until the split in 1882. The abbreviation 'the Auxiliary' is also used to refer to the WPAAPS during the pre-split period, and to the Ladies' Peace Auxiliary after 1882. Post-1882, the title Women's Peace and Arbitration Association (WPAA) was retained by Southey and the women who moved to the IAPA.

22   *Herald* (1 May 1874), p. 62.

23   *Ibid* (1 July 1875), pp. 257–8.

24   *Ibid.* (1 June 1876), p. 79.

25   Lilian Lewis Shiman, ' "Changes are dangerous": Women and temperance in Victorian England', in Gail Malmgreen (ed.), *Religion in the Lives of English Women, 1760–1930* (London: Croom Helm, 1986), p. 205.

26   *Herald* (2 July 1877), p. 263.

27   Joan E. Parker, 'Lydia Becker: her work for women', Ph.D. diss., University of Manchester (1990), pp. 20, 240; *Journal of the International Arbitration and Peace Association* (1 July 1884), p. 8.

28   *Herald* (2 June 1879), p. 263.

29   *Ibid.* (1 June 1878), p. 92; (2 June 1879), p. 264.

30   Peace Society Minute Book, 14 June 1875, 11 July 1876, 20 July 1877, PSA.

31   *Herald* (1 July 1880), p. 104.

32   Brock, *Nonsectarian Pacifism*, p. 184.

33   Peace Society Minute Book, 22 November 1881, PSA.

34   Henry Richard to Priscilla Peckover, 17 December 1881, Letter Book, PSA. First emphasis added, second emphasis in original.

35   Henry Richard to Mr J. W. Harvey, 17 December 1881, Letter Book, PSA. Richard underestimated Southey's support: a number of active members of the WPAAPS went on to hold positions in the offshoot that affiliated itself to the IAPA.

36   Peace Society Minute Book, 23 December 1881, 1 March 1882, 14 March 1882, PSA.

37   *Concord* (22 June 1892), p. 108.

38   *Herald* (1 July 1881), pp. 259–60.

39   *Ibid.* (1 July 1882), p. 90.

40   *Ibid.* (1 July 1885), p. 262.

41   *Ibid.* (1 June 1889), p. 227.

42   Peace Society Minute Book, 28 December 1888, PSA.

43 For more on Darby, see Keith G. Robbins, 'William Evans Darby', in Josephson (ed.), *BDMPL*, pp. 189–90.

44 Peace Society Minute Book, 15 March 1889, 29 March 1889, 17 May 1889, 21 February 1890, 20 March 1890, PSA.

45 M. W. Kirkby, *Men of Business and Politics: The Rise and Fall of the Quaker Pease Dynasty of North-East England, 1700–1943* (London: George Allen and Unwin, 1984), appendix; *Review* (15 April 1889), p. 187; van der Linden, *International Peace Movement*, pp. 461, 478–9.

46 *Herald* (1 June 1895), p. 217. Anne Summers, *Angels and Citizens: British Women as Military Nurses, 1854–1914* (London: Routledge and Kegan Paul, 1988), pp. 332–3; Bland, *Banishing the Beast*, pp. 95–6, 99, 103–8, 113–22; Judith R. Walkowitz, 'Male vice and feminist virtue: feminism and the politics of prostitution in nineteenth-century Britain', *History Workshop Journal*, 13 (1982), pp. 79–83.

47 *Review* (15 April 1889), p. 186; *Journal* (31 July 1886), p. 76–7.

48 Henry Richard to Mrs Southey, 5 March 1874, Peace Society Letter Book, PSA; *Journal* (23 December 1885), p. 196.

49 *Herald* (1 March 1892), p. 34. Emphasis in original.

50 See for example Document 10, Box 1, IPB 1892–1914, International Peace Movement, League of Nations Archives, United Nations Library, Geneva, Switzerland.

51 *Herald* (2 November 1885), p. 304.

5

Priscilla Peckover and
the 'truest form of patriotism'[1]

A S AN ORGANISATION with a stated commitment to absolute pacifism, the Peace Society experienced considerable difficulties in working with non-absolutists. The problems were caused by divisions over the role of Christianity in peace principles, and the question of whether some wars could be justified. Indeed, a study of the Peace Society in this period suggests that it was simply impractical to expect pacifists divided by this principle to work together. Yet the work of one of the most active women in the late nineteenth-century peace movement demonstrates that it was possible for absolute pacifists to work closely with non-absolutists, even when differences of opinion and principle occurred. Priscilla Peckover provides a key example of inter-organisational co-operation, especially in respect of the mass movement she generated: the Local Peace Associations (LPAs). Peckover's methods of working drew upon both Quaker ideals and domestic ideology. In contrast to the Peace Society's approach, which was often both defensive and, to some extent, uncooperative, Priscilla Peckover was influenced by gendered norms of behaviour which, when combined with her Quaker background and the context of the peace movement, gave rise to more collaborative and conciliatory methods. She strived to conform to late Victorian conceptions of gender roles, and in consequence, used non-confrontational methods such as compromise and co-operation instead of the Peace Society's tendency towards threats and obstruction.

The influence of gender norms is of course relevant to the other women discussed in this book, because some feminists chose to deliberately challenge such norms. As Judith R. Walkowitz has shown, the leadership of the Ladies' National Association for the Repeal of the Contagious Diseases Acts was forced to battle on two fronts, against the supporters of the Acts and the male repealers who believed women had no place in the campaign. The prospect of mixed-sex meetings, for example, was particularly abhorrent to such men. As a result, women repealers began to ally themselves with other social groups, particularly working-class men, in order to create an environment in which their campaigns and opinions would be accepted.[2] Lucy Bland has discussed similar problems operating on an intellectual rather than a practical level in her consideration of the Men and Women's Club. This Club, which consisted of radicals, socialists and feminists, accepted that men and women could meet in a private forum to exchange intellectual ideas on the state of relations between the sexes. However, many women members found after a few meetings that their opinions continued to be subordinated to those of the men and that their means of expression – particularly their use of the personal, which contrasted with the dry, legalistic style used by the men – was dismissed as subjective, unscholarly and irrelevant.[3]

While these questions of social norms were undoubtedly an issue within the feminist movement, and indeed Victorian society as a whole, such disputes operated in very specific ways for the women who were active within pacifism. As a political pressure group the peace movement prioritised the work of its male members, including, after the extension of the franchise to many working men in 1867, working-class men via Cremer's WPA. The focus on those with the political power of the ballot meant that women were neglected both as suitable targets for peace propaganda and as valid workers within the Peace Society. Peckover worked within the peace movement rather than the feminist movement, and indeed was ambivalent to the women's movement and careful to distance herself and her work from it. She was a Quaker and an absolute pacifist, yet she managed to work with non-absolutist organisations far more effectively than did the Peace Society. She brought to her peace campaigns a clear concept of 'woman's role', which embraced established gender norms by emphasising women's domestic responsibilities, and yet also challenged such norms by assuming that women should have the power to shape public opinion.

Miss Priscilla Hannah Peckover (1833–1931) was born in Wisbech, Cambridgeshire, to a wealthy family of bankers and philanthropists. She was educated privately but briefly attended school in Brighton, and on the death of her brother Alexander's wife in 1862, devoted her life to raising her three nieces. She was raised as a Quaker and went on to be recorded as a minister by her Meeting, and maintained strong family ties, although she never married. It was only in her forties that she became active in peace and reform work. The Peckover family as a whole contributed significantly to the social, cultural and economic fortunes of Wisbech, playing a prominent role in charitable and philanthropic pursuits throughout the nineteenth century. They contributed to local organisations and founded a museum and a Working Men's Club and Institute. It is a testament to the family's local influence that Peckover House remains in Wisbech today, having been bequeathed to the National Trust when the last of the three nieces, Alexa, died in 1948. In addition, a large number of the surrounding buildings, including the Friends' Meeting House, were financed by various members of the family.[4]

Priscilla Peckover's inspiration to join the peace movement came, appropriately, in 1878, just a year before her youngest niece, Anna Jane, turned eighteen. At Quaker Meetings, the eighth query from the Book of Discipline, 'Are you faithful in bearing your Christian testimony against all war?' was read out periodically. Her initial response to this query was that 'it has nothing to do with us [women]'. Shortly afterwards, she came into contact with the WPAAPS work being undertaken by E. M. Southey. On hearing that the WPAAPS had only two hundred members, Peckover was roused to become involved because 'It seemed to me a disgrace that only two hundred women could be found who believed in Peace.' Instead of waiting for members to join, she canvassed from house to house, putting together a Christian declaration against war and asking for signatories and subscriptions of one penny. The result was the formation of the Wisbech Local Peace Association (WLPA), which gained six thousand subscribers within ten years.[5] Peckover's work in Wisbech spawned other LPA branches across Britain and various parts of the world, as far afield as Japan and New Zealand. However, Wisbech LPA remained the largest branch and indeed the driving force behind the LPA movement.

In 1882 Peckover founded a quarterly journal, *Peace and Goodwill: a Sequel to the Olive Leaf*, which campaigned for the establishment of a court of nations and the reduction of all armed forces, with a view to their eventual abolition.[6] Peckover edited and indeed funded the journal for nearly fifty years, until her death in 1931. It was for the most part a single-issue, Evangelical journal, focused around Christian, absolute pacifism and the progress of the peace movement across the world. However, it also included critiques of the oppression and domination that was being practised across the British empire. Like Peckover herself, *Peace and Goodwill* bypassed questions relating to the women's movement, such as the suffrage, and argued instead that women possessed the power and influence to work for peace and international arbitration, and should not think of putting off such work until other aims had been achieved. It was intended to be the journal of Wisbech LPA, but effectively became a focal point of the entire LPA movement, alongside Peckover herself and the six thousand-strong Wisbech LPA. *Peace and Goodwill* ceased publication on Peckover's death in 1931, and the Wisbech LPA was disbanded, despite the fact that membership levels remained at around five thousand people. Peckover herself was most active in the 1880s and 1890s, travelling to international congresses and involving herself with the work of the Peace Society, its women's Auxiliary, the International Peace Bureau, and the IAPA. The onset of rheumatism at the turn of the century meant that for the last thirty years of her life travel became increasingly difficult, and her activities were gradually restricted to producing her journal and maintaining the WLPA.

Existing literature on Peckover presents her as a marginal presence within the peace movement whose politics simply echoed those of the Peace Society. Jill Liddington has argued that Peckover lacked 'a sharp analysis of British imperialism', while Peter Brock claims that her opinions 'coincided more or less' with those of the Peace Society. Martin Ceadel notes that Peckover was 'astonishingly successful' in mobilising the LPA movement, yet barely mentions her work in a study of the British peace movement spanning over four hundred pages. Paul Laity acknowledges Peckover's criticisms of imperialism but on the whole presents her as conveying an 'optimistic Christian pacifism'.[7] While Peckover allied herself with the Peace Society more closely than most other female peace activists of this period, it is important to stress that on a number of significant issues she disagreed with its aims and methods. She was also critical of the expansionist British imperialism that was being practiced across the globe, and she publicly disagreed with the Peace Society on the question of how to protest against the second Anglo-Boer war.

Although Peckover's personal focus was strongly influenced by Christianity, she supported all other associations working for peace and arbitration regardless of their religious affiliation. In a list of peace societies of Europe and America published in *Peace and Goodwill* in 1885 she noted that although the associations listed did not all take a Christian, or even a religious basis, and some combined peace work with political or religious views that others would not support, they did all see 'the great need of working towards International Peace'.[8] She was adept at collaborating with a wide variety of peace workers, including the European radicals who were the object of the Peace Society's suspicion. The sole indication of any division between Peckover and republican nationalists on the continent came in the early 1900s, when it was proposed by Gaston Moch, a member of the republican ILPL, that the International Peace Bureau (IPB) pass a resolution on the 'Right of Legitimate Defence'. This right, as drafted by Moch, affirmed the right 'possessed by every nation . . . to have recourse to arms in order to safeguard its threatened interests'. This right 'results not from the nature of the claims put forward, but from the fact that the nation under consideration has shown itself ready to submit them to a tribunal or to an arbitrator, while the opposing nation has resorted to violence'. This resolution directly conflicted with the absolute pacifist rejection of the use of force even for defensive purposes. J. F. Green, the socialist secretary of the non-absolutist IAPA, warned Élie Ducommun, the secretary of the Bureau, that English and US pacifists were unlikely to subscribe to the resolution, and Peckover cautioned him that 'If the Peace Congresses . . . begin to justify or regulate war, how could we from our standpoint continue to be incorporated in the movement'.[9]

This exchange highlighted the divisions between some British and US pacifists, and the Europeans. The ILPL and its companion organisations aimed to create the conditions under which violence at an international level could be regulated or policed. Because democratic republics were seen as the ideal, it was necessary that state power be legitimised on a defensive level for their protection. This contradicted the Christian ideology of Peckover and the Peace Society, who held that the notion of legitimate defence effectively justified war and, importantly, preparations for war. By recognising that certain conflicts could be legitimate, the Bureau would acknowledge war as a system for settling disputes. Peckover warned Ducommun that the adoption of the resolution would split the membership and require the absolutists to resign. 'Of course', she remarked, 'we do not want to compel others to come up to our standard.'[10] The resolution failed, but the debate caused great concern to British absolutists and served to remind them that, in the context of the IPB, they were the weaker partners in a republican-dominated Continental movement.

Despite the conflicts over this resolution, Peckover was prepared to engage in work with non-absolutists. In 1893, after two years of deliberations, she decided to accept the position of honorary associate to Unione Lombarda, an Italian republican nationalist peace society.[11] Yet Peckover constituted the WLPA on specifically Christian grounds, and her LPA movement was unique in Britain in taking its stand 'definitely on the Christian principles of its Declaration' to which all members were asked to subscribe.[12] This was in contrast even to the Peace Society, which had regulations for the absolutism of its Executive Committee members but none for its wider membership, other than a broad commitment to be against war and in favour of peace. In addition,

Peckover did not expect the LPAs to work only with other Christians. Although she held to her Christian principles she was also one of the strongest advocates of cooperation between religious and secular pacifist groups, supporting what Thomas Kennedy has called 'collaborative pacifism'.[13] Indeed, Peckover deliberately marketed a great deal of her propaganda at pacifist organisations in general, rather than Christian pacifists specifically. She aimed to convert people to pacifism on the basis of the need for international commitment to peace and arbitration, rather than the unchristian nature of war, and was frequently critical of the fact that many clergymen did not advocate peace principles. *Peace and Goodwill* often carried articles, usually reprinted from other journals, which questioned the commitment of Christianity to peace.[14]

It was the regional aspect of Priscilla Peckover's peace work that brought her greatest success. In contrast to the Peace Society's women's auxiliary, the WLPA was immensely successful in recruiting members. When it was founded in 1879, it had 144 members. Within a year, this figure had risen to 723 men and women; by 1883, to approximately 2,400, and by 1890 it peaked at six thousand. The membership level remained the same at the turn of the century, and by the time of Peckover's death in 1931, it had declined only slightly, to just under five thousand. The remarkable growth in membership over the first few years of the WLPA can be seen in the fact that the population of Wisbech in 1891 was only about 9,300 residents.[15] Improbably, these statistics would make around two-thirds of the town's population LPA members in 1890.

While Peckover's local influence, and that of her family, was a key factor in generating so much support, it cannot be assumed that she pressured local people to join. She noted in 1902 that she was reluctant to consciously use her personal influence in order to gain subscribers, and recalled an incident in 1879 when a farmer's wife asked for one of the declaration books. The woman returned the book to Peckover a week later with the signatures of over fifty Wisbech tradesmen's wives, 'whom', Peckover remarked, 'I should have been too timid to ask – besides having a fear that they might perhaps sign only to please me – and I wanted real conviction'.[16] Although it is likely that Peckover would have held some influence over middle-class women in particular, the huge membership of the WLPA cannot be explained by this alone. The most likely explanation is that non-residents of Wisbech were recorded as members.

There are no definitive figures on how many of Wisbech LPA's members were local men and women, but there are some indications that the practice of subsuming members from other areas under the banner of Wisbech LPA was fairly common. By the mid-1890s, Wisbech LPA consisted of around eighty sub-branches, although how many members were needed to form a 'sub-branch' is unclear (it may have been as few as one or two). In 1887, the *Herald* noted that the WLPA's list of members 'included not only their own townsmen but also many from the surrounding villages and different parts of the country, where they were not strong enough to form associations of their own'. [17] As time went on, Wisbech LPA's huge membership may have consisted of members all over the world, who were either in isolation or formed into small groups who were unable to attract sufficient interest to establish a local branch. Even so, it is remarkable that membership numbers remained stable over the forty-year period from 1890 to 1931. Neither the Anglo-Boer war, nor the First World War, nor the demographic, social and economic changes that took place over this period had more than a minor impact on subscriptions.

As may be implied by the *Herald*'s statement that the WLPA attracted 'townsmen' from other areas, it existed as a women's organisation only in the early days of its existence. Peckover's canvassing soon produced a number of men who wished to be able to join. In response, the WLPA Committee prepared a 'more detailed' declaration based on that used by William Randal Cremer's Workmen's Peace Association, which Peckover reproduced in *Peace and Goodwill*. She followed this with the disclaimer that LPA work was done on a purely Christian basis, avoiding 'any party politics and denominational differences'. The wording for the original declaration was 'I believe all war to be contrary to the mind of Christ, who says: "Love your enemies," "Do good to them that hate you, &c." and am desirous to do what I can to further the cause of Peace.' Added to this, when the Men's Wisbech Local Peace Association was created, were three principles: 'To advocate the settlement of all International disputes by Arbitration and establishment of a High Court of Nations for that purpose'; 'To place before our fellow-countrymen the danger, immorality and expense of standing armies'; and finally, 'To at all times urge upon our Parliamentary Representatives, that in the interests of civilization and humanity, it is the duty of the Government of the United Kingdom, to take the initiative in promoting International Peace, by proposing a large, mutual and simultaneous reduction of all armed forces, with a view to their entire abolition.' The declaration then pledged members 'to use every constitutional means' to achieve these aims.[18] Significantly, the separate Men's and Women's Associations were short-lived as after only a few months they found it more productive to amalgamate. Although they remained separate at

Committee level, the Associations clearly found joint meetings to be more successful than segregated ones. The WLPA remained predominantly female in membership, however, and continued to be referred to as a 'Ladies' Peace Society'.[19] There was also considerable overlap between the LPA movement and the Ladies' Peace Auxiliary of the Peace Society, both of which were led by Peckover in the period following the split with the feminist WPAA in 1882 and prior to Ellen Robinson's period of leadership, which began in 1894.

The work of Wisbech LPA, which it advocated for LPAs in other regions, included circulating tracts as well as information. One of the earliest documents it produced contained instructions on 'How to form a Local Peace Association in your own neighbourhood', which was circulated for inclusion in journals such as the *Herald of Peace*, the *Englishwoman's Review* and *Women's Work*.[20] One of Peckover's aims for the LPA movement was for it to inspire other associations which would build themselves up to the strength of the WLPA in other parts of Britain and the world. However, the movement did not take off in this way in the long term. Certainly during the early stages of the WLPA, its growth inspired similar associations in Britain and small numbers of members from abroad. For shorter periods during the 1890s there were also bursts of interest in the LPA movement, usually spurred by the prospect of war, colonial conflicts, or treaties of arbitration. But on the whole, Peckover remained the driving force in the movement.

A key factor in Peckover's belief in the importance of a local movement was her conviction that the enrolment of members was most effectively done on a local basis, due to the 'large amount of personal explanation' of the principles of peace that was needed, in addition to the 'direct appeal to conscience and good sense'. This work, requiring 'earnestness', patience and leisure time was, she concluded, best done by ladies.[21] In addition to membership canvassing, this method could be used for gaining signatories to petitions. The focus was on encouraging people to understand the principles behind the work, and in this sense petitions had a dual purpose. Not only were they expected to influence the body to which they were presented, but they also had an educative function for their signatories. 'I have a great belief', Peckover said, 'in the educating power of a petition amongst the people asked to sign it. Every one has to have the thing explained, and even the most impatient has learnt something about the reality of the movement.'[22]

These ideas illustrate how Peckover expected women's organisations to work. She put aside ambitious movements for peace, such as work at Parliamentary, national or international levels, in favour of focusing upon her immediate locality. Thus the WLPA reached prospective members directly. In relying upon women's – or rather, ladies' – leisure time, Peckover expected that the most active women in this work would be middle class. Yet the membership figures for Wisbech were so high that there must have been a sizeable number of working-class men and women involved, if only as passive members. The level of involvement the Peckovers had with Wisbech Working Men's Club, and the peace lectures that were occasionally given there, suggest that there was some involvement of working-class men in the Wisbech LPA.[23] Information on working-class women is difficult to obtain, although there is some evidence that Peckover did philanthropic work for such women in and around Wisbech, and that she involved the working classes in her campaigns. In a speech to Leeds Women's Peace Auxiliary, she argued that the working classes were more likely than the middle classes to agree that killing was wrong, and that the middle classes tended to dispute 'plain abstract truths'. 'She had not', it was reported, 'found this among the working classes'. This is supported by a later comment on petitions, when she noted that 'The working classes sign very readily only needed to be asked & know what it means [sic]'.[24]

Despite her emphasis on the importance of regional work, Peckover was keen to situate the WLPA and the LPA movement more generally within the national Ladies' Auxiliary of the Peace Society. Addressing the Auxiliary's 1884 Annual Meeting, she called for a better organisation to form the centre of the work, because effectively the 'method and impetus' of the Auxiliary was coming from Wisbech during this period. She expressed her concern that Wisbech LPA was, as a result of its size, becoming the centre of the movement, 'to which', she said, 'it has no such pretensions'.[25]

Priscilla Peckover was Evangelical in her views, and much of her focus in peace arguments was upon Scripture, which she could recite at length and often used to illustrate her points during lectures. Her energy for reform, and the process of winning converts to the peace cause, marked her out as Evangelical in her methods. Yet, as Thomas Kennedy has argued, she 'was one of the earliest advocates of cooperation between religious and secular peace groups'.[26] She had been strongly influenced by the Olive Leaf Circles begun by Elihu Burritt, and viewed her LPA movement as a revival of this, adapted to the changed needs of the late nineteenth century. This can be seen most obviously in the subtitle of her journal, *Peace and Goodwill: A Sequel to the Olive Leaf,* and the statement in its first issue that LPA work was 'a revival, on a scale adapted to the present day, of that inaugurated and sustained by Elihu Burritt'.[27] The initial aims of Peckover's movement were to circulate information and details of new publications, and to provide a point of contact for existing organisations. In this sense, the LPAs were similar to the earlier Olive Leaf Circles in that they were regional in basis and dominated by religious argument. However, Peckover was prepared to go further than the Olive Leaf women in promoting the peace movement.

Priscilla Peckover was in many ways the embodiment of the type of woman member that the Peace Society preferred. She was silent on the question of women's rights, and espoused peace on the basis of the religious arguments that the Society encouraged from its women members. On being invited to give her first public speech in 1879, Peckover later wrote that she had found it 'a *formidable* proposal to one who had never appeared on a platform'. Even two decades later, in 1901, she lamented that Bertha von Suttner was unable to attend the Glasgow Peace Congress because she felt that, in being left to represent 'women' alone, she was 'somewhat beyond my ordinary sphere', and felt 'a certain timidity, lest through any incompleteness of understanding I should fail to do the best thing'.[28] Her method of approach fitted precisely with the Peace Society's ideas of women's sphere, and the work done by Wisbech LPA to strengthen the peace movement's links with religious ministers, Sunday Schools and provincial women was entirely in keeping with the Peace Society's expectations.

Peckover was celebrated within the *Herald* as an active peace worker in 1881, at a relatively early stage in her peace work, and in 1882, when she was elected a vice-president of the Ladies' Peace Auxiliary. In 1883, a separate section of the Peace Society's Annual Report was devoted to her work, and she was invited to join the Executive Committee in 1889.[29] Her refusal to take up this offer signals her determination to involve herself in the movement in a private and, as far as possible, a non-pioneering role. Her acceptance of a vice-presidency of the Society, which entailed involvement mainly as a figurehead, demonstrates that she preferred to take a passive role in the public sphere rather than to become an active formulator of policy within the Society. However, in private Peckover enjoyed a close relationship with the Executive Committee of the Peace Society: in 1888 she recommended the appointment of William Evans Darby to the Committee. Darby took the post of secretary after Henry Richard's death, and became the Society's most influential agent until his retirement from the post in 1915. The extent of Peckover's influence on Darby can be seen in the fact that he produced a biography of her in the early 1890s.[30]

As shown in chapter 4, in the early 1880s the women's Auxiliary to the Peace Society was in a state of crisis after the split occasioned by the birth of the IAPA. Priscilla Peckover's conversion to the movement and the meteoric effect which she had upon local membership in Wisbech provided a much-needed point of focus for the Society and its reformulated Auxiliary. The reasons for her complete acceptance within the Peace Society, which was, as we have seen, conservative with respect to women, are twofold. First, her views on peace were primarily Christian and Evangelical. She therefore met the Society's requirements as demonstrated during the formation of the Auxiliary in the 1870s. Second, she was reticent, to say the least, on women's roles and, more importantly, the women's movement itself.

Although Peckover was prepared to speak in public, and her production and dissemination of *Peace and Goodwill* over nearly a fifty-year period demonstrates a need for a public platform, this did not extend to involvement in the women's movement. Peckover did not publicly criticise feminist campaigns, remaining silent on the divisive matter of the suffrage, and she argued that women had influence as citizens, regardless of their position as non-voters. She emphasised that women had influence and power by virtue of their civil and limited political rights, and therefore they did have roles to play within the peace movement. In a piece written in 1885 about the beginnings of the LPA movement, she made it clear that her first attempt at organising a local association was 'among women only' because '[t]heir influence had been hitherto but little brought out, and the very gentleness of their nature might . . . predispose them to gather round the banner of Peace and Goodwill'.[31] Thus she employed the same gendered constructions regarding women's 'nature' that were used by many feminists.

Throughout her writings Peckover stressed the importance of unity in peace work between societies, and it seems to be implicit in such statements that she was as prepared to ally with feminist groups which supported peace as she was with any other pacifist society. The strands of the women's movement with which she became involved tended to be feminist in the very broadest sense, or focused specifically around social purity. She submitted instructions on how to form a LPA to the *Englishwoman's Review* in 1880, and joined her local Women's Liberal Association and the feminist social purity society, the Moral Reform Union. She was also present at a meeting on arbitration held by the International Council of Women in 1899.[32]

However, Peckover never became actively involved in feminist causes such as political reform. In a speech in 1884, she remarked that 'She was not one of those who wanted to bring women out in an unnatural position, but she urged them to use their influence in their homes and amongst their children – not to teach them the spirit of war and retaliation, but of peace.'[33] Even as the women's movement progressed in the period up to 1914, *Peace and Goodwill* avoided questions such as women's suffrage. In the post-war period when women were granted the vote, her journal had nothing to say on the matter. This is surprising if only because, as demonstrated in chapter 2, a prominent suffragist argument for peace over the fifty-year campaign for the franchise was the idea that women would not vote for war. Regardless of her views on the rights or wrongs of women's suffrage, this was an obvious argument for Peckover to use after it was granted. Yet the content and editorials of *Peace and Goodwill* were almost exactly the same as they had been during the peak of the LPA movement in the 1890s, containing nothing that was not directly related to the progress of the peace movement proper.

Peckover did, however, advocate women's involvement in the political process. In 1885, the WLPA distributed the Peace Society's 'Appeal to Electors', which urged voters to be aware of the position that their parliamentary candidates took on peace and arbitration.[34] That a predominantly female organisation should take this step links it in some ways to the methods of the Women's Liberal Associations (WLAs), in that women could educate themselves and publicly connect themselves with the political process. The LPA movement was also reminiscent of the WLAs in the stress that was placed upon house-to-house visiting and canvassing.[35] Thus while Peckover aimed to distance herself from the women's movement, she simultaneously founded her LPA movement on the (limited) power and influence of women. Her emphasis on women's ability to influence those around them undoubtedly originated from her privileged class position. As a wealthy, upper-middle-class woman, she could believe that 'in this free country we all have a political influence . . . which cannot fail to be felt by any Government'. She viewed the LPA movement as consisting of 'individual work', because '[e]ach individual counts for something as a portion of public opinion, and each may be a centre of public opinion'.[36] This approach to the individual as having power in their own right, regardless of their civil or political rights, borrowed heavily from both Quietist Quaker theology and from liberal thinking. Peckover's construction of the individual owed much to late Victorian understandings of democratic citizenship, the belief that individuals were 'free and equal and possessed of rights deriving from their innate capacities as human beings'.[37] In the mould of the Enlightenment, an ungendered discourse of the individual was employed that was based on the concept that the individual in question was in fact male. Yet Peckover's ideas were also based on the gender neutrality of Quaker theology, in which the concept of the 'Inner Light' in human beings gave rise to the idea that individuals could overcome the imposition of gender restrictions. This individualism was of course problematic in that it took little account of class differences, and it is significant that Peckover put forward such ideas while the lower-middle-class Ellen Robinson, who is discussed in the following chapter, adopted an openly feminist agenda.

Peckover's arguments regarding women were also occasionally inconsistent. At a peace meeting in the late 1880s, Peckover remarked: 'I used to think I am only a woman and have not much with [peace]. But I know better now . . . How much more should women do, now that they are emancipated!'[38] She implied that because women were able to see themselves as centres of public opinion and as part of the public sphere, they had in effect liberated themselves. Peckover also adopted arguments that connected women's subordination with war. In response to a refusal by the German police to allow women to join a peace society at Wiesbaden, she noted that 'It is a part of militarism to deny any political influence to the gentler sex. They may suffer but not protest.'[39] This argument is much closer than Peckover's other writings on women to the arguments put forward by the more feminist Ellen Robinson, or even to Florence Fenwick Miller in the *Woman's Signal* in the late 1890s, as discussed in chapter 2. There was an explicit connection made between militarism and the oppression of women.

These ideas were echoed at a later date by one of Peckover's nieces, Alexa, in an address to a meeting of Wisbech Women's Liberal Association, which was also attended by Peckover. Alexa offered criticisms of the second Anglo-Boer war that were similar to those put forward in *Peace and Goodwill,* and emphasised that obtaining the vote for the Uitlanders was not a sufficient reason to go to war, as 'even the women themselves were outside the suffrage in Britain'. She went on to say, to some laughter, that '[a]lthough they had no vote they would not go to war about it'.[40] The political activism of women was positioned against the actions of the government and the Uitlanders, with the suggestion that women were more civilised than both because they would not entertain the possibility of going to war over an issue of political rights. Although these sentiments came from Alexa Peckover, the close working relationship between the two (Alexa was also active in the WLPA) meant that her ideas and reasoning were not so different from those of Priscilla Peckover. A clear hierarchy was presented, with peace and justice carrying more weight than the political rights of any section of society, including women. While this undoubtedly set Peckover apart from the feminist movement, it can nonetheless be seen that in some circles she was active on behalf of women. She claimed the right for pacifist women to define their own place in society, and to take their own aims and concerns into the public sphere. During the 1895 dispute over the role of Women's Yearly Meeting of the Society of Friends, Peckover 'expressed regret that women's meetings were being given up in some places, and swamped in joint conferences'. Other Friends disputed the suggestion that women's contributions were 'swamped', arguing that 'it was a privilege for women Friends, and an added responsibility, to be invited to take part in the deliberations of the meeting as a whole, on an equal footing'.[41] Peckover was, it seems, a traditionalist and a separatist, but her arguments could also be progressive: separate meetings would protect women's input and ensure them a public voice. It could be argued that, although she differed in principle from some of the aims of the feminist movement, Peckover did nonetheless work for the improvement of women's position in society.

Despite her difficult relationship with feminism, Peckover remained an independent and, on occasion, radical voice within the peace movement. For example, on the outbreak of the second Anglo-Boer war, Peckover's WLPA Committee called a meeting at which it unanimously adopted two resolutions. Firstly, it protested against 'any such thing as warlike coercion of the Transvaal Government . . . [because] a war with this small and independent state would be a blot upon England's honour'. Secondly, it registered 'an emphatic protest' against suggestions made in the House of Lords to introduce compulsory service, which it regarded as 'embodying a gross interference with the liberty of the subject and with liberty of conscience'.[42]

Wisbech LPA took this step in the face of a decision by the Executive Committee of the Peace Society not to take any action against the war, on the grounds that 'it was not clear that any useful action could be taken'. The Committee ignored letters and communications urging it to protest from Priscilla Peckover, its own president Joseph Whitwell Pease, Miss Spence (secretary of the Lincoln LPA), and Princess Gabrielle Wiszniewska of France. Peckover's letter begged the Society to protest 'by memorializing the Government or otherwise in connection with the war'. Spence asked the Peace Society to take up the cause of the Transvaal Refugee Fund, and Wiszniewska forwarded an appeal for the Widows and Orphans of Boers for insertion in the *Herald*. The Committee decided that all of these measures were 'inexpedient' and beyond the scope of the Society.[43] It was not until March 1900 that a draft memorial to the

Prime Minister was prepared, and in February 1901 the Peace Society sent memorials calling for a pacific settlement of the war to the King and to the government.[44]

In response to the war, the *Herald* had reiterated the Peace Society's opposition to all war on the grounds that it was inconsistent with the spirit of Christianity, but crucially, it also stated that the temptation which 'lovers of Peace' felt to 'do something' to avert the horrors of war could only lead to 'mischief'. Any such action was, it believed, '[m]isdirected zeal', which could actually be harmful. The Committee reported that it had given much consideration to how 'action could be attempted with any prospect of success or possibility of usefulness', but felt that there was no point in undertaking efforts for peace which would not have some concrete result.[45] This can be contrasted with the work of the IAPA over the same period. On the outbreak of war, the IAPA took part in open-air meetings to publicise its opposition, while its chairman, Hodgson Pratt, was convinced even at the start of the conflict that the war could only be brought to an end if influential people were approached and convinced of the futility of the fighting. The IAPA also co-operated with the anti-war organisations that were set up during the conflict, particularly the Transvaal Committee and the South Africa Conciliation Committee.[46] In contrast, the Peace Society deliberately distanced itself from such bodies.

Like the IAPA, Peckover's journal *Peace and Goodwill* actively promoted the peace movement from the beginning of the hostilities. It gave detailed consideration to the causes of the war, followed by a critique of Britain's record in other parts of the empire, such as India, remarking that 'It is the truest form of patriotism to do our utmost to save our country from the crime and shame of an unjust war.'[47] This comment exemplifies the pacifist revision of patriotism. While the women's movement recast patriotism in a specifically feminist light, with women embodying the morality that could revitalise the nation, Peckover asserted that pacifism was the force which would be most progressive. If the 'truest form of patriotism' was the desire to avoid 'unjust' wars, then implicitly it was this stance that would most advance the cause of humanity and also the nation. While Peckover and the women discussed in chapter 2 utilised similar motifs, i.e. the recasting of patriotism as a service to a higher ideal than that of the nation, each based it on different criteria, using pacifism or middle-class womanhood respectively as the surest means of progress.

The contrast between the editorial policies of *Peace and Goodwill* and the *Herald* can be seen in the response to an address that was issued in early 1902 from two thousand German women, led by Countess Butler-Haimhausen, to the women of Great Britain. *Peace and Goodwill* published the address in full on its front page:

> We do not approach your country with hatred or prejudice, nor from any political or national consideration. We do not enquire whether in your opinion the war carried on by your Government in South Africa is a just or an unjust one. We approach you as fellow-creatures, as sisters, as children of the same civilisation.
>
> [. . .]
>
> We know that the best and noblest among you revolt against [these horrors] as we do . . . but for this very reason we conjure you therefore Raise your voice, and save the honour of your country, your husbands, brothers and sons. DO NOT DISDAIN THE JUDGEMENT, THE OUTCRY OF THE CONSCIENCE OF THE WHOLE WORLD.[48]

This was followed by an editorial comment by Peckover supporting the German women's argument and adding, with reference to the concentration camps run by the British army: 'Have we been culpably blind as to what our officers and men were learning to do amongst semi-armed uncivilised [*sic*] races?'

With respect to the same address, identical copies of which were forwarded to all peace organisations in Britain, the *Herald of Peace* carried on its front page a paragraph that tersely stated:

> Some of our friends abroad, who undoubtedly mean well and are really desirous of promoting Peace, defeat their own purpose by the manner and spirit of their attempt. We have received a document . . . with a request that we would give it publicity. We regret that the tone of the document makes this impossible; it would only produce the opposite effect to what is sought.[49]

Even the feminist *Englishwoman's Review* (under the editorship of Helen Blackburn and Antoinette Mackenzie) refused to publish Countess Butler-Haimhausen's appeal, on the grounds that it was 'based on an entire misunderstanding of the facts'.[50] This is but one example which highlights not only the extent of Peckover's anti-imperialism when compared to the Peace Society and the feminist *Review*, but also the impartiality with which she and many of the women involved in the LPA movement met international criticism of British aggression.

In 1901, Priscilla Peckover spoke of her pleasure that the Local Peace Association was showing a 'united front' regarding the war, while the Annual Report of 1901 showed that eight thousand tracts had been sent out by the WLPA in the preceding year. This is a slight increase on the figure for 1898–99 (7,400 tracts), but a decline from the figure for 1895, when around 12,800 tracts were sent to readers. The work of the LPA was being somewhat tested by the war and the prevailing jingoism, although its membership figures did not suffer to any great degree.[51] On the resolution of the war, Wisbech LPA sent a greeting to Louis Botha (an Afrikaner general active during the war), and to the Afrikaner people as a whole, in which they expressed their 'desire for the material and spiritual welfare of those with whom our country has so recently been engaged in deadly warfare'.[52]

As noted above, the Peckover family were a powerful presence in Wisbech, yet as Quakers, they were firmly opposed to war and to any action which might support or maintain it. In addition, the WLPA had a large local membership. What then took place in Wisbech when the Anglo-Boer war broke out? The Peckovers, with the aid of the Peace Society, had successfully resisted an earlier attempt to base a militia in the town.[53] Yet during the war, Wisbech did send volunteer corps to South Africa. Their departure was marked by celebrations and public send-offs, though the local liberal newspaper, the *Advertiser*, reported these in muted fashion, noting that at the end of the day, the war was not desirable. Yet in order to justify the posting of local men to a distant war, the press had to accept the legitimacy of the battle to some degree.[54]

The *Advertiser* remained balanced in its approach throughout the war, including a discussion of the anti-war protests of Princess Wiszniewska in Paris and acknowledging the British refusal to arbitrate. It also published an appeal to the Queen from Dutch men and reviewed Alice M. Richardson's *A Quaker View of the War*. While noting hostile British responses to an appeal for peace from Swiss women, the *Advertiser* reprinted the Swiss women's reply in a neutral tone (in contrast to the *Englishwoman's Review*, which had dismissed it as inflammatory).[55] Although the Peckovers had no direct influence over the *Advertiser*, the fact that the wealthiest and most prominent family in Wisbech were not only Quakers but active pacifists must have been influential in this matter. In 1900, Peckover wrote to Élie Ducommun, secretary of the International Peace Bureau, noting that the WLPA's peace work during the war had been 'not without some result[,] locally at least'.[56] Throughout the war, Peckover's Local Peace Association movement was more persistent as a campaigning organisation than its parent body, the Peace Society, and less concerned about causing offence to pro-war sympathisers. This is perhaps because its profile was lower, as both a newer, predominantly female organisation, and one with a powerful local base.

In conclusion, Peckover established a regional movement that, while not explicitly feminist, was significant for the overall development of pacifist feminism. Her work within both the regional WLPA and the international peace movement established her among her pacifist colleagues as a woman who was competent in national and international campaigns. Although her traditionalism meant that she preferred to remain in the background of the peace movement rather than to constitute its public face, she did nonetheless demonstrate to pacifist men that women could make a useful contribution to imperial and international questions. Her Evangelical pacifism and avoidance of feminist issues gave rise to a professedly apolitical stance which could be utilised by many non-feminist women to argue that peace was a 'women's issue'.

Peckover eschewed direct control of the national Ladies' Peace Auxiliary, focusing instead on her own local movement and preferring it to be seen as one regional branch among many. But her energies were such that this movement rapidly eclipsed the national body, with the effect that Peckover became dominant in the movement despite her best efforts to encourage work among women elsewhere. This decentralised the power that had previously been held by the two-hundred-strong, London-based women's Auxiliary, and one consequence of this was that the Peace Society found it much more difficult to control the Auxiliary at either national or regional levels. The lack of conflict between the Peace Society and its Ladies' Auxiliary during this period is surely due to the fact that Peckover's aims were in many respects similar to those of the Peace Society.

Peckover worked primarily at a local level, but she showed a strong commitment to international communication and co-operation, establishing contact with many individuals across the world who affiliated themselves to her Local Peace Association. She established herself as a prominent voice of anti-imperialist, absolutist pacifism, but in practice she devoted much of her time and energy to collaborating with non-absolutist organisations. By the turn of the century, she was one of the best-known and most highly respected women in the British peace movement. Only her colleague, Ellen Robinson, surpassed her in terms of her level of activism in the British women's peace movement.

Notes

1 *Peace and Goodwill* (hereafter *P&G*) (16 October 1899), p. 97.
2 Walkowitz, *Prostitution and Victorian Society*, ch. 7.
3 Bland, *Banishing the Beast*, ch. 1.

4   *Dictionary of Quaker Biography* (hereafter *DQB*), Library, Friends' House, London; Thomas C. Kennedy, 'Priscilla Hannah Peckover', in Josephson (ed.), *BDMPL*, pp. 736–8; *Eastern Daily Press* (11 September 1931) in *P&G* (15 October 1931), pp. 101, 108–10.

5   P. H. Peckover, *Incidents in the Rise and Progress of Wisbech Peace Association* (Wisbech: W. Poyser, 1906), p. 2.

6   *P&G* (April 1882), p. 4.

7   Liddington, *Long Road to Greenham*, p. 28; Peter Brock, *The Quaker Peace Testimony, 1660–1914* (York: Sessions Book Trust, 1990), pp. 290–1; Ceadel, *Semi-detached Idealists*, p. 114; Laity, *British Peace Movement*, p. 118.

8   *P&G* (15 October 1885), p. 221.

9   Gaston Moch, transl. by J. F. Green, May 1910, Document 4, Box 193; P. H. Peckover to Élie Ducommun, 5 October 1903, Document 3, Box 42, IPB 1892–1914, International Peace Movement, League of Nations Archives, United Nations Library, Geneva, Switzerland (hereafter IPB).

10 P. H. Peckover to Mlle Montaudon, 5 October 1910, Document 4, Box 193; P. H. Peckover to Mlle Montaudon, 5 July 1910, Document 3, Box 42; see also P. H. Peckover to Élie Ducommun, 23 March 1904, Document 3, Box 93, IPB.

11 P. H. Peckover to Captain Siccardi, 21 March 1891, WLPA, Box 4, Folder 3, Swarthmore College Peace Collection, microfilm copy in Wisbech Public Library, Wisbech, Cambridgeshire; *P&G* (15 July 1893), p. 211.

12 *P&G* (15 July 1898), p. 17.

13 Kennedy, 'Priscilla Peckover', in Josephson (ed.), *BDMPL*, p. 737.

14 See for example *P&G* (15 July 1886), p. 26.

15 Frederic John Gardiner, *History of Wisbech and Neighbourhood, 1848–1898* (Wisbech: Gardiner and Co., 1898), p. 477.

16 Peckover, *Incidents in the Rise and Progress*, p. 4.

17 *Herald* (1 February 1887), p. 174.

18 *P&G* (April 1882), pp. 3–4.

19 *Ibid.* (14 July 1883), p. 75; *Herald*, (1 July 1886), p. 90; (1 April 1901), p. 48.

20 *P&G* (April 1882), p. 4; *Review* (15 June 1880), pp. 275–6; *Herald* (2 August 1880), p. 116; (1 November 1882), p. 148. The *Women's Work* was probably the *Englishwoman's Year Book: The Year Book of Women's Work*, edited by Louisa Hubbard.

21 *Herald* (1 January 1880), p. 4.

22 P. H. Peckover to F. Bajer, 13 September 1892, Document 2, Box 42, IPB.

23 *Herald* (2 July 1883), p. 253; (1 March 1888), p. 39; (1 March 1894), p. 27.

24 *Ibid.* (1 February 1880), p. 31; P. H. Peckover to Élie Ducommun, 26 January 1893, Document 1, Box 222, IPB.

25 *P&G* (15 April 1885), p. 186; *Herald* (1 July 1884), p. 83.

26 Kennedy, 'Priscilla Peckover', in Josephson (ed.), *BDMPL*, p. 737.

27 *P&G* (April 1882), p. 1.

28 *Herald* (2 June 1879), p. 264; Peckover, *Incidents in the Rise and Progress*, p. 6; P. H. Peckover to Bertha von Suttner, 4 September 1901, Box 25, Bertha von Suttner Correspondence, Fried-Suttner Papers, International Peace Movement, League of Nations Archives, United Nations Library, Geneva, Switzerland. Emphasis in original.

29 *Herald* (1 June 1881), p. 238; (2 October 1882), p. 136; (1 June 1883), p. 238.

30 *Ibid.* (April–June 1954), p. 2; P. H. Peckover to Élie Ducommun, 25 March 1899, Document 12, Box 162, IPB.

31 *P&G* (15 July 1885), p. 204.

32 P. H. Peckover to Élie Ducommun, 5 April 1899, Document 3, Box 42, IPB.

33 *Herald* (1 May 1884), p. 56.

34 *P&G* (15 October 1885), p. 217.

35 Linda Walker, 'Party political women: a comparative study of Liberal women and the Primrose League, 1890–1914', in Jane Rendall (ed.), *Equal or Different: Women's Politics, 1800–1914* (Oxford: Basil Blackwell, 1987), p. 182.

36 *P&G* (April 1882), p. 4; cutting, n.d. [Wisbech newspaper], enclosed in letter from P. H. Peckover to Élie Ducommun, 15 June 1893, Document 2, Box 71, IPB.

37 Richard Bellamy, *Liberalism and Modern Society*, p. 13.

38 *WPP* (2 March 1889), p. 6.

39 *P&G* (15 April 1893), p. 195.

40 *Supplement to the Wisbech Advertiser* (14 February 1900), p. 3.

41 *Friend* (31 May 1895), p. 358.

42 *Herald* (2 October 1899), p. 288.

43 Peace Society Minute Book, 11 August 1899, 20 October 1899, 17 November 1899, 15 December 1899, 19 January 1900, 16 February 1900, PSA; Kirkby, *Men of Business*, p. 124.

44 Peace Society Minute Book, 16 March 1900, 1 February 1901, PSA.

45 *Herald* (1 March 1900), p. 30.

46 Pamphlet for a Trafalgar Square Demonstration, 'Protest of the men and women of London against war with the Transvaal Republic', 24 September 1899, Document 1, Box 200, IPB.

47 *P&G* (16 October 1899), p. 97.

48 *Ibid.* (15 January 1902), p. 241. Square brackets and all capitals in original.

49 *Herald* (1 February 1902), p. 185.

50 *Review* (15 April 1902), p. 119.

51 *Herald* (1 April 1901), pp. 47–8; WLPA Sixteenth Annual Report, Document 2, Box 120, IPB.

52 *Herald* (1 October 1902), p. 303.

53 *Hertfordshire and Cambridgeshire Reporter*, n.d., enclosed in letter from P. H. Peckover to Élie Ducommun, 24 February 1897, Document 2, Box 121, IPB; *Herald* (1 April 1896), p. 55.

54 *Isle of Ely and Wisbech Advertiser* (8 November 1899), p. 3.

55 *Ibid.* (30 August 1899), pp. 3, 5; (14 February 1900), p. 5; (14 May 1902), p. 6; *Review* (15 January 1902), p. 47.

56 P. H. Peckover to Élie Ducommun, 5 January 1900, Document 3, Box 42, IPB.

6

Ellen Robinson: ' "United action" in Continental politics'[1]

I N LATE 1894, Priscilla Peckover handed the Ladies' Peace Auxiliary and the Local Peace Association movement over to Ellen Robinson, a fellow Quaker and long-standing colleague in the peace movement. Robinson reorganised the Auxiliary and renamed it the Peace Union, and began to work for the establishment of a union of women's peace societies across Europe and North America. This union, despite the Peace Society's reservations in relation to the IPB about linking itself with European movements, received notice in the *Herald* for its 'truly international and widely useful' work.[2]

Ellen Robinson was, like Priscilla Peckover, raised as a Quaker and came to peace work in her forties. She was notably more feminist in her politics, and spent much of her time and energy lecturing on peace to working-class men across Britain. Like Peckover, in the 1880s she established a local peace organisation, the Liverpool and Birkenhead Women's Peace and Arbitration Society (LBWPAS) which despite its name was, like Peckover's WLPA, open to both men and women. Her politics were more advanced than Peckover in that she had a strong sympathy with and interest in socialism, and a clearly defined commitment to feminism. Although both women were personally committed to absolute pacifism, they worked closely with non-absolutists in Britain and abroad.

Miss Ellen Robinson (1840–1912) was born in Derby, and raised in Liverpool. Her father was a provision merchant, and she was educated at, among other places, a Moravian school in Germany. She worked during her twenties and thirties as a private tutor, teacher and schoolmistress, and in the late 1870s opened a girls' boarding school in Liverpool with her sister, Louisa.[3] Few details remain of Ellen Robinson's family background, her early activities, or how she was drawn into peace work. She was recorded as a Quaker minister in 1885 at the age of forty-five, when she retired from her boarding school and began to give addresses on peace, at first mainly to schools and Sunday Schools. Her experience as a teacher greatly augmented her public speaking skills. Mary Lamley Cooke noted after Robinson's death in 1912 that her teaching experience, 'besides its own value, was specially calculated to develop her powers of clear thought and lucid expression, and to strengthen and enrich the faculty of sympathetic insight into the minds of others'.[4]

Robinson's first speeches were organised through the Liverpool Peace Society, a regional branch of the Peace Society. In 1885 she founded the LBWPAS as an independent and non-absolutist peace organisation, which maintained unofficial links with Peckover's LPA movement, the Liverpool Peace Society, and the central Peace Society. In addition to these societies, Robinson became involved in the work of the International Arbitration and Peace Association, the International Peace Bureau and of course the Society of Friends. She was particularly active in the campaign against the Anglo-Boer war, joining the Aborigines' Protection Society and serving on the Friends' South African Relief Fund Committee, as well as addressing meetings with the humanitarian Emily Hobhouse.[5] Robinson was involved to a limited degree in labour politics, for example, in the Adult School movement run by William Randal Cremer, and was a member of the Women's Liberal Federation.[6] During the 1890s she was a key figure in encouraging the passing of pacifist resolutions by WLA branches.[7] She also strengthened the peace movement's connections with the British Women's Temperance Association and the Labour Church. After a heart attack in 1907, Robinson found it necessary to restrict her work and turned for the remainder of her life to local politics, standing unsuccessfully as a Liberal candidate for Liverpool City Council in 1907 and being elected in 1908 onto the West Derby, Liverpool Board of Guardians.[8]

The LBWPAS, which Robinson founded with a small group of Liberal women, came into existence just a few years after Peckover's LPA movement, in late 1885. The links between Robinson and Peckover were already established, and Peckover addressed the LBWPAS's inaugural meeting. Likewise, Robinson became active in the LPA movement, helping to circulate literature among LPAs in the north of England and speaking at the Ladies' Peace Auxiliary's annual meeting.[9] In contrast to the WLPA, however, the LBWPAS remained a relatively small organisation. It had 290 men and women members in 1894, most of whom were middle-class radicals, including local clergymen and philanthropists. There was some overlap of membership with the Women's

Liberal Federation and the suffrage movement.[10] Despite this highly politicised base, in the early years much of its work was focused upon promoting peace among the clergy, schoolchildren and other (middle-class) women. Robinson was one of the few who preached on peace to working-class men.[11]

The work of the LBWPAS was regularly reported in both the *Herald of Peace* and *Peace and Goodwill*, but despite this, it never formally affiliated to either the Peace Society or the LPA movement. Importantly, it did not make the absolutist declaration against '*all* war' a condition of membership, unlike Peckover's organisation and the Executive Committee of the Peace Society, nor did it advocate the abolition of the army or navy. In fact, its aim was solely to influence public opinion against war.[12] This is despite the fact that many of its most active members were Quakers. Its president, Frances Thompson (1840–1926), was a Friend and, with Robinson, constituted the driving force behind the LBWPAS. She had been educated at the Mount School, York, and had known Ellen Robinson through the Liverpool Meeting since her youth. Thompson spent much of her adulthood nursing her elderly mother, on whose death in 1895 she moved from Liverpool to Birkenhead to live with an unmarried brother. Like Robinson, she was a vocal supporter of the new liberal Quaker theology, in particular the work of John Wilhelm Rowntree. She remained active on a local rather than a national level, and in 1899 she refused an offer by the Peace Society to appoint her a vice-president.[13] Her work, however, complemented that of Ellen Robinson, who, in addition to establishing the LBWPAS, focused on national and international peace campaigns.

The fact that both Robinson and Peckover's first work was done locally suggests that their approach differed significantly from the men's peace movements of this period. Both the Peace Society and the IAPA were founded as national societies, which later established auxiliaries across the country and, in the case of the IAPA, across Europe. But Peckover and Robinson were concerned with politics that began in the regions, aiming to change public opinion in their immediate environments in the hope that the impact of their work would then be felt on a wider scale. The social circumstances of both, particularly their status as unmarried women, tied them to their birth families and regions of origin. In addition to these regional ties, both Peckover and Robinson undertook national and international peace work during their careers, but perhaps because of their provincial status, they have often been represented in the secondary literature on the peace movement as little more than appendages to pacifist men. They have been linked with the

Peace Society in particular because of their personal perspectives of Quaker-influenced, Christian pacifism. As a result, the features that distinguished them from the central national and international organisations have been overlooked. Both women had strong opinions on peace issues, and struggled to make these heard within the Peace Society, the IAPA and the IPB. Ellen Robinson's relations with the Peace Society are particularly illuminating, as her feminist politics made her a more problematic ally than the more traditionalist Peckover.

From the establishment of the Ladies' Peace Auxiliary in the 1870s, it was clear that the Peace Society encouraged women to oppose war on primarily religious grounds, and that it sought to regulate and constrain its connections to the feminist movement and those who were active within it. Although the Peace Society's attitude to women's involvement began to improve with the appointment of William Evans Darby as Secretary, these changes occurred largely as a result of the work of individual women such as Robinson and Peckover. As a Quaker, an absolute pacifist and an eloquent and persuasive speaker, Robinson met the Peace Society's expectations of its women members, yet it is significant that the Society did not shy away from public involvement with her given that she held feminist principles. In 1890, Robinson became the first woman to address the Peace Society's annual meeting and the *Herald* announced that it was 'an innovation on previous arrangements . . . but the experience of this year['s meeting] will well warrant a resort to the ladies' help, in this direction, on similar occasions in future'.[14] Robinson was not at this stage invited to become a vice-president of the Society, like Peckover, Sarah Pease and Mrs Henry Richard, who could boast of prominent family connections. Yet the Society's acceptance of Robinson, who was active as a feminist, was a clear indication of change within the Peace Society.

Robinson's internationalism and her willingness to challenge the Peace Society's decisions can be seen in a difference of opinion that took place between Robinson and the Peace Society in 1892 over the formation of the International Peace Bureau. When the Peace Society publicly opposed the formation of the Bureau, Ellen Robinson entered into debate with the Society over their decision in the pages of the *Herald*. She argued that the Bureau was necessary as an information centre for the International Congresses, and for 'united action' between peace societies of different nations. The editor of the *Herald* responded that 'the majority of those present' at the meeting when the IPB was proposed 'were foreigners, and little acquainted with the work of the existing British and American Peace Societies, who are already performing the functions of a Bureau'. The key problem for the Peace Society, as a supposedly non-political association, was the potentially political nature of the Bureau and of some of the associations that would affiliate to it. While wishing to co-operate with such organisations, the Executive Committee deemed itself 'unable to place itself unreservedly at the mercy of "united action" [Robinson's phrase] in Continental politics, in which it would have but a minor voice, and of which it might not approve', given the *advanced* political views' of the International League of Peace and Liberty.[15] Affiliation with Europe – though not with America – was a problematic question for the Peace Society, but not for activists such as Robinson who believed collaboration to be more important than control.

When the Peace Society's Ladies' Peace Auxiliary was reorganised and transferred to Ellen Robinson in 1894, she immediately began to explore the possibilities for making the new Peace Union more international in its focus. Robinson had in fact put the proposal to reorganise the Auxiliary to Priscilla Peckover, who agreed to the transfer and supported Robinson's idea for a Union that would promote international expressions of goodwill and 'closer friendship between the . . . nations'.[16] Peckover's LPA movement had already extended its peace message to individuals abroad, but Robinson sought to continue this at an organisational level.

Robinson's international efforts began in France. In the spring of 1895, she took a letter to Marie Goegg's Paris-based La Solidarité, appealing on behalf of the British Peace Union for French women to join in the cause of peace and international arbitration. Goegg was a republican nationalist and a feminist – she was nicknamed 'pétroleuse', after the women incendiaries of the Paris Commune – and from 1868 she had been secretary of the ILPL, the very organisation that the Peace Society had denounced as too 'advanced'.[17] Robinson also met Eugénie Potonié-Pierre, co-founder of La Solidarité. Potonié-Pierre was also a radical republican, an internationalist and a feminist, and regularly berated the socialist movement for ignoring women's rights. She recognised the connections between women's rights and international politics, calling directly for disarmament during the 1890s when bodies such as the IPB had more pragmatic goals in sight, and she consistently argued that the cost of maintaining armaments was the major cause of women's oppression.[18] After meetings between Ellen Robinson and La Solidarité's republican feminists, the Women's International Peace Union (WIPU) was constituted. Over the following twelve months, women in the US, Italy, Holland, Belgium, Germany, Denmark and Switzerland heard of and joined the Union, forming branches in their own nations.[19]

In April 1896, as branches were formed in New Zealand, Sweden and Portugal, Robinson issued an appeal to all branches of the Union in which she requested them to enlist the support of Women's Associations within their respective countries, because 'societies working for the equality of the sexes can surely be brought to see that the war system necessarily leads to an inferior position for women . . . When justice is substituted for violence, then the qualities and capabilities of women will have their due appreciation in the State, and there will no longer be unequal laws for the sexes.'[20] She outlined arguments with which they could persuade humanitarian associations, such as the Red Cross, to support the Peace Union. She did likewise for societies active in rescue work (for 'fallen' women and girls), temperance societies, those working to improve women's industrial position, and women who were members of Christian Churches. The range of her argument is perhaps the clearest indication of the scope of Ellen Robinson's feminist approach to the case for international peace and arbitration.

Robinson's appeal considered the economic aspects of war, arguing that both men and women suffered financially from the cost of war and the heavy taxation it incurred. Women's inequality in paid work was highlighted with the argument that one of the reasons women were paid less was because, as they did not fight, they were thought to be physically weaker than men. The reluctance of governments to legislate against intemperance was, she argued, due to the high tax revenues that were needed to keep the war system in operation. The 'moral degradation of women' (prostitution) occurred on a greater scale in any town where there were military barracks situated, and this, she stated, was another evil that was implicitly sanctioned by governments in order to maintain standing armies. Humanitarian societies such as the Red Cross existed to alleviate the suffering of soldiers in war, and it was therefore logical, Robinson argued, for such societies to oppose war on the grounds that prevention is preferable to cure. It was only towards the end of her appeal that she turned to Christianity. 'Women who are members of Christian Churches ought not to need to be convinced that Christianity is opposed to war. Christianity is a religion of righteousness and love.'[21] Every cause for the social or political advancement of society within which women were involved could, from this perspective, be compatible with the advocacy of peace principles. Ellen Robinson sought to bring this message to as many women as possible through speaking to a wide range of audiences, including branch meetings of the Women's Liberal Associations and the British Women's Temperance Association.[22]

The effect of this activity was to subtly reposition the Peace Society's Auxiliary. While it had continued as an Evangelical movement under Peckover's secretaryship, Robinson transformed it into an international union, and distanced it from its Evangelical context by focusing more upon women and their political or philanthropic interests. By doing this without specifically altering the policy of the Auxiliary, she managed to keep it allied to the Peace Society while vastly widening the scope of its work. Even the *Herald of Peace*, which had been extremely critical of the International Peace Bureau and was reluctant to involve itself in European peace work, praised Robinson for her 'truly international' work, and appointed her a vice-president of the Society in 1896.[23]

Although she co-operated with the Peace Society, Ellen Robinson distanced her peace work from it by establishing the LBWPAS as an independent organisation and by challenging the Peace Society's attitude to the European peace movement. She also undertook campaigns against the Anglo-Boer war in concert with other organisations, such as the Society of Friends, the South Africa Conciliation Committee and the Women's Liberal Federation (WLF). The WLF emerged during the war as an outspoken opponent of British intervention in South Africa: even before the outbreak of hostilities a number of WLAs publicly called for peaceful settlement of the dispute, and later, dozens of local branches actively campaigned against the war. Prominent WLF anti-war campaigners included Mrs Stewart Brown and Kate Ryley of the LBWPAS, as well as Mrs W. P. Byles, Mary Priestman and Sarah Sheldon Amos.[24]

Like the WLF and the IAPA, Ellen Robinson organised protest meetings against the Anglo-Boer war in the hope of changing public opinion, if not government policy. She addressed a large anti-war demonstration in Liverpool in January 1900, which was attended by representatives of thirty WLA branches. The meeting unanimously carried a resolution 'which denounced Mr. Chamberlain in the most uncompromising way'. Other speakers on this occasion were WLF members Mrs Stewart Brown, Mrs W. P. Byles and Mrs Leonard Hobhouse, and the socialist feminist Isabella Ford. Ellen Robinson also brought a greeting from this demonstration to the Peace Congress of 1900.[25] The WLF's annual meeting in June 1900 provided another forum in which members could speak out against the war, and Ellen Robinson again proposed a resolution, this time emphasising the desirability of arbitration. This meeting was also addressed by Lady Carlisle and Emily Hobhouse, and (again) Mrs W. P. Byles and Isabella Ford.[26] Ford was an active campaigner against the war and frequently attended WLF meetings, though her political allegiance lay with the Independent Labour Party (ILP) rather than the Liberals. Indeed, June Hannam notes that Ford was careful to emphasise that she attended WLF meetings as a guest, rather than a member. At the annual meeting Ford put forward the distinctively socialist analysis that the war was the product of a 'commercial spirit', and the result of it would be that 'our capitalism would now find a home in the Boer States, as well as our militarism and all the splendours of our civilisation'.[27] Although the ILP tended to view imperialist wars as a product of capitalism, it also frequently relied upon anti-war arguments that emphasised Christian and pacifist ideas alongside its socialist ideology. This did not mean, however, that its socialist analysis was not a crucial element in its opposition to war. In an exchange in the pages of the *Labour Leader* in 1901, Hodgson Pratt attempted to convince Keir Hardie that a mass movement for peace was required to bring an end to the war. Hardie retorted that it was 'absurd . . . to expect peace among *brothers* who *exploit* each other!'[28]

The Anglo-Boer war confirmed Ellen Robinson's worst fears about British imperialism by demonstrating that it was motivated by militarism rather than any spirit of Christianity or civilisation. The war also highlighted the weakness of the peace movement in Britain. The failure or refusal to combine methods and resources among the Peace Society, the Peace Union, the IAPA and the Society of Friends meant that as a whole, they were powerless to combat the aggressive spirit that was dominant during the war. Robinson's commitment to collaborative work was only strengthened by this experience, as can be seen from her work with the IPB. Despite its role as a co-ordinating body, the IPB was on occasion an instrument of such conflict itself. After a difficult Peace Congress in Glasgow in 1901, at which a number of Dutch delegates expressed dismay at having to travel to Britain to discuss principles of peace and arbitration, the Bureau provoked further controversy and disagreement among its members by its choice of location for the tenth Congress, in 1902.[29] At the invitation of Prince Albert I of Monaco, it was suggested that the IPB hold the annual Congress in Monte Carlo, and that it should take place at Easter, rather than the usual autumn meeting. This was strongly supported by the republicans Gaston Moch and Charles Richet, who had close personal connections with the Prince and stood to gain personally from closer collaboration with him. The Prince's invitation was linked to his desire to establish an International Peace Institute in Monaco, with Moch as president. This was successfully done during the Congress, and the ample educational and bibliographic resources it provided soon surpassed anything the IPB could afford.[30]

Yet the suggestion that the Universal Peace Congress should take place in a principality known for its gambling, and that the IPB should change the timing of the Congress so as to fit in with the Prince's offer, caused some offence among various societies affiliated to the IPB. Prince Albert's links to Monaco's gambling interests were particularly strong because it was his own father, Charles III, who had overseen the founding of the casino in 1868. Arguments against holding the Congress in Monaco were forthcoming from societies in Britain, the Netherlands, Italy, Germany and the USA. William Evans Darby and the Peace Society objected to the suggestion at the earliest opportunity, but for the first time their position was supported by the other British members of the IPB. Ellen Robinson voted against the location and the timing of the Monaco Congress, as did Isaac Sharp and J. G. Alexander of the Society of Friends, and Hodgson Pratt of the IAPA. Ducommun and the 'advanced' members of the IPB Committee foresaw the possibility of problems, however, and manipulated the terms for the vote. They stated in the circular outlining the proposition that those who did not respond would be counted as having voted in favour of Monaco. Thus, in order for the election to go *against* Monaco, it was necessary to outnumber those voting yes and those whose votes were not received. The final result was eight votes in favour and eight against, with one notified abstention, two replies refusing to make the choice, and a total of seven Committee members who had failed to respond. Under the IPB Committee's voting system, this put the motion for Monaco at fifteen votes to eight.

There were of course complaints made to the IPB not only on the grounds that Monaco was a principality built upon gambling, but also because of objections to the way in which the IPB had arranged the vote. In addition to disputes over the counting method, it was argued that a postal vote had prevented those opposed to Monaco from making their reasons heard. William Evans Darby sent a long, formal letter to Élie Ducommun, the IPB secretary, detailing his objections regarding Monaco and the IPB's actions. Referring to the vote, he said: 'there is such a thing as the rights of the minority'. Those who had carried the decision 'by mere force of numbers . . . have imperilled the cordial relations between the friends of International Peace'.[31] Ellen Robinson made a concerted effort to heal the rift that had developed between some British IPB members and the central Committee. Like other members, she proposed that they should all abandon the 1902 Congress and let the conflicts blow over, because if half of the membership proceeded with the Monaco meeting it would invite further division. She wrote to Élie Ducommun that 'We are so sorry to act in opposition to some of our colleagues but the English societies can not take part in . . . [a Congress] held at Monaco under the auspices of its Prince.' It would be, she argued, 'most injurious to our cause', because '[t]hose who support us, are those who advocate most moral causes, and who are especially opposed to gambling at home & abroad'. Those opposed included, of course, members of the Society of Friends. Robinson went on to state that: 'There is also some annoyance felt at the Congress being hurried on for the very purpose of being held at a place to which so much objection is taken.' Allowing divisions within the peace movement to become public would also, she argued, be damaging: 'Will it not necessarily injure the influence of the Peace Congress if several important countries openly abstain from taking part in it? and will not the wisdom & judgment of the Berne Bureau be called in question by the public?'[32] Robinson and Darby's letters made no difference, and the Congress went ahead at Monaco. Rather than miss it, the IAPA decided to attend, while Priscilla Peckover's WLPA appointed the Danish peace activist Frederic Bajer (who had voted in favour of going to Monaco) as their delegate. Many other British Committee members decided that they could not attend the Congress, including Ellen Robinson and the LBWPAS, the Society of Friends and the Peace Society. Afterwards, however, business largely returned to normal. Perhaps what is most surprising is that the decision to override the wishes of a significant minority by taking the Congress to Monaco did not cause more problems than this. The following year, decisions regarding the next venue were taken as normal, and the conflict was overcome.

Throughout the 1890s there were frequent and serious disputes between Darby, the secretary of the Peace Society, and members of the IPB, including its secretary Élie Ducommun. Just a year after the IPB was founded, Darby accused Ducommun of having been 'persistently unjust and unfair to the Peace Society'. Ducommun believed – as did Hodgson Pratt of the IAPA – that Darby's 'extraordinary animosity' to the IPB suggested that he had never intended to support it.[33] In contrast, when Peckover or Robinson opposed a measure taken by the IPB the debate was invariably conducted in conciliatory but clearly expressed terms. Two factors marked Peckover and Robinson's approach as distinct from that of the Peace Society. The most important of these was the existence of prevailing gendered norms of behaviour, in which middle-class women strenuously avoided any confrontation that might imply aggressiveness or a lack of femininity. Yet Peckover and Robinson also upheld gendered ideals of women's moral mission, therefore when they disagreed with prominent male pacifists, they did so on matters of principle. The second factor must be the context of the movement in which these two women were involved. Both were acutely aware of the importance of peace and arbitration and carried this into their personal dealings as well as their public arguments. On one occasion of disagreement, for example, Robinson wrote to Ducommun that 'je n'aimerais pas qu'on penserait que dans une Union pour le Paix, on se dispute!' [I would not like it to be thought that in a Peace Union, we could quarrel!].[34]

In the context of both Quaker theology and domestic ideology, such constraints on women's free expression were justified by popularly held concepts of inner peace. The idea of the 'Inner Light' in Quakerism made an implicit connection between God, the soul, and the self, implying that through the 'light' or 'peace' that resides within, the individual can also guide others to discover their own Inner Light. Similarly, Victorian ideology of the middle-class woman as the 'angel in the house' constructed an ideal in which women were represented as more moral than men because of their seclusion from public life. They could, therefore, be an influence for good on their husbands and children. The techniques adopted by Peckover and Robinson facilitated international work as the women's peace movements in Britain quickly expanded and made useful contacts abroad, while the Peace Society became increasingly isolated and indeed began to decline in power and influence. Although Ellen Robinson challenged both the Peace Society and international organisations such as the IPB when she disagreed with its decisions, the guiding principle behind much of her work was the need for co-operation and collaboration, both nationally and internationally and between absolutists and non-absolutists.

Robinson was also active within the Society of Friends, and involved in decisions made over the status of Women's Yearly Meeting. While Priscilla Peckover argued for the continuance of separate Women's Meetings, seeing them as potentially useful for women Friends, Ellen Robinson's main focus was on the need for equality within the Society. Women, she argued, 'were either equal members, or not members of the Society at all'. She did not argue for an end to separate meetings, but she felt 'that it should be our right to have all important subjects brought before us . . . instead of its being left to the judgment of the Clerk'. The question was whether Women's Meeting was entrusted to decide its own remit, rather than have it decided for it. She added: 'We were sometimes told in Quarterly Meetings that although joint conferences were held, we were not properly constituted members of the Quarterly Meeting, and had no status. It was needful to find out what our position really was, for the benefit of those who came after us, as well as for ourselves.'[35]

As Holton and Allen have argued, women Friends were split over what kind of change was required in the organisation and administration of the Society, yet there was almost universal agreement that changes of some sort were necessary. Prominent feminists such as the Brights and Priestmans argued for the merging of the two Meetings, while more traditionalist members, such as Peckover, argued that it was only through having separate Meetings that women were able to develop the skills and confidence which made their work possible. There was clearly a whole spectrum of opinions in between, including Ellen Robinson's idea that both had a place within the Society, providing the role of each was clear. Robinson drew attention to the fact that the problem was not who took part in which Meeting, but the ambiguity over the status of the Women's Meeting and, in fact, over the status of women in the Society as a whole.[36]

While Peckover continued to work primarily at a local level, Robinson became involved on a national basis with the Society of Friends and its Peace Committee. In 1888–89 she addressed seventy meetings for the Peace Committee, in addition to her work for other associations.[37] She also contributed to theological debates within the Society. She spoke at the Manchester Conference in 1895 at which Quaker theology and its relation to social change was debated, and was one of the first female members of the Meeting for Sufferings.[38] Mary Lamley Cooke noted in her obituary of Robinson that 'it is a little difficult for the present generation [in 1912] to understand how warmly, twenty or thirty years ago, thoughtful younger Friends welcomed the clear and logical expression of broad views of Christian teaching'. Robinson had, she wrote, 'made it her duty carefully to study the best results of modern thought, so that she might be as well equipped as possible for work of such profound importance'.[39] Although Robinson was more advanced in her views and theology than women members of the Peace Society were typically expected to be, she received support and encouragement from the Peace Society in her work, as did the LBWPAS, perhaps because of the prominence of liberal Friends such as William Pollard and John W. Rowntree on the Society's Executive Committee. The Peace Society on more than one occasion claimed the LBWPAS as a formal auxiliary, despite the fact that it did not denounce all war.[40]

Ellen Robinson's competence and popularity within the international peace movement led many of its male leaders, in Britain and abroad, to acknowledge that women could contribute to political as well as religious debates on peace. However, Robinson's combination of feminism,

Quakerism and Liberalism forged a different path to that of Priscilla Peckover, by which she drew women into the public sphere within both the Meetings of the Society of Friends, and the Women's Liberal Associations. As a result, she made questions of peace, humanitarianism and international arbitration more prominent within these organisations.

On a number of occasions, Ellen Robinson argued that women's moral influence enabled them to affect public opinion. In a speech in 1890, she argued that 'Moral force is superceding [sic] physical force in family and social life, why not in international? Women as well as men are responsible for public opinion; it is our duty to combat false maxims and wrong methods.'[41] This is a restatement of the feminist conception of patriotism referred to earlier, in which women are represented as public agents embodying morality and humanity, while men are implicitly connected with the rule of physical force. Robinson's feminism led her to address these questions from a different perspective to that taken by Peckover: one took a progressive stance, the other a more traditional one. Both women, however, influenced the developing strands of pacifist feminism, albeit in very different ways. Robinson's approach was similar to the ideas of Henrietta Müller and Florence Fenwick Miller, although Robinson worked primarily within the peace movement rather than the women's movement and aimed to popularise pacifist feminist theories within this context. Peckover, on the other hand, worked almost exclusively within the peace movement, as shown for example in her reformulation of patriotism. She argued that an acceptance of pacifist ideas would lead to the reassessment of what was best for one's country and the recognition that the national interest was best served by arbitration and the avoidance of conflict. This was distinct from feminist revisions of patriotism, which focused on the effects of women's enfranchisement and argued that women would be loyal to a higher ideal, or a more moral and humane nation.

The contributions of Peckover and Robinson to pacifist feminist ideas can be seen in the impact that both had upon the roles of women within the peace movement, especially the Peace Society. By opening up new channels to women and demonstrating that they could make a useful contribution to pacifist arguments, Peckover and Robinson proved that pacifism could be a women's question and even, for some women, a feminist one.

The organisation which best blended these feminist and pacifist interests in the late-nineteenth century was undoubtedly the IAPA, which was primarily a pacifist organisation but attracted many feminist members. This association is discussed in detail in the following chapters.

Notes

1 *Herald* (1 March 1892), p. 34.
2 *Ibid.* (1 June 1896), p. 75.
3 *Dictionary of Quaker Biography* (*DQB*); Thomas C. Kennedy, 'Ellen Robinson', in Josephson (ed.), *BDMPL*, pp. 811–13.
4 *Friends' Quarterly Examiner* (March 1912), p. 148.
5 Hope Hay Hewison, *Hedge of Wild Almonds: South Africa, Pro-Boers and the Quaker Conscience, 1890–1910* (London: James Currey, 1989), pp. 65–6, 145, 353.
6 Mlle Montaudon to Ellen Robinson, 20 August 1907; Ellen Robinson to Mlle Montaudon, August 1907, Document 1, Box 162, IPB 1892–1914, International Peace Movement, League of Nations Archives, United Nations Library, Geneva, Switzerland (hereafter IPB).
7 P. H. Peckover to Élie Ducommun, 9 October 1894, Document 1, Box 225, IPB. The WLF was the umbrella organisation for WLA local branches.
8 *DQB*, based on testimony of Hardshaw West Monthly Meeting in *Yearly Meeting Proceedings* (1912), p. 271.
9 *Herald* (1 June 1886), p. 79, (1 June 1887), p. 235; *P&G* (15 January 1886), p. 234.
10 Annual Report of the LBWPAS, 1894, Document 1, Box 225, IPB. LBWPAS members such as Mrs John Ziegler, Mrs and Miss Abraham, Mrs Egerton Stewart Brown, Mrs J. Crosfield, Kate Ryley and Miss Dismore were active in the Women's Liberal Federation and the National Union of Women's Suffrage Societies. My thanks to Krista Cowman for sharing her considerable knowledge of suffragists and radicals in Liverpool in this period.
11 *Herald* (2 June 1890), p. 90; (1 June 1893), p. 248.
12 *P&G* (14 July 1888), p. 145, emphasis in original; *Herald* (2 April 1888), p. 45.
13 *Friend* (27 August 1926), p. 753; *DQB*; Peace Society Minute Book, 16 June 1899, Peace Society Archives, Fellowship House, London (hereafter PSA).
14 *Herald* (2 June 1890), p. 73.
15 *Ibid.* (1 March 1892), p. 34. Emphasis in original.
16 Ellen Robinson to P. H. Peckover, 8 October 1894, WLPA, Box 4, Folder 3, Swarthmore College Peace Collection, microfilm copy in Wisbech Public Library, Wisbech, Cambridgeshire.
17 Cooper, *Patriotic Pacifism*, pp. 39, 41; Cooper, 'Marie Pouchoulin Goegg', in Josephson (ed.), *BDMPL*, pp. 338–9.
18 Cooper, 'Edmond Potonié', and 'Eugénie Potonié-Pierre', in Josephson (ed.), *BDMPL*, pp. 763–6; *Herald* (1 July 1898), p. 88.
19 *Herald* (1 January 1896), p. 12; (1 March 1896), p. 35; (1 April 1896), p. 46; *P&G* (15 July 1895), pp. 81–3, 96; (15 October 1895), pp. 97–8.
20 *Herald* (1 April 1896), p. 46.
21 *Ibid.*
22 *P&G* (15 April 1896), p. 129.
23 *Herald* (1 June 1896), p. 75; Peace Society Minute Book, 16 June 1899, PSA.
24 The work of the WLF is only briefly covered in this book, because like the 'pro-Boer' organisations that sprang up in 1899–1900, it worked for peace primarily in response to the outbreak of war, rather than as a constant campaign issue. For more on the WLF and its rival, the Women's National Liberal Association, during the

Anglo-Boer war, see Claire Hirshfield, 'Liberal women's organizations and the war against the Boers, 1899–1902', *Albion*, 14 (1982), pp. 27–49.

25 *Concord* (February 1900), p. 97; International Peace Bureau Report, 1901, Document 11, Box 90, IPB; IPB, *Rapports sur les Manifestations de 1899 et 1900*, 1900, Document 1, Box 201, IPB.

26 Hirshfield, 'Liberal women's organizations', pp. 40–1; *Concord* (July 1900), p. 108.

27 *Labour Leader* (23 June 1900), p. 199; June Hannam, *Isabella Ford* (Oxford: Basil Blackwell, 1989), pp. 84, 96.

28 Other sections of the British left were divided over the war. A number of members, including Margaret MacDonald and Emmeline Pankhurst, resigned from the Fabian Society when it voted by a narrow margin not to make a pronouncement against the war. *Labour Leader* (27 April 1901), p. 133, emphasis in original; (14 April 1900), p. 119; see also Douglas J. Newton, *British Labour, European Socialism and the Struggle for Peace* (Oxford: Clarendon Press, 1985), ch. 5; Paul Ward, *Red Flag and Union Jack: Englishness, Patriotism and the British Left, 1881–1924* (Suffolk: Boydell Press, 1998), ch. 4.

29 Universal Peace Congress, *Proceedings of the Tenth Universal Peace Congress, held in Glasgow, 1901* (Berne and London: International Peace Bureau, 1902).

30 Cooper, *Patriotic Pacifism*, p. 82.

31 William Evans Darby to Élie Ducommun, 3 February 1902, Document 13, Box 88, IPB.

32 Ellen Robinson to Élie Ducommun, 29 January 1902, Document 13, Box 88, IPB.

33 William Evans Darby to Élie Ducommun, 8 March 1893, Document 10, Box 1; Hodgson Pratt to Élie Ducommun, 11 March 1893, IPB.

34 Ellen Robinson to Élie Ducommun, 9 December 1897, Document 2, Box 144, IPB.

35 *Friend* (7 June 1895), p. 382.

36 Holton and Allen, 'Offices and services'.

37 *Herald* (1 June 1889), p. 230.

38 Hewison, *Hedge of Wild Almonds*, p. 45.

39 *Friends' Quarterly Examiner* (March 1912), pp. 148–9.

40 *Herald* (1 June 1889), p. 230; (1 June 1891), p. 250.

41 *P&G* (15 January 1890), p. 243.

7

'Unity is strength': the International Arbitration and Peace Association[1]

HE ABSOLUTIST Peace Society dominated the British peace movement throughout most of the nineteenth century. However, its absolutism was increasingly challenged from mid-century onwards, and it became apparent by the 1870s, as a result of republican nationalist campaigns in Europe, and in Britain the rise of working men's peace groups and the growth of the women's movement, that there was also some demand for a secular peace organisation. The International Arbitration and Peace Association (IAPA), founded in 1880, was the main secular peace organisation in Britain and the one which experienced the greatest conflict with the Peace Society. Significantly, it was also the most likely of the mixed peace societies to draw in women from the feminist movement. It accommodated a variety of feminist perspectives, as well as attracting women such as Priscilla Peckover who were active within the peace movement but maintained a distance from the women's movement.

As an organisation, the IAPA drew together discourses of liberalism, socialism, Evangelicalism, feminism and internationalism, a blend that made it central to both the British and European peace movements. The IAPA acknowledged European definitions of 'just wars' and refused to be swept along in the tide of jingoistic imperialism that gripped Britain at the turn of the century. Although it was officially secular in its arguments for peace, it had many members who upheld religious and Evangelical ideas. The IAPA's arguments for equality drew in women from various strands of the feminist movement, giving rise to a range of ways of working within the organisation. Women were active as individuals, as members of the IAPA's secularist Women's Committee, and as members of its Evangelical social purity auxiliary, the WPAA (formerly the women's auxiliary to the Peace Society). In its internationalism, the IAPA was ideologically connected to movements in Britain and

Europe, as well as North America. It benefited greatly from being a new organisation. Lacking either a history of dominance within the peace movement or a background of nonconformity and defiance of the state, the IAPA was more adaptable than the Peace Society to the changes in Victorian society, and therefore it was better able to accommodate feminist thought. This chapter outlines the IAPA's contribution to the late Victorian peace movement and the role of women in its work, while chapter 8 discusses the auxiliaries – the Women's Committee and the WPAA – that were attached to it.

The birth of the IAPA was closely connected to some of the problems experienced by the Peace Society in the 1870s. It was founded in 1880 by the Peace Society's former collector, Lewis Appleton, who had been expelled from the Peace Society for misappropriation of funds. Also involved was William Phillips, who became the Association's Honorary Secretary. However, it was not until 1883, when Hodgson Pratt accepted the chairmanship of the IAPA, that it began to raise its profile and publicise its theories on peace and international arbitration.

Contrary to Peace Society suspicions, the Association did not reject Christian beliefs. During a debate with Henry Richard as to whether the IAPA was duplicating the work of the Peace Society, Pratt asked Richard what problem there could be with the IAPA if the net result was to bring more 'into the field of Christian work'.[2] However, Christianity in itself was not part of its rationale for opposing war. Rather, its principles were based upon: 'a recognition of the mutual respect and justice between nations, and on broad principles of international polity, the general adoption of which will lead to the substitution of Arbitration for War'. It professed itself to be 'unsectarian' and, like the Peace Society, in principle unconnected to party politics. Its objectives were to create 'an enlightened public opinion towards the abolition of war', to advocate practical measures for peace and 'to secure permanent relief from the crushing burden of National Armaments'. It aimed to promote: arbitration as a substitute for war; 'the establishment of a code of International Law, and an International Tribunal'; international treaties for such objects; and finally, means 'for bringing about a good understanding' between warring nations.[3]

The means by which the IAPA expected to spread its message lay in the establishment of similar organisations across Europe and the US, creating an international federation in which each association would be independent, but working with a common plan of action. It established a journal in 1884, entitled the *Journal of the International Arbitration and*

Peace Association (given the rather catchier title of *Concord* in 1887). Its work, the *Journal* argued in its first issue, 'is one in which both men and women of all classes, of all parties, and of all religious denominations may do something; each in his, or her, own sphere'.[4] From the outset, the IAPA consciously attempted to embrace women's work for peace.

The appointment of Hodgson Pratt as chairman marked a turning point for the Association. Pratt had a history of radicalism, and at the 1871 Congress of the republican International League of Peace and Liberty he had actively opposed the Franco-Prussian war. Pratt attended the ILPL's 1872 Congress as a delegate of William Randal Cremer's Workmen's Peace Association, and was put forward as a candidate for the ILPL's central Committee in the same year, although he declined to accept this offer because he refused to 'look upon the republic as neces-sary to peace' and thus endorse wars of liberation.[5] On accepting the chairmanship of the IAPA, Pratt made a number of innovative changes: he invited Henry Richard to become president of the IAPA (Richard refused), suggested an amalgamation of the Peace Society and the IAPA (negotiations were begun, but came to nothing), and provided a monthly mouthpiece for the Association by establishing the *Journal*. Pratt gradually gained the IAPA a following and membership that did not overlap with that of the Peace Society, though the relationship between the two organisations remained tense for several years. The conflict con-tinued throughout the 1880s and was exacerbated during the 1890s by the founding of the IPB. The Anglo-Boer War of 1899–1902 highlighted the tensions again, as the IAPA took an openly anti-government stance while the Peace Society refused to undertake any efforts that could not guarantee success.

Initially, the expulsion of Lewis Appleton in late 1884 from the secretaryship of the Association, followed by negotiations during 1885 on the possibility of a merger, meant that by the mid-1880s the rela-tionship was co-operative, even if it was also unpredictable. In 1886, Hodgson Pratt was invited to address the annual meeting of the Peace Society, a significant gesture of goodwill, as the *Journal* was pleased to note: 'Our Association has long been anxious for a closer union with our brethren in the great cause . . . More especially have we been anxious for brotherly relations with the Parent Society, which has for so many years had the benefit of Mr Henry Richard's able and earnest services.' The *Journal* acknowledged the continuing dominance of the Peace Society in the British peace movement as a whole, and the prominence and status of Henry Richard. It also implied that, as in any unequal relationship, it fell to the side with the upper hand to recognise the subordinate: it was therefore the privilege of the Peace Society to invite Hodgson Pratt to speak to their meeting, rather than the IAPA to invite Henry Richard to theirs. The *Journal* went on to note that 'the circumstances under which the two societies were thus represented on a common platform were of no small importance'.[6]

In contrast, the *Herald of Peace* gave no special notice to the event, but reported Pratt's remarks that 'He felt it to be a very great honour indeed to find himself on that platform on the anniversary meeting of an association which had done so much.' By 1889, relations between the two organisations had improved even further, to the degree that the *Herald* paid Pratt the rare compliment of comparing him to both Joseph Sturge and the recently-departed Henry Richard: 'Perhaps no one, since the days of the late Joseph Sturge, has devoted more personal attention, labour and money, to the arduous work of peace propagandism on the Continent. He has well followed up and maintained, in this direction, the similar efforts of the late Mr Henry Richard, MP. Mr Pratt is almost a Peace Society in himself.'[7]

Notwithstanding the different emphasis that the Peace Society and the IAPA attached to Christian pacifism, on paper the practical aims of the Peace Society and the IAPA were similar: the establishment of systems of arbitration and a court of nations, and the advocacy of mutual disarmament. Yet the two organisations worked in very different ways. During the 1880s, they were coloured by the politics of their respective chairmen, Henry Richard and Hodgson Pratt. Richard's long experience of peace work served to emphasise the dominance of the Peace Society, while Pratt's background in the co-operative movement established links for the IAPA that went beyond the peace movement into wider political circles. Membership records show that the majority of Peace Society and IAPA members did not join both societies. The primary factor affecting the relations between them was the attitudes of their leaders. The rivalry, such as it was, changed course after Richard's death in 1888. His replacement in the Peace Society, William Evans Darby, was primarily concerned with maintaining the status that Richard had obtained for the Society. It became an increasingly insular organisation towards the end of the century, and in consequence, the generation of feminists that emerged in the 1880s and 1890s were far more likely to turn to the IAPA as an effective context for their peace work than to the Peace Society.

Just as many women preferred the IAPA, European activists found a sympathy and tolerance for their views from the IAPA that was not forthcoming from the Peace Society. This is particularly clear from an analysis of the International Peace Bureau, which was intended to be a non-partisan, co-ordinating body for national peace movements. Under William Evans Darby, the Peace Society was reluctant to acknowledge or support the IPB because it included many influential members of the ILPL. Hodgson Pratt was aware that the Peace Society would be uncooperative, and during discussions on the formation of the IPB he warned Élie Ducommun, the ILPL member who became the IPB's secretary, that 'You must be prepared for *opposition*, great opposition.'[8] While Pratt did not share the ILPL's views on, for example, wars of national liberation, he was nonetheless prepared to work closely with it to strengthen the international movement.

The functions of the IPB were, among other things, to collect, catalogue and provide information and publications on peace and arbitration, and to prepare subjects for the Peace Congresses and carry out their resolutions.[9] As a transnational umbrella organisation, the IPB drew diverse groups together to exchange ideas and work collectively for peace. Delegates to the IPB's first Peace Congress in 1892 included Richard and Emmeline Pankhurst and E. M. Southey (for the IAPA), Joseph Sturge (for the Workmen's Peace Association), Mrs Henry Richard and Priscilla Peckover (both for the Peace Society and the Ladies' Peace Auxiliary), Margaret Tanner and Anna and Mary Priestman (three of a long list of delegates sent by the Peace Society) and Ellen Robinson for the LBWPAS and the Society of Friends.[10] The Congress attracted a number of prominent British pacifists, and drew workers from a wide range of peace organisations. It also explicitly targeted women.

During the 1890 and 1891 Congresses at which the idea for the Bureau was established, a number of resolutions were passed regarding women's roles in peace work. The most comprehensive of these called for:

> every woman throughout the world to sustain, as wife, mother, sister, or citizen, the things that make for Peace; as otherwise she incurs grave responsabilities [*sic*] for the continuance of the systems of war and militarism, which not only desolate but corrupt the home life of the nations ... [W]omen should unite themselves with societies for the promotion of international peace.[11]

The same resolution was passed by many individual peace societies in the months after the Congress, including for example Priscilla Peckover's WLPA. However, while it undoubtedly valued their support and contributions, the IPB could offer women little in terms of international peace work. Dominated as the Bureau was by men who could directly influence the political process in their own nations, there were few opportunities available for women who wanted to work within it. The Austrian aristocrat and novelist Bertha von Suttner was perhaps the exception to this rule, as her elite background gave her a wider sphere of influence than the middle-class women who made up the bulk of women involved in the peace movement. Suttner also had a popular anti-war novel to her name, which had established her as an authority on questions of peace and arbitration.[12]

Yet while the IPB offered few opportunities for women, it did provide a means of external support to the IAPA, which was relatively isolated in Britain due to its difficult relationship with the Peace Society. For example, during the second Anglo-Boer war, when the Peace Society resisted all calls to campaign for peace, the IAPA (along with the WLPA and the LBWPAS) developed a range of strategies, including public meetings, petitions and peace propaganda to protest against the war. The IPB assisted with these wherever it could. For example, its central Committee wrote to the British Prime Minister reminding him of the promises made by the British government at the Hague Conference only a few months earlier. A similar appeal was addressed to the twenty-five signatories to the Hague Convention, requesting that they intervene and assist in bringing about an end to the hostilities.[13] These actions followed lengthy communications between Hodgson Pratt and Élie Ducommun, in which Pratt argued that 'mere Resolutions and Addresses, signed by members of Peace Societies, [giving] continuing protestations against the Transvaal war will avail nothing'. Rather, a definite step was needed in which, 'in each country, a large number of influential persons should seek a personal interview with the Head of Government or Minister of Foreign Affairs, with the view of urging an offer of Good Offices or Mediation; – whether that offer be made by the Government in question acting alone, – or in conjunction with other Governments'.[14]

This discussion came early in the war, after a protest meeting held by the IAPA, the Transvaal Committee and the Social Democratic Federation in September 1899 had erupted into violence.[15] Members of the public attacked both speakers and pacifists attending the demonstration, and left a number of them injured. Sections of the London press had identified Hodgson Pratt and Ellen Robinson as unofficial representatives of the Afrikaners, though few papers went on to describe the riot that erupted in consequence.[16] As a result of this intimidation by sections of the general public and the popular press, Pratt contacted the IPB and suggested joint methods of protest which he believed would be more successful. Thus the IPB was used as an international point of contact, to provide support in the face of weaknesses in the British movement. This re-emphasises the idealistic construction of patriotism as an international, rather than uniquely national, identity. This was particularly important for Priscilla Peckover, Ellen Robinson and Hodgson Pratt, who were all working within a variety of contexts in Britain.

Alongside its attitude to Continental peace movements, the IAPA's second striking difference from the Peace Society was its attitude to women, and its commitment to a mixed-sex organisation. The IAPA addressed itself to women in the very first issue of the *Journal*. Almost since its inauguration it had enjoyed an organised presence of women experienced in peace work, through the affiliation in 1881 of the WPAA.[17] A four-page 'Appeal to Women on Behalf of International Arbitration' was produced by Hodgson Pratt and published by the Association for distribution among various women's societies, and was also circulated by Lydia Becker, who enclosed it in an edition of the *Women's Suffrage Journal*.[18] The republican feminist Marie Deraismes, of Paris, prepared a French translation which the IAPA circulated on the continent, and her organisation, the Société pour l'Amélioration du Sort de la Femme et de la Revindication de ses Droits, sent a letter of support to the IAPA.[19]

That women were actively included in the IAPA's work is clear from the proceedings of its annual meetings, its Executive Committee (which consisted of both women and men), its explicit inclusion of women within the Association's general work, and the content of the *Journal*. As noted in chapter 4, until the early 1890s, the Peace Society advocated women's peace work only in the context of the domestic or religious spheres, that is, among other women, children and the clergy. Women's contributions were explicitly confined and constrained. The IAPA took a less divisive stance, arguing that 'every word in the Journal should be one which men and women may express or receive without distinction'.[20] The work of women was accepted as a vital part of the whole picture. The IAPA's connections with Europe may also have affected its political perspective, as women were generally more influential within the Continental peace societies than they were within the British ones.

Concord's subscription lists for the period 1884 to 1899 show that approximately one quarter of the IAPA's five hundred members were female.[21] Some of these women members founded a separate female auxiliary to the IAPA, known as the Women's Committee, and there were also of course the members of the more independent WPAA, which had formerly been affiliated to the Peace Society. But the IAPA also had many individual women members who were influential in political and social reform. These included Mrs Ellen Sickert, who was the daughter of Richard Cobden and sister-in-law of Helena Swanwick, and Mary Costelloe, who was the mother of another active feminist, Ray Strachey, and daughter of the Quaker Hannah Whitall Smith (also a member of the IAPA, and formerly of the WPAAPS). Elizabeth Pease Nichol and Margaret Bright Lucas were two prominent feminist members (Bright Lucas was also president of the WPAA), as were Laura McLaren and Florence Fenwick Miller. Emmeline Pankhurst, then best known as the wife of the socialist Dr Richard Pankhurst, was an IAPA member, as were the Irish Unionist Isabella Tod and the American Julia Ward Howe. Constance Lloyd, better known as Mrs Oscar Wilde, was a regular speaker at IAPA women's meetings between 1884 and 1893.[22]

Many of the IAPA's women members had a high profile within society and were accustomed to the more equal partnerships that were popularised in the 1890s by the concept of the 'New Woman'. Unlike pioneering feminists of the 1860s and 1870s, for whom an equal marriage partnership was regarded as enterprising and unusual, the feminists of the 1880s and 1890s enjoyed the concept of equality in marriage as a vital component of their lives. The IAPA accorded women an equal role, given that women were still politically disenfranchised under British law. For example, its 1884 annual meeting included a woman speaker not only addressing a mixed audience but also proposing a resolution. This is in contrast to the Peace Society, who did not invite a female speaker until 1890. Women were also accepted as having a political role. After a conference in 1885 on the possibility of the peaceful settlement of disputes over the Afghan frontier, the *Journal* noted that 'many members' of the WPAA were present, and that the resolution – recommending arbitration – was forwarded to the Prime Minister.[23] This involvement of women in a predominantly male political act demonstrates that the IAPA was very different from the Peace Society in the role it accorded women.

Four women in particular became involved in the IAPA in ways that advanced both their peace work and their feminism. Isabella Tod, Florence Fenwick Miller, Laura Ormiston Chant and Florence Balgarnie were all middle-class suffragists with a background of active involvement in the feminist movement. Each had their own interests of course: Tod focused on campaigning for women's education and against Home Rule, Miller on neo-Malthusianism and new approaches to sexual politics, Chant on a reactionary form of social purity, and Balgarnie on women's suffrage and trade unionism. Their different approaches to social questions were carried over into the peace movement, as each presented different methods of working to the IAPA's meetings. Tod, for example, was an internationalist and opposed imperial expansion, though she also tolerated some forms of imperialism, for example in her opposition to Home Rule for Ireland. Fenwick Miller, as shown in chapter 2, was much more identified with conceptions of international citizenship and universalised sisterhood, while Balgarnie was implicitly critical of such ideas, locating responsibility for war in class, as well as gender terms. Chant provided the clearest example of the Evangelical feminist position, echoing the social purity interests of the WPAA. These four women can be viewed as further evidence of the diversity of feminist perspectives that was highlighted in chapter 2. Their involvement in the IAPA shows that the Association could attract feminists from a range of backgrounds and political ideologies, who were drawn to the peace movement because it supported their views on the suffrage, imperialism, social purity, education or motherhood. The IAPA's position as a flexible and broadly based organisation also meant that it was able to accommodate this range of perspectives.

Miss Isabella Tod (1836–96) was one of the most prominent feminists to regularly attend the IAPA's meetings. Tod had been a popular figure in the women's movement for nearly two decades, becoming interested in women's education and the campaign for married women's property laws at the Social Science Congress in Belfast in 1867. These interests led her into the suffrage movement, and she became a member of the Executive boards of the Ladies' National Association for the Repeal of the Contagious Diseases Acts, the National Vigilance Association and the Married Women's Property Committee. Born in Scotland but raised in Belfast, Tod's primary concern was the promotion of the interests of Irish women, and she was perhaps the most prominent Irish women's suffragist of the late nineteenth century. Her controversial commitment to Unionism emerged in 1886, after her reputation was established, when she devoted all her energies to the campaign against Home Rule, alienating many of her colleagues and, despite her Liberalism, allying herself with the Unionists.[24]

Tod maintained that her Unionism was not based on 'religious bigotry'. Rather, 'what we dread is the complete dislocation of all society, especially in regard to commercial affairs and to organised freedom of action . . . [I]t is needful to point out that the conditions of a free democracy do not exist in Ireland.' At best, she said, widespread educa-tion and training in local government would be needed before Home Rule could be attempted, and Ulster should claim 'a separate jurisdiction' in order to maintain its political freedom and its ability 'to do some good for the rest of Ireland'. During her campaign Tod befriended Millicent Garrett Fawcett, another Liberal who converted to the Liberal Unionists, and publicly disassociated herself from Josephine Butler after the latter declared herself in favour of Home Rule.[25]

There was, however, a distinct difference between the politics of Tod and Fawcett where the question of the use of force was concerned. Fawcett sympathised with imperialist arguments and supported the use of physical force in Ireland as a means of maintaining order. Tod's position regarding the empire was slightly more complex. Surprisingly perhaps, she had more than a passing interest in the work of the IAPA. She was present at nearly all of its annual meetings during the 1880s, relinquishing her role as one of its most popular women speakers only as ill health forced her to cut back on her political activities during the 1890s. Many of her speeches for the IAPA propounded comprehensive arguments for peace work, similar to the reasoning Ellen Robinson developed. She drew on notions of women's duties, of national and racial difference, human rights as against physical force, the economic implications of war, which directly hampered social progress, and the importance of equal rights not only for women but also for the 'others' upon whom Britain might be tempted to wage war.[26]

In her first recorded IAPA speech, she stated that: 'This Society invites . . . women . . . to take their full share – and that a large and definite share – in enlightening the public mind, and awakening public conscience, not only to the dangers which follow war, but also to those underlying principles of selfishness and tyranny.' This 'underlying . . . selfishness' referred to Tod's belief that politicians were, generally speaking, concerned with party political questions rather than public issues. She was a democrat at heart, and believed that the best means by which to limit war was to re-educate the public so that they would not vote for war or for inflexible, combative politicians. She employed feminist arguments of sexual difference in her contention that the infringement of human rights was inherent in the use of physical force: 'We have to fight for and protect the interests of the weak, by teaching the strong that they have no rights by virtue of their strength.' This, she said, was 'a work in which women can assist. I cannot but feel that we have the *right* to appeal . . . in this matter.'[27]

Her arguments, as these quotes show, were focused on a conception of women's rights and duties that was typical of the women's movement at this time. Her speeches and publications on women's suffrage drew on ideas of justice, on women's rights as citizens of the state, and particularly on the separate spheres ideology of women's moral and spiritual superiority. Yet Tod also employed anti-imperialist rhetoric in conjunction with her feminist and Unionist principles. At the IAPA's fourth annual meeting in 1885, she criticised the war system in all its forms, stating that whether it was a great war or 'one of those wretched little wars, as they were called', in which Britain 'had been often engaged, threatening and overbearing races which we were pleased to think inferior to ourselves', women nonetheless, on any prospect of war, stopped their social and philanthropic reforms until peace was restored. Hence war impoverished all social work, and had ramifications far beyond the financial cost of the military conflict. It was not only damaging in the sense that it hampered social progress, but its effects were felt doubly because increased taxes were levied and resources wasted 'on needless warlike enterprises'.[28] Thus there was economic damage done to a nation by engaging in war, and moral damage as a result of their indifference to the deaths of the enemy. In line with her views on the importance of an educated and democratic electorate, Tod concluded that 'by far the highest and broadest aim of [the IAPA] . . . is not the external one, but the inculcating of regard for the equal rights of others, and the exercise of unceasing personal self-control over all personal, class, and party impulses'.[29] This was a position that was in complete harmony with her opinions on the suffrage.

A striking contrast to Tod's position can be found in the arguments of another speaker for the IAPA, Florence Fenwick Miller. Originally qualified in medicine, Miller was one of the earliest women journalists, the biographer of Harriet Martineau and editor of the feminist journal the *Woman's Signal*. She was also no stranger to controversy. In 1877 she supported Annie Besant's popular distribution of a pamphlet on contraception, and as a member of the London School Board her support was publicised and much criticised. She was the only feminist to publicly express her anger at the Ripper murders in London in 1888, naming them as not isolated events but part of the constant and increasing cruelties against women which were, to make matters worse, treated leniently by the (male) judiciary. Despite her outspokenness, her debating skills meant that she was in constant demand as a public speaker. Possessing 'aggressive body language and verbal style', Fenwick Miller and her lectures were very much 'part of the spectacle of London life in the eighties, provocative signs of modernity and vibrant radicalism'.[30]

By the 1890s, Fenwick Miller was one of the most prominent feminists of her generation to develop internationalist ideas of pacifist feminism. Like many of the women involved in the IAPA, she was critical of jingoistic imperialism and aggressive militarism. Like many Victorian feminists, she blended ideas of progress and rationalism with a feminist sexual difference perspective, to argue that women's status in society improved as civilisation progressed. Yet importantly, she applied these ideas directly to an international rather than a national stage. In arguing that the 'women of the whole world' were beginning to form a united sisterhood and overcoming the 'barbarism' of military societies, she connected feminism with pacifism on a global scale, implying a course of progress and evolution throughout history where earlier feminists such as Caroline Ashurst Biggs and Lydia Becker had relied on more static constructions of 'nature'.[31] While this approach highlighted the universalism of her feminism, it was nonetheless a dramatic leap to take from a Victorian feminist perspective.

Fenwick Miller was therefore an obvious choice for the IAPA's annual meetings, and her controversial approach compensated for her low level of involvement in the IAPA's work. Fenwick Miller disagreed with Isabella Tod's decrying of the 'war spirit' discussed above, arguing that combating war required the same martial spirit of the 'noble warrior'. She emphasised the unpopularity of peace principles, saying that, particularly in the sphere of politics, 'if a man or a woman wanted the reputation of being a practical politician . . . they had better leave this question alone'. In order to have such an impracticable question as peace recognised in politics, it must be fought for by those who believed in it: 'let us look to our principles being carried out, and if not, *fight* for those principles, although [you belong] . . . to a Peace Society [*sic*]'.[32]

This combative approach was reflected in Fenwick Miller's other arguments on women and peace. For example, she used the popular approach that women suffered more in wars than did men, because while '[i]t was true that men had to bear arms in the field of battle . . . who would not rather go into the fight and share its dangers and glories and successes, than stay at home anxiously waiting lest they should hear of the death of those nearest and dearest'.[33] In the differences between the arguments of Fenwick Miller and Tod, there are parallels with the debates that raged within the suffrage movement, both during the 1880s and 1890s, and during the early twentieth century as a result of the methods of suffragists and, later, suffragettes. Fenwick Miller's combative approach and Tod's emphasis on the need for self-control echo suffragist debates on tactics within this period, over issues such as the refusal to pay taxes and the inclusion of married women in the franchise. There were perpetual disagreements over whether methods that exploited power relations were necessary in order to effect change, or whether a reformulation of the use of power on all levels was required. The contrasting feminist philosophies of direct action and the use of force, as against restraint and passive resistance, were a continual source of friction.[34]

The third example of a prominent feminist who regularly spoke at IAPA meetings is Mrs Laura Ormiston Chant. As discussed in chapter 4, Chant was one of the first women to be appointed a vice-president of the Peace Society, in March 1889. But before this date she spoke on a number of occasions at IAPA events, including the annual meetings of 1886 and 1887. Linda Walker credits Chant with helping to 'formulate the moral basis of Liberal feminism', and as noted earlier, her primary area of interest was in social purity campaigns, although she was also an active suffragist.[35] Like Isabella Tod, she took a strong line on personal morality, although she went further than Tod in her campaign to improve and purify public life. Her interests in this respect were similar to those of the Moral Reform Union (MRU). Like the MRU, in 1888 Chant protested against Sir Charles Dilke's candidacy for a position on London County Council because Dilke had been named as correspondent in a divorce case in 1885.[36] Chant was also an engaging and controversial lecturer: in 1888 Henrietta Müller termed her 'the most popular of our lady speakers'.[37]

During the late 1880s, Chant conducted a relentless campaign to make the streets of London safer for women. However, in her terms this meant ridding them of prostitutes so that 'respectable' women could use public spaces unmolested. Unlike many of her contemporaries, including Josephine Butler, Chant endorsed the middle-class philanthropist's view of the working class as '"child-like" and in need of direction', though she was also highly critical of the (sexual) leisure pursuits of the male aristocracy. Seen by critics as a dangerous example of the 'New Woman', it is nonetheless clear that although she tried to rid the streets and public entertainment sites of prostitutes, her ultimate aim was in fact to transform these sites so that women could move freely in them without fearing attack or loss of respectability. As Lucy Bland notes, the public arena in the 1880s was 'reserved for men and those women who "immorally" serviced them', so in trying to change the nature of the public sphere, Chant was in her own terms attempting to free women from repression. She curtailed prostitutes' liberty by attempting to eliminate their public presence, but argued that this was necessary because under the existing state of affairs, firstly, her own liberty (and that of respectable women like her) was being curtailed as a result of prostitutes' freedom, and secondly, prostitutes' liberty was infringed because, she argued, 'vice in itself is a colossal injustice'.[38] Of course, the prostitutes, and many other philanthropists who were seeking to 'help' them, such as Josephine Butler, did not see the problem in quite these terms.

Chant's arguments on behalf of the peace movement reflected her moral purity feminism. She particularly favoured maternalist arguments for peace, telling the IAPA's 1886 annual meeting that she 'could not imagine a mother looking on placidly at the number of men who were trained in the world for no other purpose than to be run through by bayonets'. Like Isabella Tod, Chant argued that education could be used as a means to prevent war, and that boys needed 'a different education ... beginning it in the nursery', so that they 'should not be taught to find pleasure in those toys which men suffer for afterwards'. By this means, she argued, 'women could do a great deal ... to help forward the great cause'. Indeed, it was on women's 'own inner moral sense that the world would rely' to reach higher levels of civilisation.[39] These arguments exemplify the Evangelical moral purity stance on peace, with its distinctive focus on the luxuries of resourceful middle-class motherhood and unceasing moral improvement.

A clear contrast to Chant can be found in another advocate of education who spoke for the IAPA, Miss Florence Balgarnie (1856–1928). Balgarnie had more in common in terms of politics and ideology with Florence Fenwick Miller than she did with Laura Ormiston Chant or Isabella Tod. She was based in Scarborough, but of Irish descent, and was the daughter of a Congregationalist minister. She had been educated in London and Germany, was a member of the School Board in Scarborough for two years in the early 1880s, worked as full-time secretary to the Central National Society for Women's Suffrage, was co-founder of the Women's Trade Union Association, and in 1894 became secretary of the Anti-Lynching Committee. Balgarnie was also a member of the Men and Women's Club, a radical, elitist club of twenty members that ran for four years in the late 1880s to discuss 'the mutual position and relation of men and women'.[40] Like the Ashursts, she had great respect for Mazzini, and also for the writings of Ruskin.

In defining women's emancipation in a paper read to the Men and Women's Club in 1888, Balgarnie argued that the first step must be economic independence for women, followed by the control of (men's) passion by the use of reason. She rarely felt happy as part of this Club, however, and revealed to Henrietta Müller in an interview the following year that 'Fine ladies make me nervous ... I do not prefer speaking at drawing-room meetings. I am more at home when addressing working people, especially working men.' The drawing-room atmosphere of most women's peace meetings clearly did not appeal to her. She preferred an environment in which real debate took place: 'When the audience is either sympathetic, or directly antagonistic, one's ideas flow forth easily, and the listeners seem to inspire one.'[41]

In keeping with this preference for lively listeners, rather than the restrained reading or speaking that characterised drawing-room meetings, Balgarnie's arguments on peace education focused on the sort of opportunities that would have been available to working-class children, instead of (like Chant) drawing on the experience of the middle classes: the working-class home had no nursery or toy soldiers. Balgarnie highlighted the issue of discipline and argued that it was in the (mis)use of punishment that aggressive behaviour was learnt. In educating working-class children, 'the master or mistress, . . . being a bigger animal, could exert more physical power . . . instead of appealing to a child's common sense'.[42] She emphasised the class differences in education during this period, showing that among the working as well as the middle classes, belligerent behaviour was learnt and had direct effects in adulthood.

Balgarnie also drew on Ruskin in her arguments against war. Borrowing from his lecture on war in *The Crown of Wild Olive*, she argued that women were partly culpable for war because of their lack of interest in peace questions. Following Ruskin, Balgarnie used the same assumption of what might be called the false consciousness of middle-class women that was used by many speakers and writers who argued that women and peace were inherently linked. War was, she said, nothing but 'a sorrow and an affliction to woman', yet women appeared to have no sympathy for the cause of peace. Instead, they were 'dazzled' by the red coats of the military.[43] In a paraphrase of Ruskin, she raised a laugh from the audience by saying that 'If only the women of England could be made to feel half as much for the horrors of a great battle, as they cared for the smashing of their best tea-things at home, we should very soon see war cease.'[44] From Ruskin, these arguments appear misogynist in their emphasis, coming as they do at the end of a long lecture on men's role in war, at which it is concluded that war is 'wholly' the fault of women, who 'are too selfish and too thoughtless to take pains for any creature out of your own immediate circles'.[45] Yet for Balgarnie, who was more comfortable debating among working people than giving a formal speech to a large, middle-class meeting, such an argument had a very different impact, and it is likely that as an experienced public speaker she was aware of this. A critique of the idleness and political ignorance of middle-class women could be used to much greater effect by a woman than by a man. Balgarnie's exploitation of this is confirmed by the fact that she does not actually reference Ruskin in her speech, instead presenting her ideas as an outgrowth of her experience.

In addition to the 'modernity and vibrant radicalism' that these four women represented, they brought a range of finely honed speaking and debating skills to the IAPA meetings.[46] Isabella Tod's and Laura Ormiston Chant's middle-class philanthropic backgrounds contrasted with the working-class women's concerns which Florence Fenwick Miller and Florence Balgarnie attempted to represent. Isabella Tod's critiques of expansionist imperialism and her opposition to the use of violence and physical force contrasted with Fenwick Miller's combative and controversial approach to the question of how to achieve peace and arbitration. All four women introduced feminist arguments of sexual difference through, for example, Chant's analyses of maternalism and education, and Balgarnie's conflicting critique of idle middle-class womanhood and domesticity. Their involvement with the IAPA demonstrates that, within some contexts, the various strands of the women's movement could be brought into dialogue with one another. The abstract question of peace, and women's relationship to it, was addressed in many different ways. Chant drew on quasi-essentialist ideas of woman's innate moral nature, while Tod represented moral behaviour as a universal human aspiration. The agnosticism of Miller and secularism of Balgarnie provided a strong contrast with Chant, an Evangelical preacher. In addition, Tod's Unionism set her apart from the Home Rulers who dominated the IAPA. Yet all four women found common ground within the Association, accommodating as it did Evangelicals and secularists, neo-Malthusianists and social purity campaigners.

Despite the divergent interests within the peace and feminist movements of the late Victorian period, it was possible to formulate co-operative and collaborative approaches through which many diverse interest groups could unite to express common aims. By the turn of the century, the IAPA was working with absolute pacifists, Continental nationalists, socialists and feminists, all of whom had different conceptions of what peace meant and how it might be achieved. To further illustrate the range of ways in which women worked for social progress through the IAPA, the following chapter examines the work of its two single-sex auxiliaries, the Women's Peace and Arbitration Auxiliary, which seceded from the Peace Society and affiliated to the IAPA in 1881–82, and the Women's Committee, which was established in 1887.

Notes

1 *Concord* (18 June 1890), p. 77.
2 *Journal* (30 November 1885), pp. 187–8.
3 *Ibid.* (1 July 1884), p. 2.

4 *Ibid.*, p. 4.

5 Van der Linden, *International Peace Movement*, pp. 925–6.

6 *Journal* (31 May 1886), p. 53.

7 *Herald* (1 June 1886), p. 76; (1 January 1889), p. 167.

8 Hodgson Pratt to Élie Ducommun, 30 September 1891, Document 2, Box 1, IPB 1892–1914, International Peace Movement, League of Nations Archives, United Nations Library, Geneva, Switzerland (hereafter IPB). Emphasis in original.

9 Élie Ducommun, 'Report on the work of the International Peace Bureau from 1 January 1891 to 31 January 1893', Document 1, Box 38, IPB.

10 W. Gilliver to Élie Ducommun, 11 August 1892; P. H. Peckover to Élie Ducommun, 19 July 1892; Isaac Sharp to Élie Ducommun, 5 August 1892; W. E. Darby to Élie Ducommun, 23 July 1892; J. F. Green to Élie Ducommun, 28 July 1892 and 12 August 1892; M. L. Cooke to Élie Ducommun, 8 August 1892; list of delegates, 21 July 1892; Document 3, Box 64, IPB.

11 International Peace Bureau, *Resolutions of the Eight Universal Peace Congresses 1889–1897*, n.d., 29, Document 9, Box 58, IPB.

12 For more on Suttner, see Brigitte Hamann, *Bertha von Suttner: A Life for Peace* (translated by Ann Dubsky) (Syracuse, New York: Syracuse University Press, 1996); Beatrix Kempf, *Suffragette for Peace: the Life of Bertha von Suttner* (translated by R. W. Last) (London: Oswald Wolff, 1972); Caroline E. Playne, *Bertha von Suttner and the Struggle to Avert the World War* (London: George Allen and Unwin, 1936).

13 Élie Ducommun and others, 15 May 1900 and 25 May 1900, Document 4, Box 201, IPB.

14 Hodgson Pratt to Élie Ducommun, 1 January 1900, Document 5, Box 200, IPB.

15 Pamphlet for a Trafalgar Square Demonstration, 24 September 1899, 'Protest of the men and women of London against war with the Transvaal Republic', Document 1, Box 200, IPB. The Transvaal Committee was an offshoot of the Transvaal Independence Association, founded in 1881. Dominated by radicals, its work fed into that of the South Africa Conciliation Committee. Interestingly, its chairman was J. Passmore Edwards of the Peace Society, and its treasurer, Dr G. B. Clark, was a member of the IAPA. Stephen Koss (ed.) *The Pro-Boers: The Anatomy of an Antiwar Movement* (London: University of Chicago Press, 1973), p. 3.

16 *Concord* (October 1899), pp. 165–7; (November 1899), pp. 180–1 in Cooper, *Patriotic Pacifism*, pp. 104, 176.

17 Peace Society Minute Book, 22 November 1881, 19 June 1882, PSA.

18 *Journal* (1 July 1884), p. 7.

19 *Concord* (22 June 1892), p. 114; (April 1893), p. 74. Patrick Kay Bidelman, 'Marie Desraismes', in Josephson (ed.), *BDMPL*, p. 208;. Hause with Kenney, *Women's Suffrage and Social Politics*, p. 8; Moses, *French Feminism in the Nineteenth Century*, pp. 179–84.

20 *Concord* (17 March 1891), p. 47.

21 Total IAPA membership was about four hundred people, with an additional circulation of the *Journal* to subscribing non-members of about one hundred. *Concord* (1884–1899); see also J. Frederick Green to Élie Ducommun, 21 September 1898, Document 7, Box 19, IPB.

22 *Concord* (18 March 1890), p. 39; *Journal* (23 December 1885), p. 196.

23 *Journal* (15 April 1885), p. 102.

24 See Maria Luddy, 'Isabella Tod', in Mary Cullen and Maria Luddy (eds), *Women, Power and Consciousness in Nineteenth Century Ireland* (Dublin: Attic Press, 1995); Heloise Brown, 'An alternative imperialism: Isabella Tod, internationalist and "Good Liberal Unionist"', *Gender and History*, 10: 3 (1998), pp. 358–80.

25 I. M. S. Tod, *Northern Whig* (17 June 1886) in Luddy, 'Isabella Tod', pp. 221–2; see also Tod in *Northern Whig* (26 May 1887) in Luddy, 'Isabella Tod', p. 223; Sandra Stanley Holton, *Suffrage Days: Stories from the Women's Suffrage Movement* (London: Routledge, 1996), pp. 45–7; Walkowitz, *Prostitution and Victorian Society*, pp. 124, 126–7; Helen Blackburn, *Women's Suffrage: A Record of the Women's Suffrage Movement in the British Isles, with Biographical Sketches of Miss Becker* (London: Williams and Norgate, 1902), pp. 127, 130, 141, 209.

26 *Journal* (15 August 1887), p. 85; *Review* (15 January 1897), pp. 58–63; *WPP* (12 October 1889), p. 1. For more on Fawcett, see Rubinstein, *A Different World for Women*, p. 115.

27 *Journal* (1 June 1884), p. 11. Emphasis added.

28 *Ibid.* (31 July 1885), p. 137.

29 *Concord* (17 March 1891), p. 45.

30 Walkowitz, *City of Dreadful Delight*, pp. 66–7, 235; Bland, *Banishing the Beast*, p. 193.

31 *Woman's Signal* (21 January 1897), p. 40.

32 *Journal* (31 July 1885), p. 137. Emphasis added.

33 *WSJ* (1 September 1883), p. 165; see also (1 July 1882), p. 105.

34 See chapter 9 for a fuller discussion of this. *WSJ* (1 January 1889), pp. 4, 8–14.

35 Walker, 'Party political women', p. 177.

36 *Ibid.*, pp. 176–7; Walkowitz, *City of Dreadful Delight*, p. 126; Bland, *Banishing the Beast*, p. 105.

37 *WPP* (1 December 1888), p. 1.

38 Bland, *Banishing the Beast*, pp. 106, 118, 121.

39 *Journal* (31 July 1886), p. 76.

40 Bland, *Banishing the Beast*, pp. 3, 18, 30–1, 37; Hollis, *Ladies Elect*, pp. 134–5; Vron Ware, *Beyond the Pale: White Women, Racism and History* (London: Verso, 1992), pp. 209–11, 217–18; Marian Ramelson, *Petticoat Rebellion: A Century of Struggle for Women's Rights* (London: Lawrence and Wishart, 1967), p. 96; Philippa Levine, *Victorian Feminism 1850–1900* (London: Century Hutchinson, 1987), p. 115; *Review* (15 April 1889), p. 186.

41 *WPP* (16 March 1889) in Bland, *Banishing the Beast*, p. 44; Walkowitz, *City of Dreadful Delight*, p. 68.

42 *Journal* (31 July 1886), pp. 76–7.

43 *Ibid.*

44 *Journal* (31 July 1886), p. 77; John Ruskin, *The Crown of Wild Olive: Four Lectures on Industry and War*, 3rd edn (Orpington, Kent: George Allen, 1889), p. 169.

45 *Ibid.*, p. 169.

46 Walkowitz, *City of Dreadful Delight*, p. 67.

8

Awakening women:
pacifist feminism in the IAPA

HE IAPA had a women's auxiliary almost from the date it was founded, as between 1881 and 1882 a number of women in the Peace Society's Auxiliary attempted to formally attach their organisation to the IAPA. When matters reached a head in April 1882, the Auxiliary split, with one organisation – the Women's Peace and Arbitration Auxiliary (WPAA) – attaching itself to the IAPA, the other reconstituting itself and remaining with the Peace Society. The social purity politics and Evangelicalism of the WPAA did not appeal to other women members of the IAPA, however, and a second female auxiliary was founded in 1887, titled the Women's Committee. This chapter considers why such an inclusive organisation as the IAPA had two separate female auxiliaries, and examines the politics of each.

An article by Hodgson Pratt published in *Concord* in 1888 dwelt at length on women's relationship to peace, and their special qualities that would be of use in the movement. Unlike the Peace Society, he assumed women's rights as a given. Pratt wrote: 'To women, growing stronger in the best kind of influence over men, through their wider training and acquirements, and the recognition of their *right* to a greater part in the world's affairs – to women we look for help to reach that new world.'[1] Although he believed that there should 'be no peace society without its women's branch', Pratt also questioned the wisdom of having a separate 'Women's Column' in *Concord* and separate auxiliaries, such as the Women's Committee and the WPAA.[2] He reminded the readers of *Concord* that:

> women as well as men sit on the Executive Committee; and some of us think that every word in the Journal should be one which men and women may express or receive without distinction . . . Some of us doubt whether greater identification of the two branches of the

human family in all thought and work is not desirable, rather than this tendency to separateness.[3]

The issue of mixed sex versus separate women's organisations was not generally a matter for debate within the peace movement, although as previous chapters have shown, the Peace Society was very specific about the role its women's auxiliary should take. The IAPA, however, was more flexible. Its approach to women's involvement meant that separate spaces for women did not necessarily marginalise them, but could instead offer greater opportunities for debates and meetings in which women managed and conducted their own affairs. They could then focus on those aspects of the peace movement that were of greatest interest to them. The WPAA, for example, was particularly concerned with social purity questions and its members often raised these within discussions on peace and pacifism. But within the IAPA, and again in contrast to the Peace Society, women had the opportunity for involvement in its Executive Committee. Many members of its other women's auxiliary, the Women's Committee, were involved in both the separatist and the mixed-sex aspects of the Association.

Whether separate organising was compatible with the peace movement was less a matter for debate than in other areas of the women's movement, because there was not the same degree of ideological conflict between the social constructions of 'women' and 'peace' as there was between, for example, 'sex' and 'class'.[4] Women were often represented in their traditional role as mothers, and pacifist feminists frequently emphasised the special reasons why women as a sex would benefit from an end to war – usually via the argument that women suffered through losing husbands and sons – but there was also great interest in ungendered questions of international arbitration and conflict resolution. Auxiliaries such as the Women's Committee engaged with similar arguments to the mainstream peace movement, and *Concord* regularly carried a 'Women's Column' that covered publications or speeches on peace questions that would have been of equal interest to men and women readers. It seems that separate women's auxiliaries were required by women members because these provided them with the space to debate the theory and practice of the peace movement, while also enabling them to explicitly draw connections with other issues of interest, such as – in the case of the WPAA – sexual morality and social purity.

The WPAA affiliated itself to the IAPA in 1881 and finally separated from the Peace Society in the summer of 1882. E. M. Southey and the other women who constituted the WPAA after the split with the Peace

Society were overwhelmingly based in London and, perhaps surprisingly, were mostly Quakers. Under Southey's leadership, the WPAA in its new guise was as energetic in its peace work as it had been when part of the Peace Society. In 1884, Southey responded to an article in the IAPA's *Journal* by John Noble, which gave 'Twelve Reasons in favour of Arbitration as a Substitute for War in the Settlement of International Disputes'. She requested no less than two thousand copies of the article for circulation, suggesting that although the WPAA's work was not being reported in detail in the *Journal*, it was nonetheless continuing apace.[5]

In 1885, Southey began the production of her own journal, *The Olive Leaf*. Its first issue contained a brief history of the development of the WPAA, beginning with the Olive Leaf Circles, the 'step in advance' made by the formation of the women's auxiliary to the Peace Society in 1874, and the decision in 1882 that 'it was thought desirable to work independently of the Peace Society, but, at the same time, in harmony with them'. A desire was expressed to 'co-operate heartily with every kindred society' working for peace, while the *Journal* acknowledged the assistance the WPAA had provided to the IAPA at conferences and meetings. It was noted in the *Journal* that *The Olive Leaf* was not devoted exclusively to peace questions, having a much wider scope that included the 'moral and social welfare' of the nation. The Peace Society's publication, the *Herald of Peace*, gave *The Olive Leaf* a much briefer notice, detailing its price and publisher and remarking that it 'contains very useful information'. Mrs Southey was nonetheless recognised by the Peace Society as 'an earnest worker in the cause'.[6]

In keeping with this mood of conciliation, in the late 1880s the factions that had dominated the British peace movement for nearly ten years began to temporarily break down. As the prelude to a cross-organisational 'Great Peace Demonstration' in the summer of 1889, a meeting of the Moral Reform Union (MRU) was held at the house of its secretary, Thomazine Leigh Browne, in March of that year.[7] The membership overlap between the MRU and the WPAA was considerable. Leigh Browne was a member of the WPAA throughout its 1874–90 lifespan, and was also a member of the MRU and the Social Purity Alliance (SPA). She may have been influential in calling the meeting, but why it was held under the auspices of the MRU rather than as a peace meeting is unclear. It is possible that the WPAA offered the most obvious common ground between the Peace Society and the IAPA, blending as it did the moral and religious concerns of the older organisation and the radicalism of the new. The meeting saw widespread co-operation between members of different peace societies, despite the fact that the main concern of the MRU was the promotion of social purity.

The Moral Reform Union was the most feminist of the social purity organisations of the late nineteenth century. Established in 1881 by Browne, it survived until 1897 and its membership averaged 150 men and women, peaking at 177 in 1889–90 when Helen Taylor took over as secretary.[8] It was concerned with education, rather than legal reform or repeal, and its professed aims were to 'collect, sell, distribute, or publish Literature for Moral Education', to study all matters affecting 'the moral welfare of the young', and to work to reform 'public opinion, law and custom on questions of sexual morality'.[9] It opposed free love, and any form of state-regulated prostitution, and argued that girls under the age of eighteen should not be held responsible for any 'immorality' that was visited upon them. It was divided on the question of divorce, but in agreement that judicial separation should be sufficient in the face of an 'unhappy marriage'.[10] Pamphlets and tracts produced by the MRU focused on the Contagious Diseases Acts, the poor moral standards of public figures, and the need to eradicate sexual double standards.[11] It had strong links with the Social Purity Alliance, an anti-CD Act organisation founded by William Shaen that aimed to promote self-control among men so that prostitution would become unnecessary. For just under a year the MRU shared in the production of the SPA's journal, the *Pioneer of Social Purity*.

As an organisation, the MRU attracted a curious mix of people. Many of its members were political radicals, often involved in repeal organisations such as the Ladies' National Association. While such men and women were undoubtedly concerned with the MRU's first two aims of protecting the moral welfare of the young and publishing material on moral education, they were also concerned with carrying out practical measures for reform of ideas on sexual morality, particularly the sexual double standard. Other members, however, were clearly more concerned with moral reform than with promoting debate on such controversial subjects as sexual morality. For example, Priscilla Peckover was a MRU member, but did not argue for the reform of sexual morality in her own publications.[12] The more radical members of the MRU included: Henrietta Müller, editor of the *Women's Penny Paper*; Kate Biggs, sister of Caroline Ashurst Biggs; Helen Taylor, suffragist and step-daughter of John Stuart Mill (and the MRU's honorary secretary for four years); James Stansfeld, MP and campaigner against the Contagious Diseases Acts; his wife, Caroline Stansfeld (formerly Ashurst, aunt of Kate and Caroline Biggs); and William Shaen. It attracted many of the feminists who were active in the IAPA including Isabella Tod, Laura Ormiston Chant and Florence Balgarnie, as well as Isabella Ford, Anna Swanwick, who was president of the IAPA's Women's Committee, and a number of women who were members of the WPAA, including E. M. Southey.[13] These connections were the means by which Helen Taylor, as the MRU's honorary secretary, was drawn into work for the WPAA. In 1881, when the WPAA had attached itself to the IAPA but had not yet formally severed its ties with the Peace Society, Helen Taylor spoke at the WPAA annual meeting alongside Margaret Bright Lucas on 'the impotence of mere force . . . as compared with the slower but more thorough con-quests of moral persuasion'.[14] She also prepared a paper that was read at the 1893 International Congress of Women in Chicago by Marie Fischer-Lette of Berlin, another active IAPA member.

The MRU's March 1889 meeting of peace activists was an unpreced-ented and unusual occasion, characterised by caution. The resolutions passed were innocuous enough, and had clearly been designed so as to promote agreement from all perspectives. The first resolution, protest-ing against the expansion of the navy, was proposed by Priscilla Peckover and seconded by E. M. Southey of the WPAA; a second, expressing satisfaction with the progress of peace on the Continent, was proposed and seconded by Monica Mangan, secretary of the IAPA's Women's Committee, and William Evans Darby, secretary of the Peace Society; while the final resolution, requesting a petition to the government urging mutual disarmament across Europe, was moved by George Gillett of the Peace Society and seconded by Mrs Charles Mallet of the Women's Committee of the IAPA.[15]

The fact that the members of the various peace societies were meet-ing in the name of the MRU, and that the Peace Society was only just beginning to open its executive ranks to women with the appointment of four female vice-presidents, suggests that significant changes were taking place, perhaps occasioned by the recent appointment of Darby to the Peace Society on the recommendation of Priscilla Peckover. Within only a few months, in the summer of 1889, this new approach of co-operation and collaboration was publicly affirmed at a 'Great Peace Demonstration' held in St James' Hall, London. It was organised by a sub-committee of the Peace Society, aided by Southey and the women of the WPAA, and there was also collaboration with the IAPA and the Women's Committee. Those attending included Margaret Bright Lucas for the WPAA, Darby for the Peace Society, Hodgson Pratt for the IAPA, Thomazine Leigh Browne for the WPAA and MRU, William Randal Cremer for the Workmen's Peace Association, E. M. Southey for the

WPAA and Monica Mangan for the Women's Committee. Reports of the meeting appeared in both the *Herald* and *Concord*, and focused on the address given by the main guest, Laura Ormiston Chant, who emphasised the need to influence children against war, the horrors of war, and the need for the public to take a stand on behalf of peace.[16]

Within a few months of this meeting, however, further changes took place in the life of the WPAA. In response to a suggestion by Hodgson Pratt, the WPAA amalgamated with the other female auxiliary to the IAPA, the Women's Committee. Just a few months later, E. M. Southey retired from peace work. The WPAA Committee presented her with an illuminated address, which expressed their appreciation of 'her deep and untiring devotion to the Peace cause', and recognised 'her earnest and her zealous services . . . during the last sixteen years'. It also voiced the 'mingled feelings' with which WPAA members viewed their recent amalgamation with the Women's Committee.[17] These 'mingled feelings' were borne out over the following years. The new organisation was dominated by the Committee's methods and principles, which were not, as we shall see, entirely in step with those of the WPAA.

The Women's Committee was characterised by secularist politics, which placed it much closer to the IAPA in terms of ideology than the WPAA ever pretended to be. The Committee attempted to ally itself with prominent feminists, but at the same time distanced itself from campaigns that it deemed controversial. It worked primarily with the Women's Liberal Associations, the Women's Co-operative Guild and the education branches of co-operative societies.[18]

The Committee was formed in November 1887, and aimed to make the work of the IAPA more widely known, promote the study of questions of 'international concord', reform the teaching of children regarding war, promote the spirit of friendship toward 'foreign peoples', and 'especially . . . [awaken] WOMEN to a clearer perception of the evils of militarism'. It explicitly invited 'women of all countries, without distinction of class, party or creed' to join, a policy, it might be said, that closely echoed that of the IAPA.[19] The formation of the Committee had been prompted by the Executive Committee of the IAPA, who called a meeting in late 1887 which was attended by fifty women. The IAPA's 'Appeal to Women' had been reprinted, and they were 'anxious to obtain for it a wide circulation'.[20] Miss Anna Swanwick, suffragist and prominent translator of Goethe and Æschylus, accepted the presidency of the Committee, and Miss Monica Mangan was appointed its secretary.[21] In February 1888 *Concord* published details of two vice-presidents, one of whom was perhaps a surprising choice: Mary, Lady Hobart, and Millicent Garrett Fawcett.[22]

Fawcett's jingoistic imperialism and her support for rule by force have been discussed earlier in this book. Her commitment to the vice-presidency of the Committee appears to have been somewhat half-hearted. There is no record of her attending IAPA or Women's Committee meetings, although she sent written apologies for her inability to attend on at least four occasions, and finally resigned the vice-presidency in early 1889.[23] Monica Mangan's appointment as secretary was, however, a crucial one. She became an active and prolific member of the Committee and a translator of European peace articles for publication in *Concord*.[24] An anonymous letter in *Concord* in February 1889 noted that 'I am certain that the Committee could not have been carried on at all without [her] . . . devotion and energy.'[25]

In 1890, Mangan contributed a page-long article on 'Women and Peace' to *Concord*, in which she discussed the indifference of many women to peace work. Some, she considered, took peace either to mean something very 'indistinct' (such as, for example, inner peace or tranquillity) or they assumed it to mean absolute pacifism, rather than the adoption of practical steps to encourage arbitration between nations. Here, she may have been referring to the WPAA and the Peace Society respectively. The moral reform focus of the WPAA allied it much closer to the concept of an inner peace, which would then permeate and transform society, than to arguments for arbitration or international tribunals. The Peace Society, of course, had a public reputation as an absolute pacifist body, one of its chief signifiers of difference from the IAPA. Mangan went on to argue that although women had much improved their 'intellectual advancement' in recent years – and here she recognised that these improvements had also been condemned by many women – it was nonetheless still a common 'feminine characteristic' to exhibit 'an essential and deeply-rooted Conservatism . . . [and] a certain lack of mental perspective'. During war, women flocked to nurse the wounded, 'but it does not occur to the majority to ask, "Need there *be* any wounded?"'[26] Women, Mangan argued, failed to think about the consequences of war, but once they realised that war was wrong they possessed an inherent duty to effect change by speaking and acting upon their principles.

Her arguments in this piece and in other speeches and articles reproduced in *Concord* suggest that Mangan was a secularist, although she did address the role of Christianity in war by reminding Christians that peace should appeal equally to 'the Christian and the friend of Humanity', because 'in the belief of one, souls so hastened into another world are often unprepared to die; and, according to the other, they are cut off, and pass into the cold night of oblivion before their time'.[27] When she first addressed the IAPA's annual meeting in 1892, she explained the strength that the 'London Secularists' had given to the work of the Women's Committee, and acknowledged the input of the women of the Society of Friends, who largely constituted the membership of the WPAA.[28] This classification epitomises the differences between the two auxiliaries. Mangan's use of secularist ideas located her ideologically with the Committee, whereas Evangelicals such as Southey and the Quakers who made up the WPAA preferred moral and religious arguments.

Mangan used free trade and Cobdenite arguments for peace rather than religious ideas. She held that 'prosperity would result from the interdependence of nations . . . [F]ree commercial relations, international education, and other ideals – in a word, all which tends to the unity of man – would sweep away the prejudices founded upon the self-seeking fostered by diplomats.'[29] She clearly had more in common with the radicalism of Hodgson Pratt and the IAPA than with the 'peace through moral reform' message of the WPAA. Mangan's role within the Women's Committee ended after only a few years, however. She married Hodgson Pratt in late 1892, and although she continued to attend peace meetings, the greater part of her time was taken up with the demands of marriage and motherhood. The couple retired from peace work and moved to France in 1899, when the chairmanship of the IAPA was taken up by Felix Moscheles.

The Women's Committee's first report was published in *Concord* in July 1888, and showed that it had been working closely with the Women's Liberal Associations (WLAs), a fact emphasised by their invitation of the WLA Committee member, Eliza Orme, to the IAPA's annual meeting in 1888.[30] The Committee offered to give lectures on peace and arbitration to WLA meetings, and asked the WLAs if one or two members from each would join them in promoting peace. Connections between the Committee and WLAs developed further over the following months, as a number of the members clearly overlapped. In addition to lectures in Bristol arranged by Eliza Orme, Emilia Monck (a member of the Women's Committee and the Chelsea Liberal Association) arranged similar meetings, as did Committee members Marion Mills and Miss Ravenstein, who had links with Brixton Liberal Alliance.[31]

For a short period, the Women's Committee's small member-ship was fairly active. In 1888, it held meetings that were addressed by Mrs Oscar Wilde, Mrs Stuart Downing and Florence Balgarnie, among others. Mrs Wilde focused upon the influence that women had over men, as wives, sisters or friends, and the influence that mothers had over children. She concluded that the family was the 'unit of the nation', and much work could be done by 'the preservation of peace in the family'. Florence Balgarnie, in contrast, spoke about the bodies that supported war, 'monopolies, the military, and the Government classes', while Mrs Downing stated that the Committee did not believe in the 'extreme' peace principle (absolute pacifism), nor did it wish for the obliteration of armies and navies. Indeed, it could see the 'wisdom of maintaining [these] . . . in a state of efficiency'. Instead, its purpose was to educate people and public opinion in different nations, so that they would prefer to settle disputes by 'rational' means. She concluded that 'we know that information as to the objects of the Association is the only thing needed to make it successful'.[32] Women's role was therefore to be patient and calm enough to put the message across successfully.

Despite this encouragement, the Committee cannot have worked as well as it was originally hoped. At the February 1889 annual meeting, Hodgson Pratt proposed that the Women's Committee amalgamate with another society. He sent the meeting a list of twenty-two suggestions for its future work, which included international education, International Conferences of Women, the formation of a sub-committee to supply articles to the press, correspondence with existing women's committees with a view to holding local conferences, and consideration of whether the Committee would be 'stronger and more successful' if it was to constitute itself independently of the IAPA. The Committee's response came within a year, when it amalgamated with the WPAA, to become known as 'the Women's Committee of the International Arbitration and Peace Association'.[33]

The amalgamation raises the question of why the Women's Committee was established separately from the WPAA to begin with. As shown in chapter 4, the WPAA's feminist leanings were unacceptable to the Peace Society, but in the context of the IAPA it seems to have been its Evangelical social purity stance, rather than its feminism *per se*, which was problematic. Certainly it seems to have been insufficiently politicised for those who made up the Women's Committee, as Monica Mangan's use of Cobdenite arguments, and her rejection of the search for 'inner peace' as a road to international peace, suggest. The problem was not one of absolute pacifism against pragmatism, as characterised by the conflicts between the Peace Society and the IAPA, but a distinction in the way that ideas of the domestic sphere were used. The WPAA explicitly argued that moral purity was a prerequisite for peace. The Women's Committee, by contrast, echoed the secularist ideas and political liberalism of the IAPA.

After the amalgamation, the new committee was dominated by the ideals of the old Women's Committee. It continued the co-operation with Women's Liberal Association branches, and relied increasingly on Cobdenite free trade arguments for peace. The social purity stance which had dominated the WPAA was entirely absent, although there were attempts by both auxiliaries to highlight the connections between the two organisations and their previous methods of work. For example, shortly after the amalgamation, Elizabeth Colgate, an Evangelical and a member of the WPAA since 1874, submitted a short account of Elihu Burritt's Olive Leaf Circles to *Concord* along with a letter sent in 1853 from the late Richard Cobden to 'Mrs C.', a convenor of an Olive Leaf Circle. The same letter had appeared in an early number of the *Women's Suffrage Journal*. It was a message of encouragement to women engaged in peace work, in which Cobden stated that: 'All I desire to impress upon you is the value of your own labours.' He continued: 'As a busy and practical politician . . . nothing is so calculated to nerve our arms, and impart confidence to us in the struggle of public life, as to know that the active sympathy of the ladies is on our side.'[34] Colgate concluded by noting that the letter showed that the peace cause had very much advanced since the days of the Olive Leaf Circles, but that much remained to be done. The letter, and Colgate's message, suggested that the Committee's interest in Cobden could be blended with the old-fashioned respectability and domesticity of the Olive Leaf Circles, an aspect that appealed to the WPAA members. But the peace movement had changed dramatically since the days of Cobden and the Olive Leaf Circles, leaving little common ground between the religious and the secular organisations. Colgate's message was not sufficiently nuanced to speak to the feminist, suffragist principles of the WPAA, which were also increasingly distant from the Olive Leaf Circles. The amalgamation of the Women's Committee and the WPAA ultimately failed, and the WPAA members disappeared from active work within the IAPA, a process which was hastened by the fact that the WPAA had lost both its chief organiser and its president since Mrs Southey's retirement and Margaret Bright Lucas' death in 1890.

The work of the Women's Committee slowed down considerably after 1892, probably as a result of E. M. Southey and Monica Mangan's retirement from peace work. *Concord* frequently reported the work of the LBWPAS, but there was little recorded on the activities of the Women's Committee. Even the more active women who constituted the Committee continued to work for the IAPA and contribute to its funds, rather than maintaining their own organisation.

In relation to feminism, the IAPA accommodated many different perspectives, from social purity campaigners who aimed to redefine motherhood, to secularists and neo-Malthusianists who saw arbitration and internationalism as evidence of the progress of civilisation. The Evangelical moral reformers who comprised the WPAA argued that if higher standards could be brought about in terms of relations between the sexes, then there would be an increase in social justice and universal peace would be attainable. In contrast, the Women's Committee relied on arguments of social justice through democracy and international co-operation. Within the IAPA, the diversity of its auxiliaries was tolerated and indeed encouraged, with the result that several strands of pacifist feminism can clearly be seen to emerge by the end of the century.

Chapter 9 pursues this question of diversity within the feminist movement by examining the International Council of Women, in particular the problems it encountered in recruiting women to work for peace.

Notes

1 *Concord* (16 May 1888), p. 199. Emphasis added.

2 *Ibid.* (22 June 1892), pp. 103–8.

3 *Ibid.* (17 March 1891), pp. 46–7.

4 Hannam and Hunt, *Socialist Women*, ch. 4.

5 *Journal* (1 July 1884), p. 9; (September and October 1884), p. 30; (1 December 1884), p. 48.

6 *Ibid.* (24 October 1885), p. 171; *Herald* (2 November 1885), p. 305. *The Olive Leaf* existed for at least three years, but is unlikely to have lasted longer than the turn of the century, as a journal with a similar name was founded by the Peace Society in 1903. MRU, Sixth Annual Report, May 1888, Fawcett Library, London, p. 8.

7 Also known as Mrs S. Woolcott Browne. See also Hollis, *Ladies Elect*, pp. 317–19; Sheila Jeffreys, *The Spinster and Her Enemies: Feminism and Sexuality 1880–1930* (London: Pandora Press, 1985), p. 19.

8 MRU Eighth Annual Report, June 1890, Fawcett Library, p. 10; Jeffreys, *Spinster and her Enemies*, pp. 18–22.

9 MRU, insert, First Annual Report, April 1882, Fawcett Library.

10 T. H. Browne, insert, MRU, Eighth Annual Report, June 1890, Fawcett Library.

11 MRU, Pamphlets and Leaflets, 1883–88, British Library, London.

12 MRU, Thirteenth to Fifteenth Annual Reports, 1894–97, Fawcett Library.

13 Other members were Ada Brocklehurst Hack, Sarah Hill, Annie Peppercorn and Louisa Wates. The MRU's paid secretary, Miss F. E. Albert, also attended WPAA meetings. MRU, First Annual Report, 1882, Fawcett Library; *Review* (15 September 1876), p. 411; (14 October 1876), p. 461; (14 March 1885), pp. 135–6; *WSJ* (1 November 1876), p. 155.

14 *Herald* (1 July 1881), p. 259.

15 For more on Mrs Mallet, see *WPP* (14 November 1891), pp. 883–4; *Concord* (19 May 1890), pp. 59–61.

16 *Herald* (1 June 1889), p. 227; *Concord* (18 June 1889), p. 72.

17 The ten women signatories to the address were nearly all members from the days when the WPAA was attached to the Peace Society. They were Jane Auckland, Thomazine Leigh Browne, Eliza Cole, Elizabeth Colgate, Ada Brocklehurst Hack, Sarah Hill and Annie Peppercorn. The newer members were Sarah Cattle, Marion Mills of the Women's Liberal Federation, and Louisa Wates. [*Concord* (17 November 1890), p. 126; *Herald* (1 December 1890), p. 170.] Mrs Southey continued a low-key career after her retirement, attending the Rome International Peace Congress in 1891 and establishing a 'Women's Local Peace Committee'. At the turn of the century she moved from London to Brighton and established a small social purity organisation called the Guild of St John. This organisation encompassed the sexual morality aspects of the MRU, as well as anti-vivisection and vegetarian arguments, temperance and pacifism, with the rationale that ridding the world of 'Social Evils' would bring about peace on earth and 'The world-wide patriotism of the Prince of Peace'. The Guild included Marion Mills, another IAPA and WLA worker, as chairman, and survived until at least 1911. E. M. Southey to Élie Ducommun, 13 August 1901, and 'The Guild of St John' flyer, Document 1, Box 86; E. M. Southey to A. Gobat, 8 April 1911, Document 10, Box 109, IPB 1892–1914, International Peace Movement, League of Nations Archives, United Nations Library, Geneva, Switzerland; *Concord* (October 1894), p. 131.

18 *Concord* (18 December 1889), p. 135.

19 *Ibid.* (15 November 1887), p. 122.

20 *Ibid.*

21 Mary L. Bruce, *Anna Swanwick: A Memoir and Recollections, 1813–1899* (London: T. Fisher and Unwin, 1903).

22 *Concord* (16 February 1888), p. 163.

23 *Concord* (15 March 1888), p. 174; (20 July 1888), p. 229; (16 March 1889), p. 34.

24 *Ibid.*, various editions (1888–91).

25 *Ibid.* (19 February 1889), p. 21.

26 *Ibid.* (September and October 1890), p. 106. Emphasis in original.

27 *Ibid.*, pp. 106–7.

28 *Ibid.* (22 June 1892), p. 108.

29 *Ibid.* (16 May 1891), p. 81.

30 *Ibid.* (20 July 1888), p. 233. For more information on WLAs, see Walker, 'Party political women', pp. 165–9.

31 *Concord* (20 July 1888), p. 246; (15 August 1888), p. 253.

32 *Ibid.* (16 May 1888), pp. 203–4.

33 *Ibid.* (19 February 1889), p. 21; (16 March 1889), p. 34; (18 April 1890), p. 52.

34 *Concord* (17 March 1891), pp. 46–7; *WSJ* (1 March 1871), p. 29.

9

'A new kind of patriotism'?[1]
British women in international politics

P REVIOUS CHAPTERS have outlined the diverse contexts in which reformulations of patriotism and citizenship emerged. The feminist movement produced arguments based on 'separate spheres' ideologies which held that women's contribution to the public sphere would bring an increased recognition of humanity in international relations. In contrast, peace workers such as Priscilla Peckover based their arguments on how a full understanding of pacifism would lead to a revision of what was understood by the 'best interests' of the nation. The methods of organisation used by Priscilla Peckover, Ellen Robinson and the IAPA were arguably more collaborative than those of the Peace Society, because they managed to work with people and organisations with whom they had political or ideological differences. This chapter considers the issues involved in collaborative organisation in greater depth, with reference to the International Council of Women (ICW). The ICW was founded in 1888, and was intended to provide a point of international contact and focus for the feminist movement. It grew steadily across the globe and continues to function today, maintaining a formalised structure built upon the model established in its early years.

Even in its first decades, however, patriotisms and nationalisms intruded on the ICW in unexpected and often counter-productive ways. For example, the International Council of Women found that some potential members were hostile to the prospect of organising internationally. In 1890, Millicent Garrett Fawcett put it to the secretary of the ICW that the British and US women's movements could have nothing to learn from one another. When the issue of peace work was raised at the 1899 Congress it was widely accepted as a worthwhile principle, yet when the ICW tried to transform argument into practical work, it met with considerable opposition and inertia at national levels. In addition to disputes over if and how such work could be practical, member

Councils tended to prioritise other issues, such as domestic politics, over foreign concerns. Particularly during periods of international conflict, National Councils fell back on conventional constructions of patriotism and (often temporarily) withdrew from international peace work. The ICW had great difficulty deciding how best to campaign for women's interests in an international context.

The ICW was originally conceived of in 1882, and thus preceded by a number of years the growth in international women's organisations that took place in the early twentieth century. It was undeniably important in the development of an international movement for women's rights, and in 1899 became the first international women's association to identify itself with the peace movement. Here, the focus is on the formative years of the Council, and how it established strategies for international work. Central to its methods were broad principles of peace and arbitration, and the means by which these principles were adhered to are discussed to illustrate the conflicts that were inherent in international feminist organisation.

The ICW was originally intended to be an international suffrage association. The idea came from the US suffragist, Elizabeth Cady Stanton, during a tour of Europe in 1882. She put the idea to a meeting of suffragists in Liverpool in 1883, who passed a resolution agreeing 'that union is strength and that the time has come when women all over the world should unite in the just demand for their political enfranchisement'.[2] Committees were appointed for centres in the US (with three members), London (ten members, including some of the most prominent names of the women's movement[3]), Manchester (sixteen members, again including many well-known names[4]), Bristol (three members), Scotland (three members, Priscilla Bright McLaren, Elizabeth Pease Nichol and Eliza Wigham), Ireland (two members, Isabella Tod and Anna Haslam) and finally, France (four members). This meeting created the circumstances for domination of the Council by British suffragists, in particular the radical suffragist wing of the women's movement, which has been explored by Sandra Stanley Holton. Holton suggests that moderate suffragists such as Lydia Becker were sceptical of the proposal and even envious of Stanton and Susan B. Anthony's leadership. She argues that the radical suffragists, and Ursula Bright in particular, may have gone along with Stanton's idea as a means of achieving prominence over the moderates.[5]

The momentum of the 1883 meeting was soon lost, however. Perhaps this is unsurprising for a movement that purported to be international but contained only forty-one individuals from five nations (three if England, Scotland and Ireland are counted as the UK). The Council at this stage provides a clear example of how the term 'international' was often applied to any group comprised of more than one nation, without necessarily taking account of the distinct methods of working that an association of many different nationalities would require. The US National Woman Suffrage Association (NWSA) attempted to develop the movement by inviting the European members to its 1884 annual meeting. Not surprisingly, very few could attend, although many wrote to express their sympathy.[6] Little was done to publicise the movement internationally or to consider how it could be more effectively organised. The US and British suffragists were using methods based on facilitating *national* organisation, rather than applying new methods that might draw nations together, and thus the Committee was inactive until it was resurrected by US suffragists in 1887.

May Wright Sewall (1844–1920) had, as secretary of the NWSA in 1884, witnessed the first attempt to set up an international movement, and it was she who proposed a second attempt in anticipation of the fortieth anniversary of the conference for women's rights at Seneca Falls, New York in 1848.[7] During the debate on her resolution, it became clear that the NWSA was firmly split into two groups: older activists who wanted to limit the international meeting to those who advocated women's suffrage; and younger women who wanted to extend the plan to include women working for 'all lines of human progress'. The younger members won the argument on the grounds that 'many organizations of women still holding aloof from suffrage allowed their very existence to the changes in public opinion, and in law wrought by the suffragists' and 'that in many countries the ballot is not recognized as an instrument of legitimate power in the hands of either men or women'. These principles, decided as they were by one body of US suffragists, formed the basis of the inaugural meeting of the International Council of Women, which took place – again in the USA – the following year.[8]

In the process of organising this convention, and after contacting over one hundred US women's organisations, Sewall became convinced that a change in direction was necessary, and that:

> what was needed . . . was to bring them [women] together under conditions which would show them that however different in traditions, in wealth, social position and in religious and political opinions they might be, they were all *equally* related to larger interests; that indeed the likenesses existing among the most different classes of women were larger than the differences among the same classes.[9]

Thus, the congress was designed so as to convince women that they were essentially the same, and to provide them with common ground in order to ensure the success of the meeting. This, Sewall has argued, became the 'dominating idea', and as Stanton and Anthony recognised, it was Sewall who then pressed the case for a permanent International and (US) National Council of Women.[10]

The British presence in Washington was influenced primarily by national considerations, involving, firstly, the changing nature of the suffrage movement, and secondly, the scandal occasioned by the citing of Sir Charles Dilke as third party in a divorce case. In 1888, the same year as the ICW Congress, the Central Committee of the National Society for Women's Suffrage (CCNSWS) split into radical and moderate factions as the result of a disagreement over the constitution of the Society. Under the radicals' new rules, all Central Committee decisions were binding on the regional Committees, and any organisation that had women's suffrage as one of its aims, rather than its primary aim, could affiliate to the Society. This would in effect have allowed Women's Liberal Federation branches to affiliate to the CCNSWS, a proposal to which Conservative and Liberal Unionist suffragists were vehemently opposed. The drive for the new rules was led by Mrs Frank Morrison and Leonard Courtney, and was supported by many of the IAPA women discussed in chapters 7 and 8, including Laura Ormiston Chant and Florence Balgarnie. Indeed, Balgarnie became secretary to the new society, which was renamed the Central National Society for Women's Suffrage (CNSWS). Simultaneously, however, a moderate minority led by Millicent Fawcett and Lydia Becker seceded to re-convene the CCNSWS based on the old rules. The regional suffrage Committees were split in their affiliations, with some refusing to affiliate to either of the central Committees, which remained separate until they re-united in 1900.[11]

Perhaps more important than these divisions over the suffrage was the social purity aspect of the women's movement. It was this, combined with the autonomy of the regional suffrage Committees (as established under the 'old rules') that affected Helen Taylor's decision not to attend the Washington Congress. Taylor had been booked and advertised to speak, and was also expected to address a Senate Committee on women's suffrage with Elizabeth Cady Stanton. Yet the still autonomous Newcastle National Society for Women's Suffrage had nominated Dilke's sister-in-law, May Ashton Dilke, as a delegate to the Congress. On hearing this, and understanding that under the existing rules she had no power of veto, Taylor refused to attend the Congress in any capacity. For Stanton and Susan B. Anthony, organisers of the Congress, this was a considerable blow. No amount of pleading or cajoling could change Taylor's mind. Stanton wrote to her shortly before the Congress, 'Do you think the sainted John Stuart Mill if pledged to go to a great International Congress would have declined at the last minute because Sir Charles Dilke was to be there? On the contrary would he not have felt it more imperative to do his best to see that England was grandly represented.' She continued, 'You are extensively advertized & you cannot in honor now decline.'[12] Yet Taylor did not attend.

Laura Ormiston Chant, who with Alice Cliff Scatcherd and May Ashton Dilke, was one of the few British delegates to go to Washington in 1888, noted later that her position at the Congress had been severely curtailed by the moderates in the CCNSWS. She was initially invited to attend the Washington Congress as the CCNSWS delegate. However, the Manchester, Belfast, Bristol and Birmingham Committees objected to any delegates being sent to Washington, and at a CCNSWS meeting the decision to send delegates was rescinded on the motion of Helen Taylor. Chant went instead as a delegate for the radical Edinburgh Society on the suggestion of Priscilla Bright McLaren. When asked on her arrival why she was not representing her local Committee, she replied that 'the women of the Edinburgh National Society were enthusiastic and strong enough to do what the Central Committee were unable to do'.[13] Thus, divisions at the national level directly hampered the international work of British feminists.

Consequently, and perhaps predictably, the Congress was dominated by women from the USA, although there was some representation of European women and a sole participant from beyond North America and Europe, Pandita Ramabai Sarasvati, who presented a paper on 'The Women of India'.[14] The one hundred women who presented papers came from only seven different nations. Following a Committee on Organisation, consisting of as many international members as the Congress could muster, it was agreed to formally constitute a National and International Council. Only one member, Alice Scatcherd, dissented from the proposal to form an international council and supported a national body only.[15] Most histories of the ICW begin with this 1888 conference, although Leila Rupp acknowledges the importance of the 1882 meeting. Despite the fact that there was no active body in existence between 1882 and 1888, the longevity of the idea in the minds of Stanton, Anthony and Sewall is a testament to their commitment to the concept of international organisation.[16]

The ICW constitution, as decided by the Congress in 1888, began as follows:

> We, women of all Nations, sincerely believing that the best good of humanity will be advanced by greater unity of thought, sympathy and purpose, and that an organized movement of women will best conserve the highest good of the family and of the State, do hereby band ourselves in a confederation of workers to further the application of the Golden Rule to society, custom and law: DO UNTO OTHERS AS YE WOULD THAT THEY SHOULD DO UNTO YOU.[17]

This focus on the 'best good of humanity' resembles the feminist redefinition of patriotism discussed in previous chapters, in which women's interests were argued to be allied to humanity as a whole rather than the nation. The ICW took the practical implications of these arguments to their logical conclusion, however, in its focus on unity between women of different nations. The rejection of women's suffrage as a campaign issue led to something of a vacuum in terms of the ICW's aims, and as a result, the stated aims were ambiguously defined as the establishment of greater communication between women's organisations and the consideration of questions related to 'the welfare of the commonwealth and the family'.[18]

This equivocation was largely because the ICW intended to be open to women's organisations of any political or ideological perspective. The general policy of the International Council held that it was:

> organized in the interest of no one propaganda, and [has] no power over its auxiliaries beyond that of suggestion and sympathy; *therefore*, no National council voting to become auxiliary . . . shall thereby render itself liable to be interfered with in respect to its complete organic unity, independence or method of work, or shall be committed to any principle or method . . . beyond compliance with the terms of this constitution.[19]

In practice, however, the Council lacked focus in its aims and politics, and therefore attracted few prominent feminists. Some of the National Councils, particularly the British branch, even tried to exclude suffragists from international meetings, and as a result the blandness and ambiguity of the ICW's aims was not seriously challenged.

At the 1888 Congress, Fawcett was elected in her absence to the presidency of the new ICW by the US members of the nomination committee, on the grounds that she had written to the Congress on behalf of the National Vigilance Association expressing her 'warm sympathy' and conviction that 'by intercommunication of the two nations, much mutual assistance can be given'.[20] Sewall put this appointment in writing to Fawcett, and after a considerable delay received the reply that Fawcett would not have time to undertake the duties of president. It was agreed between Frances Willard, the temperance advocate, and May Wright Sewall that the most important work of the US National Council was to establish at least one National Council of Women (NCW) abroad, so that the US branch would no longer be *de facto* the International Council. With this in mind, Willard began a correspondence with Fawcett and received what she took to be an agreement that Fawcett would begin organising a British Council and reconsider accepting the presidency of the ICW.

The US National Council received an invitation to an international women's congress in Paris in July 1889, and used this opportunity to promote the Council idea, with May Wright Sewall presenting a paper on the issue.[21] However, the congress resulted in the foundation of a Conseil International Permanente des Femmes which, crucially, was not a French National Council of Women and did not affiliate with the ICW. Sewall's trip to Europe had another motive though, as she arranged a meeting with Fawcett in a final attempt to persuade her to accept the presidency. Although there were many prominent British feminists who had shown an interest in the ICW, none of these appear to have been approached by Sewall, who insisted that Fawcett should be president. Fawcett was young, but not a 'New Woman', and she had some degree of acceptability within the establishment. Yet Fawcett proved highly resistant to joining the ICW, and at her meeting with Sewall in the summer of 1890, Fawcett finally admitted that she did not believe that conditions in Britain were 'ripe for federating the existing organizations of women'. Further, to Sewall's 'utter disappointment', Fawcett said that she felt it 'quite impossible that English and American women should have anything in common, the conditions of their lives and the purposes of their respective societies being so different'.[22]

The first triennial meeting of the US NCW in 1891 officially recognised that it was still, in effect, also the ICW, as no other National Councils had yet been formed. It had been planned to hold the first quinquennial congress of the ICW in London in 1893, on the assumption that a British NCW would by then be established. This was now accepted to be impossible, and the 1893 meeting was moved to Chicago, where it could be held in conjunction with the World's Exposition. In 1892, a preliminary address was issued for the Chicago Congress that called on women from all nations to communicate with the ICW, and, if possible, to attend the Congress. This address increased the international character of the work to some degree, as correspondence was established with small numbers of women in Central and South America, Asia and Australasia. The 126 women's organisations represented in Chicago came from sixteen different countries, which was a substantial improvement on the 1888 meeting. But the most active nation in the Chicago Women's Congress, aside of course from the US, was in fact England, which sent no less than thirty delegates, including Laura Ormiston Chant, Jane Cobden Unwin, Lady Henry Somerset, Mrs Bedford Fenwick and Florence Fenwick Miller.[23] Also present was Lady Aberdeen, who was representing Irish women's work at the World's Fair, and spoke briefly at the ICW meeting to represent the Society for Promoting the Return of Women to all Local Governing Bodies, the Women's Liberal Federation of Scotland, and the Women's Franchise League of England.

At the close of the Congress, when the time came to elect new officers, the names of Lady Henry Somerset and Lady Aberdeen were put forward for the presidency. It was still seen to be essential to establish a British NCW, so that the next congress could be held in London. Lady Aberdeen was elected by a slim margin, and although she knew little about the constitution or aims of the Council, she accepted the post after some correspondence with Rachel Foster Avery, the ICW's secretary.[24] Lady Aberdeen's appointment altered the face of the ICW, as in her politics she trod a fine line between Whiggery and Gladstonian Liberalism, rather than feminism as such. A prominent feminist like Lady Henry Somerset would have made an effective president, but as her record in the temperance movement showed, her commitment to women's suffrage and her autocratic methods of working may have worked to the detriment of the ICW's long-term development. In contrast, Lady Aberdeen had a recent history of conciliation in her work as president of the Women's Liberal Federation, which had split over the issue of women's suffrage. Despite working for some years to keep the WLF united, a minority of members who believed that the WLF should support anti-suffrage Liberals withdrew in 1892 to found the Women's National Liberal Association. Lady Aberdeen worked to keep the suffragist WLF loyal to the Liberal party, and to minimise its desire to use the suffrage as a test question for Liberal parliamentary candidates.[25] She brought these diplomatic skills to her presidency of the ICW, recognising that its success depended on the establishment of as many National Councils as possible and the adoption of a moderate programme that would minimise dissent. Her three terms of presidency (she headed the ICW from 1893 to 1899, 1904 to 1920 and 1922 to 1936) saw the ICW transformed from the suffragist project of Sewall, Stanton and Anthony into a much more wide-ranging, if perhaps also less controversial, forum that was embraced by women across North America and Western Europe.[26]

The presidency gave Lady Aberdeen the responsibility for the organisation of the 1899 Congress in London. This was effectively the inauguration of the ICW as an international movement, yet Lady Aberdeen's absence from Britain during the run-up to the Congress (she and her husband were based in Canada from 1893) meant that there were considerable problems in organising a NCW for Great Britain. Lady Aberdeen decided that the National Union of Women Workers (NUWW) should become the National Council, rather than any 'newer body which might be formed for the purpose', but she experienced considerable difficulties in persuading the NUWW Committee to reorganise itself into Britain's NCW.[27] The National Union of Women Workers was a loose federation of charitable and social purity groups that held annual conferences across the UK. Lady Aberdeen's 1888 conference on 'Women's Work' in Scotland had provided the blueprint for the subsequent NUWW conferences, which began in 1889. The conferences were effectively a meeting point for regional groups, and it was not until 1895 that a national governing body was officially established. The NUWW's suitability as a National Council lay in its role as an umbrella group for a large number of affiliated regional societies, and the fact that Lady Aberdeen had long-standing connections with it. Yet its Committee could see no reason why it should subordinate itself to the ICW, and before agreeing to organise the 1899 Congress it demanded full power to decide both the subjects for discussion and the speakers. It was still arguing this point and requesting that the ICW's constitution be altered accordingly into the summer of 1897.[28] The NUWW's concerns seemed to be based on how the potentially divisive issue of women's suffrage was to be addressed, and their desire to ban from the Congress any discussion of marriage, divorce or 'New Woman ideas'. The NUWW supported a limited women's franchise only, and as a result of conflicts with the National Society for Women's Suffrage, the latter subsequently withdrew as an affiliated member of the NUWW.[29] The conflicts between the NUWW and other British feminists, as well as its disputes with the ICW, were the principal reasons for the postponement of the Congress from its original schedule of summer 1898 to one year later, in July 1899.[30] As late as 1897 the NUWW and ICW could not agree the terms for federation as a National Council, until in October the NUWW's Central Committee decided to form the National Council of Women of Great Britain and Ireland (NCWGBI) themselves, rather than waiting to reach agreement with the regional groups. The ICW approved this proposal in early 1898.[31]

During the 1890s the NUWW was dominated by moderate reformers and contained few leading feminists. As Florence Fenwick Miller re-marked during the NUWW's transferral to NCW status in 1898, its Committee had only one nonconformist member, Mrs Alfred Booth, and the Council was from the outset acknowledged to be 'essentially a Christian organisation'.[32] However, the separate sub-committee that made the arrangements for the 1899 Congress included not only NUWW Committee members such as Mrs Louise Creighton, wife of the Bishop of London, and Mrs Alfred Booth, but also socialists Margaret MacDonald of the Independent Labour Party and Dora Montefiore of the Social Democratic Federation (SDF). MacDonald was a NUWW member, but as Hannam and Hunt note, divisions within socialist politics between the ILP and SDF strongly influenced the involvement of socialist women at this time.[33] While women from a wide range of political organisations attended the 1899 Congress, they did not become involved in the ICW or NCWGBI's work in the longer term. Instead, the NCWGBI continued the NUWW's focus on philanthropy and social, rather than political, reform. Arbitration was not on the NCWGBI's list of suggested topics for the 1899 Congress, and it appears to have been only reluctantly accepted by them for inclusion. It was not until 1908 that the NCWGBI began to concern itself with questions of peace, arbitration and international affairs.[34]

However, the importance of the 1899 Congress should not be under-estimated, as it effectively set the standard and style for ICW meetings until the mid-twentieth century. Lady Aberdeen's influence was signific-ant in this respect, as she was also the main organising force in the ICW until her final retirement from the presidency in 1936. By the time of the 1899 Congress there were nine nations officially affiliated to the ICW: the USA, Canada, Britain and Ireland, Germany, Sweden, Denmark, Australia, New Zealand and the Netherlands.[35] In addition, the 1899 Congress included women from twenty-eight countries. Each of the nine NCWs presented a report on its work to date, as did women from Finland, Belgium, Italy, Russia, France, Norway, India, South Africa, Argentina, Palestine and Persia. The inclusion of South Africa on this list is highly significant given the absence of South African delegates from the 1899 Hague Peace Congress, and the outbreak of the Anglo-Boer war just months after the ICW and Hague Congresses. The ICW Congress was dominated by a large demonstration in support of peace and arbitration, and the Standing Committee on this issue that was set up as a result was the first to be formally established by the ICW.[36]

Leila Rupp has discussed how the ICW emphasised its internationalism at Council meetings by focusing upon the national characteristics of each nation present. The focus was from the outset placed upon the complementarity of nationalism and internationalism. Yet as Rupp has emphasised, these terms held intensely different meanings for women newly freed from – or indeed, still under – regimes of imperialist domination than they did for those from countries where national self-determination could be taken for granted. Where there was conflict, it was more likely to be over the role of national identities in the Council than the meanings or uses of internationalist ideas.[37] Unlike later organisations such as the Women's International League for Peace and Freedom, the ICW was not formed specifically with the pursuit of peace on its agenda, but rather, during its founding years (1888–99), women's love of peace was assumed, and their work for other causes such as education and the suffrage was expected to form their sphere of practical work. Hannam and Hunt note the irony that the issues the ICW was concerned with – social reform, the family, maternity and childcare – were very similar to those that the early twentieth-century Socialist Women's International and its British section focused upon. Yet socialist women rarely engaged with questions of pacifism and internationalism in the 1890s, and even in the years leading up to the First World War, there were few attempts to consider the implications of internationalism for socialist feminist politics.[38] Non-socialist feminist organisations such as the ICW assumed a connection between women and peace that drew on maternalist ideas as well as constructions of innate sexual difference, but there was a stronger emphasis in the ICW on relational feminism, or women's relationships to others, than on equal rights feminism or abstract ideas of equality.

The assumption of a 'natural' relationship between women and peace meant that the ICW, through its resolutions and its Standing Committee, did not actually expect its members to undertake political work for peace, but instead to co-exist in peaceful co-operation while they pursued their different aims. This is shown in an early statement issued by Sewall before the founding congress of 1888, which was disseminated widely across Europe on her visit the following year. It argued that there should be more National Councils because:

> Women have never yet united in large numbers save for good purposes; it is safe to predict that they never will. Their isolation from one

another is in the interest of brute force; their combination means a dominance of peace and spiritual power, the purification, the protection and coronation of the home; the home is the shrine for whose sacred sake all that is good and true on earth exists.[39]

This was in many ways a radical statement. Sewall's focus on women's isolation from one another was an area of concern for many feminists. She implicitly equated brute force with men and masculinity, and although her argument rested on assumptions of biological determinism, her analysis of warfare as a factor that divided women and prevented equality – between nations, as well as between men and women – was in some ways an astute criticism. The conflation of women's nature with pacifist ideals was an argument used by many feminists, but Sewall's statement was distinctive in that it identified an external factor, 'brute force', which was opposed to and, crucially, responsible for women's lack of access to power. However, Sewall's insight in this statement belied the conservatism that became evident within the Council by the end of the 1890s.

In the opening address by Lady Aberdeen at the 1899 Congress, when she had been ICW president for six years, there was an immediate emphasis on the importance of patriotism and national identity. '[W]hat we desire', she said, is 'that our National Councils may in very truth be *national* in character.'[40] At the special meeting on peace and arbitration, the resolution proposed and carried by the meeting was: 'That the International Council of Women . . . take steps in every country to further and advance, by every means in their power, the movement towards International Arbitration.' In support of the motion, there were addresses by women including May Wright Sewall, Ellen Robinson, Mme Selenka of Germany, Mme Waszklewicz von Schilfgaarde of the Netherlands and Marya Chéliga of France.[41] (Robinson attended as a delegate of the International Peace Bureau, who had been contacted by the ICW and invited to send a woman speaker.)

While the latter four women were highly active in the peace movement and the International Peace Bureau, it was the addresses by Aberdeen and Sewall that gave greatest insight into the reasons why the ICW had concerned itself with peace. Aberdeen, having drawn upon the commonplace argument that women generally suffered more from war than did men, went on to suggest that: 'We women of this day are learning a new kind of patriotism – we are learning to covet for our countries that they shall emulate one another as to which can do the most for the good of the world, and as to which can do the most to maintain the peace of the world.' This 'new kind of patriotism' was a response to the 'narrow patriotism' of the past, which 'women have done much to keep alive' by 'exalting their own country at the expense of others'. Now, she said,

> bound together in national and international ties by the 'Golden Rule' [Do unto others as ye would that they should do unto you], we should glory in a newer and fuller and more beautiful patriotism, which lacks nothing of the force of the old, but which transforms it . . . whilst giving it at the same time a worldwide field for the exercise of its new found power.

Aberdeen asserted a patriotism that was based on humanity, yet also assumed that women would 'give to [their] own country [their] heart's first and truest devotion'.[42] Internationalism in the ICW may have meant the recognition of women's common humanity, but it always came second to nationalism.

May Wright Sewall's support of the peace resolution gave greater consideration to the international aspect of the Council's work. She proposed a peace banner, inscribed with the symbols of all the National Councils, which would 'become ultimately the recognised international banner under which all nations of the world shall assemble, feeling that they have never come under the best inspiration of their own respective flags, until, with their own colours, the banner of peace is unfurled'.[43] The role of peace, according to Sewall, was to motivate national feeling as the consequence of a secure (peaceful) international situation.

The ICW aimed to attract as much attention as possible in the international press, and thus it was no surprise that the celebrated novelist Bertha von Suttner was invited to address its 1899 peace meeting. Germany had formed a NCW in 1897, but Austria, France and Switzerland had organised nothing by 1899. Suttner was consulted by Lady Aberdeen regarding which European peace women should be invited to the meeting, and Britain's NCW even proposed Suttner for the presidency of the ICW.[44] It appears that Suttner refused the offer of nomination, and in the event, she was unable even to attend the ICW meeting. It took place in London over the same dates as the Hague Peace Conference, which Suttner was attending as a press correspondent. At the last minute, she was prevented from travelling to London due to health problems, and her paper had to be read to the meeting by Mrs W. P. Byles. Suttner's paper summarised the progress being made at the Hague, and ended with the hope that:

> The women who, from all parts of the world, have come to this Congress, will . . . zealously and unanimously join in the work for peace, for they are the courageous representatives of right, freedom and ethical

progress. But I wish that the words which are spoken in this hall may reach our sisters outside, and that all mothers and wives – be they feminists or not, be they members of peace societies or not – may be roused to the duty of the present time.[45]

While Suttner recognised that women did not constitute a single unified force, she nonetheless suggested that those present had a duty to bring their skills to bear on the wider world. Her comments were remarkable for two further reasons. Most obviously, she made an early use of the term 'feminism', which suggests that she believed the ICW to be specifically feminist. Secondly, she raised the issue of sisterhood, and while referring to women collectively as 'sisters' in a rhetoric sense, relied on real rather than imagined familial relationships in arguing that the women who had a duty to work for peace were in fact mothers and wives, rather than women as individuals in their own right.

The Congress passed the peace resolution unanimously, and much enthusiasm was expressed for the potential contribution that the ICW women could make to the promotion of peace. Yet subsequent events showed that they had been overly optimistic. The chairmanship of the Committee was placed in the hands of the British NCW, and Lady Aberdeen (who was replaced as ICW president at this Congress by May Wright Sewall) was elected as the chair of the Peace Committee. Her involvement in it was short-lived, however, as the outbreak of the Anglo-Boer war, combined with her husband's role in government, led her to resign in 1900. It was the responsibility of the British NCW to find a replacement, so Mrs Alfred Booth was appointed. However, she resigned for similar reasons in 1901, and incredibly, the NCW Executive was unable to find a replacement.

It seems to have been impossible for the Council to find any Executive members who were prepared to promote peace during the Anglo-Boer war. For women who were located outside the peace movement and the various liberal and socialist anti-war movements, patriotism was defined as loyalty to the nation, rather than the alternative formulations discussed throughout this book. It was left to May Wright Sewall, as ICW President, to take up the Peace Committee's work. She apparently found that 'the wars that were then going forward in three continents involving nations in which there were affiliated Councils, made it apparently impossible' to undertake any peace work. These difficulties led to a greater awareness of the problems of recruiting politically active women who might subsequently find that their duties in respect of the Peace Committee clashed with other commitments, particularly, as Sewall put it, with 'her personal interests or the personal interests of the men of her family'. It was concluded that although women from politically active families were 'of vast value' to the ICW in other ways, Sewall 'had found it impossible that they should be useful' in regard to peace and arbitration campaigns. The failure to find a replacement chair for the Peace and Arbitration Committee meant that it remained without a leader, 'and [was] consequently practically non-existent' for three years, until May Wright Sewall resigned the ICW presidency and took up the chairmanship.[46]

Despite these very practical problems, the rhetorical commitment to 'peace' and women's 'natural' relationship to it remained. Lady Aberdeen and Bertha von Suttner spoke again on the question of peace at the 1904 ICW meeting, and May Wright Sewall pointedly referred to her mission to keep the National Councils actively supporting the peace resolution. The result of the 1899 resolution, she told the 1904 Universal Peace Congress, 'was what may be called an educational campaign participated in with greater or less sincerity and zeal by the different national organizations within the International Council'.[47] Sewall's approach, of all the Executive officers and National Councils, was perhaps the most internationalist. In 1909 she was still attempting to draw others into her vision of what could be achieved by international work between women, and commented, in a retrospective study of the work done between 1899 and 1904, that 'The National Councils had not yet come into an understanding of what is meant by International [sic] coöperation.' They were, she noted, failing to unite with other National Councils when circumstances demanded. This failure would appear to be a consequence of the ICW's focus on international and national organisation in combination. Any effort towards international work had to originate from the International Council, as the National Councils were each focused upon their internal work. Sewall's approach to the method and form of working did not change, however. She still aimed to prove that the 'necessary condition of the further progress of civilization' was the evolution of 'a peaceful method for settling national differences which shall be compatible with national dignity'.[48] The emphasis continued to be on further entrenching national identity, albeit making it perhaps less militaristic, rather than creating strategies that would encourage international identity or affiliation.

Another factor inhibiting peace work was the presence of an active international peace movement. Lady Battersea, president of the NCW of Britain, replied to Sewall's request for NCW reports on peace work that: 'we think it better for ourselves to leave the organization of demonstrations to the various Peace societies which are established and actively working among us'.[49] This response was to some degree a result of the moderate nature of the British NCW, but it also illustrates the awkward position in which all the National Councils were placed when asked to implement a resolution of international scale in a national context. Two National Councils (Argentina and Switzerland) refused to involve themselves in peace work because they believed this would mean implicit criticism of women in other nations who were affiliated to the ICW. But the majority of responding Councils (eight in total) argued that while they were in general sympathy with 'the cause of Peace', they saw little useful work that could be undertaken. Very few of the National Councils were working with, or through, the established peace movement. Their members typically had limited experience and knowledge of the peace movement, and little interest in working within it. Yet, as the popularity of the 1899 peace resolution showed, they did share a generalised commitment to a state of peace, which, while based mainly on rhetoric, nonetheless offered an analysis of war in gendered terms.

The ICW relied almost entirely upon rhetorical devices which linked cultural constructions of 'women' to abstract ideals of peace, including concepts of spiritual or moral 'inner peace'. Related to this was the problem that international organising was generally of an abstract nature. It had no visible boundaries or permanent location, and relied upon identifiable core members and organisations to create the sense of an imagined international community. Its work was not helped by its initial attempts to change its president and therefore its headquarters every five years. It quickly found that the only way for the Council to progress was to have a long-term president steering its direction, and this was one of the main reasons why Lady Aberdeen was repeatedly re-elected to the presidency. International meetings provided a sense of achievement and connection, though the primary ties between ICW members remained national in basis. It is also possible that patriotism (as it is conventionally defined) hindered international work. The ICW held internationalism as an ideal, but it also tied individuals closely to their own national identity and origins. For women working for social or political change within their own nations, an international movement was in some ways superfluous, because the issues under debate were mainly domestic questions such as education or employment, which were highly culturally specific. Therefore it was difficult for members to feel that they had a stake in the work of women of other nations. They were not working for an internationally located goal, such as the promotion of arbitration or the resolution of conflict. Shortly after the 1899 ICW Congress, Teresa Wilson, Lady Aberdeen's corresponding secretary, initiated a discussion with the International Peace Bureau and suggested that the ICW might make it possible for internationally organised societies to federate with the ICW in the same way as the National Councils. The idea came to nothing, but the possibility briefly existed for an organisation that combined national and international methods of work.[50]

Although the ICW provided a space in which international organisation could be imagined, it was limited in its impact upon feminism in Britain. By the late 1890s it had been transformed from its origins as a radical suffragist movement into a social reform organisation. As a result, the internationalism that formed part of the feminist politics of some Victorian women did not find a means for expression within the ICW. It was restricted both by its internal dynamics and the logistical problems of working internationally. However, despite its conservatism and the emphasis that was placed on homogeneity, it did offer a formal arena within which British feminists could work to establish international networks.

Notes

1 Lady Aberdeen (ed.), *The International Congress of Women of 1899: Report of Transactions of the Second Quinquennial Meeting, held in London, July 1899* (London: T. Fisher Unwin, 1900), p. 217.

2 May Wright Sewall, *Genesis of the ICW and the Story of its Growth, 1888–1893* (privately published, ICW, 1914), p. 2; National Woman Suffrage Association (NWSA), *Report of the International Council of Women assembled by the National Woman Suffrage Association, Washington, DC, US of America, March 25 to April 1, 1888* (Washington, DC: Rufus H. Darby, 1888), pp. 9–10.

3 Clementia Taylor, Margaret Bright Lucas, Helen Taylor, Henrietta Müller, Caroline Ashurst Biggs, Charles and Laura McLaren, Eliza Orme, Rebecca Moore and Harriet Stanton Blatch. Sewall, *Genesis*, p. 2.

4 These included Jacob and Ursula Bright, Mr and Mrs J. P. Thomasson, Margaret E. Parker, Mrs Oliver Scatcherd, Walter and Eva McLaren and Lydia Becker.

5 Holton, *Suffrage Days*, p. 65; Sandra Stanley Holton, 'To educate women into rebellion: Elizabeth Cady Stanton and the creation of a transatlantic network of radical suffragists', *American History Review*, 99 (1994), p. 1125; Sandra Stanley Holton, 'From anti-slavery to suffragette militancy: the Bright circle, Elizabeth Cady Stanton and the British women's movement', in Caroline Daley and Melanie Nolan (eds), *Suffrage and Beyond: International Feminist Perspectives* (Auckland: Auckland University Press, 1994), pp. 213–33.

6 Sewall, *Genesis*, p. 3.

7 International Council of Women, *Women in a Changing World: the Dynamic Story of the International Council of Women since 1888* (London: Routledge and Kegan Paul, 1966), p. 123; Michael A. Lutzker, 'May Wright Sewall', in Josephson (ed.), *BDMPL*, pp. 875–6.

8 Sewall, *Genesis*, pp. 6–7; see also Leila J. Rupp, *Worlds of Women: The Making of an International Women's Movement* (Princeton: Princeton University Press, 1997), pp. 15–22.

9 Sewall, *Genesis*, p. 10. Emphasis added.

10 *Ibid.*

11 Other IAPA members who were prominent in the formation of the 'new rules' society included: Mary Costelloe, Jane Holah, Margaret Bright Lucas, Florence Fenwick Miller, Henrietta Müller, Eliza Orme, Richard and Emmeline Pankhurst, Annie Peppercorn, Ellen Sickert, Hannah Whitall Smith, E. M. Southey and Mrs Wates. Those who re-established the 'old rules' society, the CCNSWS, included Louisa Bigg, Isabella Ford, Anna Swanwick and Isabella Tod. *WSJ* (1 January 1889), pp. 4, 8–14; Rubinstein, *A Different World for Women*, pp. 132–3; Holton, *Suffrage Days*, chapters 3 and 4; Ramelson, *Petticoat Rebellion*, pp. 94–6.

12 Elizabeth Cady Stanton to Helen Taylor, 6 March 1888, sheet no. 251, vol. 13, Mill-Taylor Collection, London School of Economics and Political Science, London.

13 *WSJ* (1 January 1889), p. 12. See also Holton, *Suffrage Days*, pp. 64–5, 74–5; Holton, 'From anti-slavery to suffrage militancy', p. 227.

14 Burton, *Burdens of History*, pp. 118, 120; Antoinette Burton, 'Colonial encounters in late-Victorian England: Pandita Ramabai at Cheltenham and Wantage, 1883–6', *Feminist Review*, 49 (Spring 1995), pp. 29–49.

15 Sewall, *Genesis*, pp. 15–16, 39; NWSA, *Report of the ICW*, pp. 30, 449.

16 Rupp, *Worlds of Women*, p. 15; Aberdeen, *Report of Transactions*, p. 53; ICW, *Women in a Changing World*, p. 14.

17 ICW, *Women in a Changing World*, p. 329; Maria Ogilvie Gordon, *Histories of Affiliated National Councils, 1888–1938* (privately published by the ICW, 1938), p. 14.

18 ICW, *Women in a Changing World*, p. 329.

19 Sewall, *Genesis*, p. 19. Emphasis in original.

20 Millicent Garrett Fawcett and Annette Bear to the ICW, in NWSA, *Report of the ICW*, p. 290.

21 This congress was attended by many of the radical suffragists who had been involved in the original idea for an international organisation in 1882. They included: Jacob and Ursula Bright, Walter and Eva McLaren, James Stansfeld, Elizabeth Blackwell, Florence Balgarnie, Mrs Ashton Dilke, Emilie Ashurst Venturi, Henrietta Müller, Sarah Sheldon Amos, Josephine Butler and Monica Mangan and Hodgson Pratt of the IAPA. *Actes du Congrès International des Œuvres et Institutions Féminines* (Paris: Bibliothèque des *Annales Économiques*, 1890), pp. 529–30.

22 Sewall, *Genesis*, p. 37. First two quotations from Sewall, third credited to Fawcett. Rubinstein notes that the latter quotation has 'the authentic ring' of Fawcett, and cites a remark made three years later by the American temperance campaigner Frances Willard, that she believed Fawcett 'considers America to be on some other planet, . . . she evidently looks upon the Republic across the water through the wrong end of her telescope – if indeed she ever look [*sic*] at all'. Fawcett later chaired a suffrage meeting at the ICW's 1899 Congress in London, but otherwise she kept a distance from the work of the ICW. Rubinstein notes that, although she accepted the presidency of the International Woman Suffrage Alliance in 1904, Fawcett was for much

of her life indifferent to international work. The only exception appeared to be where it explicitly concerned the campaign for the vote. Rubinstein, *A Different World for Women*, pp. 76, 137, 202–3.

23 May Wright Sewall (ed.), *The World's Congress of Representative Women: A Historical Resumé* (Chicago and New York: Rand, McNally and Company, 1894), pp. 20, 23, 33, 395; Sewall, *Genesis*, pp. 49–53, 60.

24 Lord and Lady Aberdeen, *We Twa: Reminiscences of Lord and Lady Aberdeen* (London: W. Collins and Co., 1925), p. 295.

25 Hollis, *Ladies Elect*, pp. 57–65; *Woman's Herald* (14 May 1892), p. 8.

26 Doris French, *Ishbel and the Empire: A Biography of Lady Aberdeen* (Oxford: Dundurn Press, 1988); Marjorie Pentland, *A Bonnie Fechter: The Life of Ishbel Marjoribanks, Marchioness of Aberdeen* (London: Batsford, 1952); *Concord* (22 June 1892), pp. 103–8; ICW, *Women in a Changing World*, pp. 126–7; Rupp, *Worlds of Women*, p. 15; Sewall (ed.) *World's Congress*, p. 19.

27 Lady Aberdeen, *The Canadian Journal of Lady Aberdeen, 1893–1898*, ed. John Saywell, (Toronto: The Champlain Society, 1960), p. 205; ICW, *Women in a Changing World*, pp. 19, 219.

28 *Woman's Signal* (3 November 1898), p. 280; Gordon, *Histories*, p. 69; Aberdeen, *Report of Transactions*, p. 109; ICW, *Women in a Changing World*, pp. 221–5; National Union of Women Workers (NUWW) Minute Book, 7 October [1897] and 11 March 1898, National Council of Women of Great Britain (hereafter NCWGB), London Metropolitan Archives, London.

29 NUWW Minute Book, 20 January 1897, 7 April 1897, 5 May [1898], NCWGB; French, *Ishbel and the Empire*, p. 193.

30 ICW, *Women in a Changing World*, p. 20.

31 Aberdeen, *Report of Transactions*, p. 88.

32 *Woman's Signal* (3 November 1898), p. 280.

33 Hannam and Hunt, *Socialist Women*, pp. 170, 174–5; Aberdeen, *Report of Transactions*, p. 18.

34 Gordon, *Histories*, p. 69; Aberdeen, *Report of Transactions*, p. 109; ICW, *Women in a Changing World*, pp. 221–5; NUWW Minute Book, 7 October [1897] and 11 March 1898, NCWGB.

35 Aberdeen, *Report of Transactions*, pp. 11–12.

36 ICW, *Women in a Changing World*, pp. 21, 23.

37 Rupp, *Worlds of Women*, pp. 122, 129.

38 Hannam and Hunt, *Socialist Women*, pp. 171, 181, 196.

39 Sewall, *Genesis*, p. 43.

40 Aberdeen, *Report of Transactions*, p. 46. Emphasis in original.

41 *Ibid.*, p. 232.

42 *Ibid.*, pp. 52, 217–18.

43 Sewall in *ibid.*, p. 235.

44 Lady Aberdeen to Bertha von Suttner, 27 April 1899, File 102, Box 13; Teresa Wilson to Bertha von Suttner, 28 March 1899, Box 21, Bertha von Suttner Correspondence, Fried-Suttner Papers, International Peace Movement, League of Nations Archives, United Nations Library, Geneva, Switzerland.

45 Suttner in Aberdeen, *Report of Transactions*, p. 230.

46 May Wright Sewall (ed.), *The International Council of Women from 1899 to 1904: Report of Transactions, Berlin, June 1904* (Boston, USA: by the author, 1909), pp. 75, 200–1.

47 Sewall in Universal Peace Congress, *Official Report of the Thirteenth Universal Peace Congress, held at Boston, Massachusetts, USA, October 3rd to 8th, 1904* (Boston: the Peace Congress Committee, 1904), 132; Maria Ogilvie Gordon, *The International Council of Women and the Meetings of the International Congress of Women in Berlin, 1904* (Aberdeen: Aberdeen Free Press, n.d. [1904]), pp. 6–7.

48 Sewall, *ICW from 1899 to 1904*, pp. 43–4, 75.

49 *Ibid.*, p. 71.

50 Teresa Wilson to Élie Ducommun, n.d., and 29 May 1899, Élie Ducommun to Teresa Wilson, 6 May 1899, Frederic Bajer to Élie Ducommun, 16 January 1899, Document 6, Box 231, IPB.

Feminist responses to the second Anglo-Boer war, 1899–1902[1]

T HE VARIOUS PACIFIST feminist discourses discussed in this book co-existed and to some extent competed with one another, a phenomenon seen particularly clearly during the final years of the study. An examination of the responses to the second Anglo-Boer war of 1899–1902 illustrates how nationalist and imperialist campaigns could challenge feminist arguments regarding women's unique role in the nation. The Anglo-Boer war concludes the period under discussion in this book, and is considered at length here because it was as controversial within the feminist movement as it was in the wider political landscape. A study of the arguments of Josephine Butler, Emily Hobhouse and Millicent Garrett Fawcett demonstrates that liberal and imperialist discourses strongly influenced the feminist responses to the war, and highlights not only the divisions within feminism at the turn of the twentieth century, but also the problematic impact of the Anglo-Boer war on the peace movement itself.

The Anglo-Boer war was distinctive in Victorian Britain as a conflict with a white, Christian and quasi-European population. The war was one-sided, although the Afrikaners' initial numerical superiority, combined with their familiarity with the geography and climate, meant that it was a long drawn-out conflict that concluded with a protracted period of guerrilla warfare. It was the tactics utilised in the final stages of the war, from December 1900, that received the greatest criticism from the British anti-war movement. Kitchener's policies of farm-burning and internment of Afrikaner women and children in concentration camps were intended to make survival impossible for the guerrillas. In practice, they not only further angered them, but they relieved them of family responsibilities and possibly facilitated the continuation of the resistance. The internment of women and children meant that the war was divisive for the British feminist movement, and produced a range of responses, both pro- and anti-war, due to Victorian feminism's complex relationship to liberalism and imperialism.

The most public feminist involvement in the Anglo-Boer war came from two women who were prominent in nineteenth-century feminism, and one who was entirely unknown. Josephine Butler, a highly regarded feminist who campaigned against the Contagious Diseases Acts in the 1870s and 1880s, published a long essay on the conflict, *The Native Races and the War*, in which she sympathised with the Afrikaners' situation but ultimately supported the British war effort on the grounds that it was undertaken for the protection and liberation of native South Africans. Millicent Garrett Fawcett, then *de facto* leader of the women's suffrage movement and a supporter of the use of physical force in the British empire, was selected by the War Office in 1901 to lead the government enquiry into conditions in the concentration camps. Emily Hobhouse, who had been active in the women's movement only briefly prior to the war, travelled to South Africa in 1900 to distribute aid in the concentration camps. Although it was her thorough and public criticism of the camps that led to the establishment of the Commission on which Fawcett served, Hobhouse herself was publicly snubbed and pilloried for her 'pro-Boer' stance and criticism of the government. For the peace movement, she quickly became the heroine of the conflict. This chapter examines Butler, Fawcett and Hobhouse's wider attitudes to war, imperialism and race, and considers the contribution each made to debates on the Anglo-Boer war.

Josephine Butler (1828–1906) came from a prosperous Liberal background. Her father, John Grey, had been active in the anti-slavery movement, the campaign against the Corn Laws and the agitation for the 1832 Reform Bill. His influence on Josephine is confirmed by the fact that she regularly drew upon anti-slavery language in her feminist arguments. In 1852 she married George Butler, and the pair moved in conservative, academic circles, often finding themselves marginalised for their liberal views. In the late 1860s, Butler was drawn into the campaigns for both women's suffrage and higher education. She was best known, however, for her leadership of the campaign to repeal the Contagious Diseases Acts. After Butler won repeal of the Acts in the UK, she extended the campaign to India in the 1890s, where governmental and military regulation of prostitution was more acute. The two greatest influences on Butler's arguments were Liberalism and Evangelical Anglicanism. Although she was perhaps closer in feminist politics to earlier campaigners like Barbara Leigh Smith Bodichon and Jessie Boucherett, whose main concerns were education and employment policies, her ideas on the sexual double standard shifted the grounds of feminist debate from a strictly liberal analysis towards a more comprehensive view of women's oppression within economic, political and sexual power structures.[2]

With the outbreak of the Franco-Prussian war in August 1870, Butler took a public stand against war, collecting an international petition of protest against the conflict and against war in general. It was signed by women only, and Butler argued in a letter to the Peace Society journal, the *Herald of Peace*, that 'I have less sympathy with the graceful charities of the scraping of lint and making of bandages than I have in woman's endeavours to make war hated as a crime.'[3] While Butler continued to support anti-war campaigns, she did little in the years after the Franco-Prussian war to draw attention to the peace movement itself. This is possibly because the Peace Society had decided to drop its opposition to the Contagious Diseases Acts, arguing that Butler's campaign was opposed only to the CD legislation, and not to standing armies or the mechanisms of war they enabled. In any case, Butler's work against the Acts soon took up all of her time. She often compared her mission to end the state's partial regulation of prostitution to her father John Grey's work against slavery.[4] Abolitionist ideas on slavery also informed her stance on war. For example, during the American Civil War both Butler and her husband supported the war, believing that it was right for the North to fight against slavery, and twenty years later Butler supported Home Rule for Ireland on similar abolitionist grounds. She argued that the British had kept the Irish in a position of subservience that was, particularly during the nineteenth century, 'a condition of slavery', and emphasised that she was using the term 'not sentimentally, but in a strictly legal sense'.[5]

In the period before the Anglo-Boer war, Butler had been 'pro-Boer', viewing the British forces as oppressors of the Afrikaner republics. However, she changed her mind after the outbreak of hostilities, and began to publicly support the government on the grounds that the British forces were fighting for the emancipation of native South Africans. Taking a pro-government stance brought her into conflict with many of her colleagues, although for the first time it led her into a close and sympathetic relationship with Fawcett. In addition to Butler's abolitionist principles, she opposed military intervention and upheld what might be termed Evangelical imperialist ideas, as she strongly believed that Britons had a mission to win converts to Christianity across the globe. Butler envisioned a Christian utopia in which 'race prejudice' and other social evils, such as war, would be history:

> We all wish for peace; every reasonable person desires it ... But *what* Peace? It is the Peace of God ... We do not and cannot desire the peace which some of those are calling for who dare not face the open book of present day judgment, or who do not wish to read its lessons! Such a peace would be a mere plastering over of an unhealed wound, which would break out again before many years were over.[6]

The attainment of a lasting peace was therefore dependent upon the acceptance, on individual and collective levels, of Christianity. This model of Evangelical imperialism was exemplified in the final sentence of *Native Races*, in which Butler argued that 'Race prejudice is a poison which will have to be cast out if the world is ever to be Christianized, and if Great Britain is to maintain the high and responsible place among the nations which has been given to her.'[7] She envisioned a world in which racial discrimination had no place, but Christianity regulated this utopian vision. The purpose of the empire was to spread Christian religion, and Butler believed – contrary to her own evidence, at times – that if both native races and imperialists were genuinely Christianised, then 'race prejudice' would be eradicated. This entailed the conversion of native races, but crucially, it also required a re-education of white Europeans with regard to their Christian responsibility.

Butler argued that the Anglo-Boer war was ultimately about slavery, attempting in *Native Races* to trace its origins over the centuries leading up to the conflict. From the British perspective, she held that the government had been inconsistent and unhelpful in its policies, altering them according to conditions at home and party preferences. Although she had been an admirer of Gladstone, she was critical of his foreign policy, arguing that 'the interests of the native races have been too often postponed to those of the ruling races'. Butler's longstanding opposition to war and her commitment to international co-operation were overruled on this occasion in favour of physical force. She wrote 'It can hardly be supposed that I underrate the horrors of war. I have imagination enough and sympathy enough to follow almost as if I beheld it with my eyes, the great tragedy which has been unfolded in South Africa.'[8]

Butler's concept of Evangelical imperialism was based primarily upon conversion rather than force. For example, writing in 1887 of Britain's record in Ireland, she asked:

> On what basis does our Empire stand? Very largely on that of conquest. Tell me what warrant there is in the teaching of Christ for the assertion of the righteousness of conquest? ... At the slightest provocation or resistance to our arms, were not unresisting races destroyed, their poor huts blown into the air by our guns, and their

women and children included in our righteous massacres? . . . To speak
of the sacred inviolability of our Empire in all its length and breadth,
and of the possible disruption of the Empire as something too terrible
to contemplate, is a weakness and a folly in face of the teaching of
Christianity, and the prophetic words of its Author.[9]

Yet while Butler condemned imperialism where it relied upon force, she
accepted to some degree the need for the displacement of native populations, arguing in *Native Races* that: 'The great blot on this necessary and
natural expansion [of the British empire] is the record (from time to
time) of the displacement of native tribes *by force and violence*, when
their rights seemed to interfere with the interests of the white man.'[10]
Displacement was not in itself unethical, but the use of force was. Butler
went to great lengths to publicly sanction the British intervention in
South Africa not, she argued, because she supported the Conservative
government's aggression, but because she believed it was necessary
to make a stand against Afrikaners' unjust treatment of native South
Africans. British rule would, she believed, be more just to all than
Afrikaner rule: 'it is not magnanimity nor brutality on the part of
individuals which are in dispute. Our controversy is concerning the
presence or absence of Justice among the Boers, concerning the purity
of the Government and the justice of their Laws, or the reverse.'[11] For
Butler, they were not fit to govern, in contrast to the British. Her
published opinion as given in *Native Races* was supported by a private
letter sent to Millicent Fawcett, enclosed with a copy of the book.
'The Boers', she wrote, '"only ask to be let alone" – a modest request.
Thieves and burglars also ask only to be let alone.'[12] Butler's only
hope for an improvement in the rights of native South Africans was 'the
re-establishment of peace under the principles of British rule'.[13]

Butler reproduced the prejudice that was widespread in British
culture in the late 1890s, contrasting the British with the Afrikaners and
presenting the view that the latter were 'as a race . . . an extraordinary
instance of an arrested civilisation, the date of stoppage being some-
where about the conclusion of the seventeenth century'. However, her
arguments regarding native South Africans were more radical than
the prevailing jingoism of the day, in that she focused upon the civil
rights due to them. She argued for '*Equality of all before the Law*',
although she specifically excluded 'social equality' from this, arguing
that it belonged 'to another region of political ideas altogether'. Her
arguments for fair treatment were comparatively radical, although they
were also carefully circumscribed. Native South Africans should be
enfranchised, she suggested, but not 'too early'. Likewise, it might be

advantageous to apply an education test, or proof of 'a certain amount of civilization and instruction'.[14]

Native Races was written early in the course of the war, and published in mid-1900, before the concentration camps were introduced. Antoinette Burton has suggested that it was therefore a product of the popular jingoism of late 1899 rather than a reaction to the later (and more controversial) conduct of the war.[15] Indeed, it makes a comparison with Hobhouse and Fawcett's responses problematic. But the evidence suggests that if anything, Butler became more pro-war and less sympathetic to the Afrikaners as time went on. In 1899, she had expressed the hope that the Afrikaners 'may be sufficiently beaten to be induced to lay down their arms, and that we may offer them *peace* on just and reasonable terms, and that they will settle down under British rule'. In 1900, she was relatively tolerant: 'I cannot find it in my heart to criticize the character of the Boers at a time when they have held on so bravely in a desperate war, and have suffered so much. There are Boers and Boers, – good and bad among them, – as among all nations.' In 1901, when Kitchener's policies of farm-burning and internment were under way – although perhaps significantly, before Hobhouse's account of the concentration camps reached the British public – she described British military manoeuvres as 'the work of the Holy Spirit'. By 1902, when both Hobhouse's and Fawcett's reports were publicly available, her concern was with 'the Satanic devices and the powers of hell which are arising to dispute with us the true possession of S. Africa'.[16] Despite the conduct of the British, Butler's compassion for the Afrikaners appeared to diminish as time went on.

Native Races came in for much criticism from the peace movement, for the principal reason that its arguments strengthened the pro-war party and therefore could prolong the war.[17] Butler argued that it was a 'just war' because it was on behalf of native South Africans, but she did not give full consideration to the use that could have been made of the arbitration process, which might have avoided the need for war. It could therefore be implied that she interpreted peace to mean an abstract concept of a Christian utopia, rather than a state of consensus that could be achieved through international diplomacy. As a result her arguments found supporters among more jingoistic imperialists, such as Millicent Fawcett.

While Butler and Fawcett were long-serving members of the feminist movement, Miss Emily Hobhouse (1860–1926) was an unknown, middle-aged Englishwoman, albeit from an established family. Her uncle was Lord Hobhouse, and in the late 1890s she became increasingly drawn into Liberal political circles, beginning a friendship with Leonard and Kate

Courtney. It was Leonard Courtney who, on the outbreak of war in 1899, persuaded Emily to become involved in the South Africa Conciliation Committee (SACC), a body primarily concerned with pressing for formal negotiation to bring the war to an end. The SACC occupied the middle ground of the anti-war movements, accepting that unilateral British withdrawal and peace at any price were unrealistic aims, but nonetheless hoping to save South Africa for the empire and indeed to save the empire itself by building it upon mutual trust and loyalties.[18]

Hobhouse accepted a position as honorary secretary of the women's auxiliary to the Conciliation Committee. This mostly consisted of a separate circle of women to the existing peace movement (Ellen Robinson being a prominent exception), although the arguments used regarding imperialism, physical force and natural justice were in many ways similar. In 1900–1 Hobhouse travelled to South Africa, funded by the SACC, to distribute aid to those involved in the war. Her report of conditions in the concentration camps was the cause of much controversy in Britain, and brought about the 1901–2 Commission of Inquiry that was led by Fawcett. Although Hobhouse's conclusions were similar to those reached by Fawcett's Commission a year later, the two women were very different in their emphasis. Hobhouse's outspokenness and criticism of the British government meant that she was treated as a traitor in Britain. During an attempt to visit South Africa for the second time, in late 1901, she was arrested by the military before even disembarking from the boat, and had to be forcibly carried onto a boat returning to Britain.

Hobhouse was clearly a thorn in the side of the establishment. Yet her own political views were overshadowed by, firstly, her insistence that her work in South Africa was not political, and secondly, the other members of the Conciliation Committee, who appeared to hold similar views and were more prepared to speak publicly on political matters. In claiming to be apolitical, her approach was reminiscent of women philanthropists of the nineteenth century who focused on material aid and relieving poverty, although she also questioned politicians and ministers on the legitimacy of government and military policy. She was one of few women at this time to argue that they had a role to play as *women* in the conduct of the war. The war was presented as not only an imperial problem, but also an international one, because of the Afrikaners' close ties with the Netherlands. Both Hobhouse and Fawcett were therefore drawn directly into the masculine sphere of foreign politics.

Hobhouse's relationship to feminism was a complex one. Her connections with some of the most prominent anti-war Liberals, such as the Courtneys, meant that she would have been exposed to feminist activities and ideas. For a brief period before the war she undertook research for the Women's Industrial Council into employment legislation, and she advocated public women's meetings as an effective means of protest against the Anglo-Boer war.[19] But she attempted to publicly maintain a position that was independent of both the women's movement and the Liberal party, relying on the argument that her work was humanitarian in basis. Although Hobhouse did not explicitly criticise the 'gendered order of society' as such, she did concern herself with the impact of gender constructions on traditionally private and individual concerns. Thus Philippa Levine's broad definition of feminism, as outlined in the introduction, might encompass women such as Hobhouse.[20] Certainly, her attempts to provide Afrikaner women with a public voice were consistent with the belief that they had the right to a greater degree of control over their own situation.

Her methods were also unconventional. As Hobhouse's biographer, John Fisher, notes, 'she was ready to make use of politicians after her own fashion – as they were of her, after theirs'. When pitted against the military and the government in late 1901, she resolved: 'I will be very polite, very dignified, but in every way I possibly can, a thorn in the flesh to them.'[21] She gained access to British officials in South Africa through her aunt Lady Hobhouse's influence, and access to Afrikaner refugees and victims of the farm-burning through her 'pro-Boer' colleagues. Her impartiality in giving aid – she provided aid to both Afrikaner families and British troops – also extended to those she informed of the problems in the camps. She was as open with 'pro-Boer' friends in Cape Town as she was with the military and the SACC in Britain, and unsurprisingly, this made her many enemies within the government and the army.

Hobhouse may have exploited her family connections and her links with Members of Parliament in order to gain access to the government, but the end she had in sight was the more humane treatment of victims of war, and women and child victims in particular. In claiming the right to define her role as a British humanitarian abroad, she indirectly advanced the position of women within government by prompting the Commission of Inquiry into the camps, although this of course had a very different agenda to that of Hobhouse. Hobhouse's response to the war was based on similar liberal ideas to those of Josephine Butler, particularly the belief that moral laws should apply to nations as much as they did to individuals. And like Butler, Hobhouse was concerned about the treatment of native South Africans, and the Afrikaners' hostile attitude towards them. During her 1900–1 trip to the Cape, as well as trying to publicise the poor conditions in the camps in which the

Afrikaners were being kept, Emily asked Lady Hobhouse to use her influence to have representatives sent out from either the Society of Friends or the Aborigines' Protection Society to investigate the camps in which the black population were confined. She had heard enough about the conditions in the camps to know that intervention was urgently needed, but she also believed that if she became involved she might alienate the Afrikaners whom she was trying to help. Her time in South Africa convinced her that any aid would have to be administered separately, but her efforts to enlist an organisation to do this proved fruitless.[22]

On Hobhouse's return to Britain, she managed to get the conditions she had discovered in the camps publicised, albeit against some opposition. Public meetings had to be cancelled because of government resistance, and it was ultimately through the efforts of David Lloyd George, who raised the matter in Parliament, that a full public discussion was initiated. As a result of this adverse publicity, in early July the War Office began to consider sending a committee of women out to visit the camps and produce a report. Hobhouse would have been an obvious candidate for such a role if she had not been so outspokenly critical in her earlier work. It was essential for the government that they pick a political ally, and Millicent Garrett Fawcett's Unionist politics stood her in better stead with a Conservative government than did Hobhouse's Liberalism.

Fawcett was active in the women's movement from the late 1860s until her death in 1929. She was strongly influenced by liberal economic and political ideas, taking many of her early views from the work of John Stuart Mill, and was one of the few late Victorian feminists to be uninfluenced by, and indeed indifferent to, Evangelicalism. Most active in the suffrage movement, she was also involved in campaigns for equal education and employment opportunities for women, and in certain strands of the social purity movement. She became the dominant force in the suffrage movement in the 1890s, and her influence was further enhanced in 1897 by her role in the amalgamation of the CCNSWS and CNSWS into the National Union of Women's Suffrage Societies.[23] She was a supporter of imperialist expansion and, if necessary, the use of force. Following the declaration of Liberal support for Home Rule for Ireland in 1885, Fawcett split from the Liberal party, believing them to be 'false to the very essence of liberalism'. She joined the Liberal Unionists and opposed Home Rule on the grounds that it was 'absolutely contrary to the interests of the British Empire and of the Irish themselves'.[24] She reportedly perceived little difference between the Liberal Unionists and the Conservatives, and resigned from the Women's Liberal

Unionist Association in 1904 when the Unionists rejected free trade. Fawcett later remarked that 'I am not a Protectionist and therefore cannot be a Conservative. I am not a Home Ruler and cannot be a Liberal. And I cannot join the Labour Party because I am not a Socialist.'[25] In discussions on the empire and women's suffrage, she often emphasised the importance of order, arguing in 1890 that 'the women of the country [were] an immense and very valuable Conservative force in the country ... There were many things ... which convinced women of the value of order, and which brought home to them the fact that order was essential to liberty.'[26]

Fawcett's imperialism was of the jingoistic type that became popular in the last years of the nineteenth century. She resisted discourses of pacifism and internationalism, although – as in her 1888 letter to the International Congress of Women – she paid lip service to peace ideals, adhering to the broad concept that a state of peace was preferable to a state of war and arguing for international co-operation between women's suffrage movements. Yet her views brought her into conflict with pacifist women. In 1888, Fawcett's support for peace and arbitration led her to accept the position of vice-president of the Women's Committee of the IAPA, but she did not involve herself in the work of this organisation and resigned her post in early 1889. In 1890, Fawcett refused to accept the presidency of the International Council of Women on the grounds that she felt it to be impossible that any international work among women could be productive. By the turn of the century, she had come to represent a strongly nationalist and imperialist discourse, and it may be no coincidence that Fawcett's reputation and influence within the feminist movement grew just as liberal anti-imperialism gave way to the jingoism of the 1890s. As noted in chapter 1, Fawcett's commitment to physical force as an effective and legitimate means of power meant that her arguments on the suffrage sidestepped the physical force objection. This was ultimately an argument that, given Fawcett's support for imperial force, she was unable to answer satisfactorily, although she could use arguments on the legitimacy of the Anglo-Boer war to support her position on women's suffrage. In arguing that the political rights of settlers in South Africa were important enough for Britain to go to war, she made the denial of the vote to British women even harder to defend.[27] She had, in effect, a vested interest in supporting the war.

Fawcett was invited to take part in the Commission of Inquiry into conditions in the concentration camps in mid-July 1901 (she was later appointed its president), as a result of a review she provided for the *Westminster Gazette* of Emily Hobhouse's report of her trip to the camps.

Fawcett's review picked out the positive comments within Hobhouse's report and scarcely touched on its more offensive or disturbing contents, going on to excuse the failings of the camps as 'part of the fortune of war'.[28] Her appointment to the Commission shows not only that she was a known and trusted political figure from the establishment's point of view, but also that as a staunch imperialist who fully supported the war, she could be relied upon to report on events in the camps from the perspective required by the British government.

Ray Strachey noted in her biography of Fawcett that 'it was an unprecedented thing for an official commission on whatever subject to consist only of women', and that as a result, Fawcett had 'no hesitation whatever' in accepting the appointment.[29] Her two British colleagues in the Commission, Lucy Deane and Alice, Lady Knox, were selected by the War Office and introduced to her at their first meeting with the minister, St John Brodrick, on 20 July. Deane was an experienced factory inspector, while Knox was the wife of one of Kitchener's senior officers in South Africa – hardly an impartial choice. Fawcett later noted in her diary that Knox viewed the Afrikaners as socially equivalent to 'where the Scottish people were 200 years ago'.[30] At the meeting on 20 July, Brodrick used the occasion to outline the aspects of the camps that the women were requested to investigate, and to inform them 'of the advisability of working *with* the authorities', an intimation that an approach like that of Emily Hobhouse would not be acceptable. The project was to be, in effect, a Royal Commission in all but name, placing considerable responsibility on the part of Fawcett and her colleagues to demonstrate that women could be trusted with such work, and implicitly therefore, to produce a report acceptable to the government. Fawcett read Hobhouse's report of the camps before arriving in South Africa, and was also requested by Josephine Butler to 'be on the lookout' for the army's attitude to 'the moral question she has worked for', and so a section on morals and discipline in the camps was built into the report.[31]

Fawcett had become an outspoken supporter of Josephine Butler after the Contagious Diseases agitation, but, as Barbara Caine has argued, there was a tension in Fawcett's politics between the liberal focus on national political activities and her feminist analysis of sexual politics, in which she was determined to attack the pervasive sexual double standard. Caine documents Fawcett's vehement opposition to sexual immorality among those in public life (particularly her disapproval of Harry Cust and eventual hounding of him out of office), which mirrored her concern with the sexual conduct of the inmates of the concentration camps.[32] She was greatly concerned with male sexual immorality, but less interested in the effects of war, and as a result it appears that she condemned sexual violence but took a more lenient view of the physical violence that was being practised by the British against the Afrikaners.

While Hobhouse's account of the Afrikaner women and children in the camps differed greatly from that offered by Fawcett, there were a number of points of agreement. Both women highlighted the large numbers of children in the camps, the foul smell and lack of hygiene, the shortage of water for drinking, cooking and washing, and the rapidity and ease with which diseases spread through the camps. Yet there was a fundamental disagreement over the status of the inmates. For Hobhouse and the 'pro-Boer' and peace movements, these were concentration camps and the men, women and children contained in them were prisoners. For Fawcett and the government, they were refugees who came to the camps for protection 'against the Kaffirs', rather than the British.[33]

The Commission and its final report were indebted to, and in many ways a governmental response to, Hobhouse's earlier criticisms. While Fawcett disagreed with some of Hobhouse's suggestions, she nonetheless read her report closely before arriving in South Africa, and worked from it when ascertaining if and to what degree the camps had improved over the months since Hobhouse had visited them. It is surely significant that the major omission from Fawcett's report, that of any study of camps set up for native South Africans, was also an omission made – consciously and for specific reasons – by Hobhouse.

Fawcett's final report outlined three areas of investigation: to determine how British charity could best be distributed in the camps; whether alterations in the organisation of the camps were desirable; and whether the geographical location of the camps was acceptable. All three issues responded to recommendations in Hobhouse's report, but the Commission was clearly biased in its conclusions. Criticism was directed against the camp superintendents, not the government or its policies, and implicitly against Hobhouse herself, as it was argued that 'private charity' was unnecessary and that the inmates of the camps were well provided for, even including the provision of 'luxuries' for the sick. This said, the report was not the whitewash that it had been expected to be, and in places it was explicitly critical of material conditions or individuals. Yet as a document it reflected the imperialist ideology of its authors. In explaining the high death rate in the camps, the three reasons given were: the 'insanitary condition of the country caused by the war'; causes 'within the control of the inmates of the camps'; and causes 'within the control of the administration'. The first two causes clearly absolved the British government of any responsibility, and, indeed, went some way to arguing that the Afrikaners were faring far better for having access to British medical care. With regard to the first reason, it was argued that: 'More is being done for them in camp, ten times more ... than could have been done for them had they remained on their fathers' farms.' The second argument, that Afrikaner women in particular were killing their infants through ignorance of medical procedures, put the case that camp superintendents were daily having to 'wage war against the insanitary habits of the people'. This placed only a fraction of the responsibility for the high death rate upon the British government, and even then criticisms were directed at past mistakes, such as the failure to appreciate the distinctions required between the treatment of women and children and the treatment of soldiers, and the sites on which some of the camps had been located. The central thread of the report was that 'we feel that in some camps there has been a tendency on the part of the officials to sink to a low standard of order, decency, and cleanliness in these matters, rather than to face the constant wear and tear involved in insisting on a high standard'.[34] The military was criticised for failing in Britain's imperial mission to elevate and civilise.

To conclude, it is notable that both Butler and Hobhouse concerned themselves with the native population, although Hobhouse's comments were kept private. Hobhouse was clearly the most 'pro-Boer' of the three, and the only one who was not an established figure in the women's movement. Butler was initially sympathetic towards the Afrikaners, but publicly critical of their treatment of native South Africans. Fawcett, in contrast, ignored the existence of a black population and disparaged the Afrikaners, particularly the women, for their supposed ignorance, lack of hygiene, and independence of mind. Fawcett received recognition from the establishment for her report, while Butler was shunned by her abolitionist colleagues because she supported the government. Hobhouse was treated as a traitor within Britain, although her actions, particularly during her deportation from Cape Town in 1901 when she had to be bodily carried onto the boat to depart, made her a heroine among British pacifists and anti-imperialists, and of course among the Afrikaners.

It has been argued, particularly with respect to the First World War, that war accelerates and crystallises social development, and as a result British women have made significant advances in wartime.[35] The Anglo-Boer war may be seen as a precursor to this trend. It saw the prominent involvement of two women, Fawcett and Hobhouse, in foreign and imperial affairs, a sphere that was typically defined as exclusively masculine, and the appointment of the first all-female government Commission, undoubtedly an important milestone. While Fawcett had always been something of an establishment figure, her leadership of the Commission ultimately reinforced this reputation and strengthened her standing within both the feminist movement and political circles generally. She was one of the first feminists to be drawn into the masculine sphere of foreign politics, albeit in a feminised, domestic role – that is, her ability as a woman to investigate other women and children. Implicitly, Fawcett's jingoistic, imperialist brand of feminism was legitimised by her appointment to and role in the Commission, while Butler's Evangelical imperialism and Hobhouse's humanitarian focus were marginalised. Hobhouse also moved beyond the domestic sphere into foreign politics, and managed to be influential even as she was excluded from the establishment, for it was unarguably her report on the concentration camps that led to the government investigation. Her involvement in this respect illustrates how a role could be carved out for women *as* women, within war and international politics.

Notes

1   In keeping with modern usage, the term 'Afrikaner' is used throughout instead of 'Boer', except in reference to the war itself and to 'pro-Boer' political opinions. The latter developed as a specific cultural meaning during the course of the war, which was distinct from pacifist, anti-militarist or humanitarian perspectives.

2   Jenny Uglow, 'Josephine Butler: from sympathy to theory (1828–1906)', in Dale Spender (ed.), *Feminist Theorists: Three Centuries of Women's Intellectual Traditions* (London: Women's Press, 1983), pp. 146–7; Caine, *Victorian Feminists*, ch. 5.

3   *Herald* (1 September 1870), p. 112.

4   Antoinette Burton, '"States of injury": Josephine Butler on slavery, citizenship and the Boer War', in Ian Christopher Fletcher, Laura E. Nym Mayhall and Philippa Levine (eds), *Women's Suffrage in the British Empire: Citizenship, Nation and Race* (London: Routledge, 2000), pp. 20–2.

5   Josephine Butler, *Our Christianity Tested by the Irish Question* (London: T. Fisher Unwin, n.d. [1887]), p. 36.

6   Josephine Butler, *The Native Races and the War* (London: Gay and Bird, 1900), p. 148.

7   *Ibid.*, pp. 152–3.

8   *Ibid.*, pp. 28, 146.

9   Butler, *Our Christianity Tested*, p. 28.

10 *Ibid.*, 140. Emphasis added.

11 Butler, *Native Races*, p. 118.

12 Butler to Fawcett, 20 June 1900, quoted in Laura E. Nym Mayhall, 'The South African War and the origins of suffrage militancy in Britain, 1899–1902', in Fletcher, Mayhall and Levine (eds), *Women's Suffrage in the British Empire*, p. 6.

13 Butler, *Native Races*, p. 5.

14 *Ibid.*, pp. 63, 132–3. Burton notes that growing numbers of native Cape South Africans already had the vote at this time. Burton, 'States of injury', p. 28.

15 *Ibid.*, p. 21.

16 Josephine Butler, letter fragment, October 1899, in *ibid.*, p. 22; Butler, *Native Races*, p. 118; Butler to Miss Forsaith, 12 February 1901; and Butler to Miss Forsaith, 1 July 1902, in Burton, 'States of injury', p. 22.

17 *Concord* (August 1900), p. 126.

18 Koss (ed.), *The Pro-Boers*, p. xxv.

19 A. Ruth Fry, *Emily Hobhouse: A Memoir* (London: Jonathan Cape, 1929), p. 69; John Fisher, *That Miss Hobhouse* (London: Secker and Warburg, 1971), p. 67.

20 Levine, *Feminist Lives in Victorian England*, p. 2.

21 Fisher, *That Miss Hobhouse*, p. 111; Emily Hobhouse to Leonard Hobhouse, 29 October 1901 in Fry, *Emily Hobhouse*, p. 171.

22 See for example Paula M. Krebs, ' "The last of the gentleman's wars": Women in the Boer War concentration camp controversy', *History Workshop Journal*, 33 (1992), pp. 38–56; Claire Hirshfield, 'Blacks, Boers and Britons: the anti-war movement in England and the "Native Issue", 1899–1902', *Peace and Change*, 8 (1982), pp. 21–34.

23 Rubinstein, *A Different World for Women*, pp. 132–8.

24 Millicent Fawcett, 'Women in English Politics', *Forum* (December 1892), p. 454, in Rubinstein, *A Different World for Women*, p. 138; Caine, *Victorian Feminists*, p. 211.

25 Rubinstein, *A Different World for Women*, pp. 182–3.

26 *Englishwoman's Review* (15 October 1890), pp. 372–5.

27 Strachey, *The Cause*, p. 288.

28 *Westminster Gazette* (4 July 1901), in Brian Roberts, *Those Bloody Women: Three Heroines of the Boer War* (London: John Murray, 1991), p. 177.

29 Ray Strachey, *Millicent Garrett Fawcett* (London: John Murray, 1931), in Roberts, *Those Bloody Women*, pp. 182–3.

30 Millicent Garrett Fawcett, 22 July 1901, diary, p. 7. Three South African women were also selected for the Commission: Dr Jane Elizabeth Waterson, a physician, relief worker and imperialist; Dr Ella Campbell Scarlett, another physician, dubbed 'headstrong' by Fawcett; and a nurse, Katherine Brereton. Fawcett, 14 August 1901, diary, p. 40; Roberts, *Those Bloody Women*, pp. 183–5.

31 Millicent Garrett Fawcett, 20 July 1901, diary, pp. 4–5. Emphasis in original.

32 Caine, *Victorian Feminists*, pp. 199, 231–3.

33 St John Brodrick in *The Times* (25 May 1901), in Roberts, *Those Bloody Women*, p. 166.

34 Millicent Garrett Fawcett (President), *Report on the concentration camps in South Africa, by the Committee of Ladies appointed by the Secretary of State for War; containing reports on the camps in Natal, the Orange River Colony, and the Transvaal* (London: HMSO, 1902), Cd 893, GB/106/7/MGF/90/B/1, Fawcett Library, London, pp. 4, 15, 18.

35 See, for example, Christine Bolt, *The Women's Movements in the United States and Britain from the 1790s to the 1920s* (Hemel Hempstead: Harvester Wheatsheaf, 1993), ch. 6; Renate Bridenthal, 'Something old, something new: women between the two world wars', in Bridenthal, Koonz and Stuard (eds), *Becoming Visible*, pp. 473–97.

Conclusion

Within the historiography of pacifist feminism, there has been a general reluctance to look further back than the First World War. The wide range of literature on the Victorian women's movement which has been produced over the last twenty years has either neglected the fact that many feminists were active in campaigns for international peace, or has listed 'peace' as a women's issue during the late nineteenth century without offering any further analysis of how women were involved, or what they did in this connection.[1] The obvious exception is Jill Liddington's The Long Road to Greenham, a valuable longitudinal study that emphasises the development of women's peace politics from 1820 to the mid-1980s.[2] The Long Road to Greenham gives an overview of many of the central events in the period with which this book is concerned, though of necessity it covers the period only briefly. It is hoped that this book has added to Liddington's work, to suggest that while some Victorian women were highly active specifically in relation to peace work, there were also a large number of feminists who incorporated pacifist ideas into their wider political analysis of women's position. Feminists' ideas of their role within the empire, their eligibility for citizenship and their suitability to act as moral guardians in public life, all made use in varying ways of gendered understandings of the role of force and the relevance of pacifist strategies such as arbitration. As a result, peace ideas had a pervasive influence on the Victorian women's movement.

Recent works by Sandi E. Cooper and Leila J. Rupp have also addressed some of the issues with which this book is concerned. Cooper's articles on European pacifist women provide an international context for the British women who are discussed here.[3] Her examination of the role of women within the Continental peace movement has highlighted trends of liberal internationalism and republican or radical internationalism. She notes that 'those who complained in later years that the movement was timid, passive and negative were luxuriating in selective memory, if not historical amnesia'.[4] Her studies of women's peace work in Italy, Switzerland, the Netherlands and Austro-Hungary provide a useful means of comparison with Britain, although the British peace movement differed significantly from that of the Continental Europeans in its approach to women's pacifism. Leila J. Rupp has focused on the growth of international women's organisations, beginning with the International Council of Women in 1888 and continuing into the twentieth century with the International Woman Suffrage Alliance and the Women's International League for Peace and Freedom. Although she does not focus in detail on Victorian feminism or the interrelations between women's individual efforts and the formal associations with which they became linked, her work demonstrates that the twentieth-century international women's movement had clear origins in the late nineteenth century. Rupp has examined the challenges of maintaining a national identity during international work, describing how some women attempted to transcend national allegiances, while others, such as the International Council of Women, held that nationalism and internationalism could be complementary.[5]

Victorian conceptions of national identity were closely linked to Britain's status as an imperial power. Antoinette Burton's *Burdens of History* has convincingly argued that in Victorian Britain, nation and empire were effectively one and the same, and allegiances to each were 'concentric and mutually dependent'.[6] She has shown how the construction of the imperial nation was reliant on an external 'other' against which it was defined, suggesting that this conflation of the nation and the empire gave feminists the means to argue that their role in the nation amounted to a responsibility for the race and indeed the empire itself.[7] Yet while Burton has demonstrated that national and imperial superiority were closely connected to 'separate spheres' arguments of women's moral superiority, there is little consideration in her work of how far the various strands of feminism contested these discourses. Imperial feminism was an important component of the Victorian women's movement, but there were also dissenting voices. Where British feminists put forward anti-imperialist or internationalist arguments, they frequently attempted to question the legitimacy of the British imperial nation, and to challenge nationalist and imperialist ideas.

This book has sought to demonstrate that there were distinct pacifist feminist arguments from as early as the 1870s. Henrietta Müller's *Women's Penny Paper* and Florence Fenwick Miller's *Woman's Signal* advanced ideas which connected women's suffrage and the advent of peaceable international relations, for example in assertions that 'there is more international feeling between the women of the world at present than between any section of men'. Fenwick Miller's ideas of 'a sisterhood of women' which 'must make for peace and for union throughout the world' implicitly established in feminist discourse an essentialist assumption that women were unified in their interests as a result of their common biological and social experiences.[8]

Like feminism, pacifism in this period was in no way unified in its politics or methods. While some of the women who were involved in the work of the Peace Society attempted to keep the peace movement distinct from the feminist movement, there were nonetheless important areas of overlap. E. M. King, for example, was active in the campaign against the Contagious Diseases Acts and founded the short-lived London branch of the Women's International Peace Association in 1873. She publicly argued as early as 1872 that women should be afforded 'the right to be heard or represented' in the settlement of international disputes.[9]

Victorian feminists, of course, used arguments of patriotism in the service of other causes. Florence Balgarnie, for example, argued at a suffrage meeting in 1884 that 'We, women, live in the country, we are citizens of the country, and we, women, I venture to say, love our country. It is because we do love our country, because we are patriots just as much as men are patriots that we wish for the change that we may share in the government of our country.'[10] While this argument employed the revised version of patriotism discussed earlier in this book, in its solely feminist interpretation it neglected the role of physical force in women's subordination. A purely feminist approach was limited in the degree to which it could address the use of governmental power, and particularly in how it approached questions of empire and nationalism. The introduction of critical perspectives on the use of physical force, whether against regions of the empire or against other nations, opened up the issue of governmental power to feminist debate. This is not to suggest that pacifist feminism was in some sense superior to other forms of feminism, but rather it shows that pacifist feminist perspectives were strategically useful for the Victorian women's movement because they could serve to advance feminist debate.

The implications of these developments were significant for early twentieth-century feminism. Although the women's movement experienced dramatic shifts in policy and emphasis during the early twentieth century, and pacifist arguments changed drastically in the face of the total war of 1914–18, it can nonetheless be argued that the theoretical and political development of pacifist feminist ideas during the late nineteenth century laid much of the groundwork for these new internationalist movements.[11] Thus, although there is no historiography which connects pacifism to feminism before 1914, many of the feminists who were active in political campaigns in the final decades of the nineteenth century were also involved in the peace movement. The wide range of perspectives taken by feminists on the uses of physical force included: free trade radicalism, which was expected to make relations between nations more equitable and therefore peaceful; anti-expansionism, as demonstrated by Isabella Tod's promotion of enlightened international relations combined with a socially responsible imperial nation; maternalism, or the argument that mothers' roles as socialising agents meant that they had a responsibility to inculcate a respect for moral, rather than physical force in their children; Evangelical pacifism, as seen in Priscilla Peckover's arguments that the promotion of peace was an essential component of Christianity; feminist internationalism, as seen in Henrietta Müller and Florence Fenwick Miller's concept of a sisterhood of women across the world; abolitionism, or the argument (most typically by Josephine Butler) that the empire should be based on the peaceful conversion of subject peoples to Christianity; and finally, the jingoistic imperialism of women such as Millicent Fawcett, who did not incorporate critiques of the use of force into their feminism and argued instead that the demonstration of women's capacity for citizenship required their acceptance of the need for physical force in international and imperial relations.

From these perspectives, four distinct strands of pacifist feminism can be identified, all of which drew upon established traditions of political or religious thought but applied feminist perspectives on the use of force to these ideas. These were free trade radicalism, moderate internationalism, Evangelical feminism and international citizenship. Free trade ideas were common until the early 1890s, and can be seen most clearly in the arguments of Lydia Becker and Caroline Ashurst Biggs. For example, in response to the Turkish invasion of Bulgaria in 1876, Becker argued that the Bulgarians were entitled to 'security for life and liberty, and opportunity for the development of their industry and culture'. These ideas incorporated concerns with political representation through arguments that 'If the [British] nation is in any way responsible for the maintenance of the power which has committed the atrocities . . . women cannot free themselves from their share in such responsibility.'[12] Evangelical social purity feminists such as Laura Ormiston Chant developed comparable reformulations of patriotism, using maternalist rhetoric to argue that 'We talked about [the military] . . . being the defenders of our country, but the defence of our country was to recognise the whole humanity of the world.'[13] E. M. Southey used similar concepts, phrasing her arguments in terms of 'The world-wide patriotism of the Prince of Peace'.[14] The social reformer Lady Aberdeen argued in 1899 that 'We women of this day are learning a new kind of patriotism – we are learning to covet for our countries that they shall emulate one another as to which . . . can do the most to maintain the peace of the world.'[15] This moderate internationalism drew heavily upon alternative visions of patriotism, as did a speech given by Mrs W. P. Byles in 1904 when she argued that 'It is the duty of all peace reformers to try to generate, by word and act and vote, a new patriotism; and the duty especially lies heavily upon us women to nourish a nobler patriotism.'[16] The common ground between these liberal perspectives and their Evangelical equivalents described above was a vision of universalism, a humanity that transcended all other considerations.

Primarily, however, it was conceptions of international citizenship that gathered pace in the twentieth century and became more readily identified with feminist argument. Virginia Woolf's classic reformulation of women's nationhood in *Three Guineas* epitomised this approach, and popularised the idea that women experienced their nationalism and patriotism in very different ways than did men. Ideas of women's international citizenship had their origins in late nineteenth-century feminisms. As early as 1870, Lydia Becker argued 'the womanly spirit of courage, patriotism, and self-devotion . . . is of no particular age or country'.[17] In 1904, Jane Addams – then only beginning upon her career as a pacifist – was described by Lucia Ames Mead as a follower of the principle: 'My country is the whole world.'[18] This phrase was coined by Thomas Paine in *Rights of Man*: 'My country is the whole world, and my religion is to do good.' It was modified and used during the nineteenth century by abolitionists such as William Lloyd Garrison, who provided the phrase: 'My country is the world, my countrymen are mankind.'[19] These sentiments were echoed by Becker and other late Victorian feminists in relation to 'women' but it was not until 1938 that Virginia Woolf memorably prefaced the statement with the words 'as a woman': 'as a woman, I have no country. As a woman I want no country. As a woman my country is the whole world.'[20]

Woolf's *Three Guineas* included an analysis of women's historical exclusion from citizenship rights, and argued that 'the very circumstances of female upbringing and education, or disenfranchisement and domestication . . . [gave] women a completely different perspective on such basic masculine concepts as patriotism and loyalty'.[21] The text called upon 'women' as a group to take the position of 'outsiders' and resist nationalist and (traditional) patriotic ideologies.[22] The emotive nature of the phrase 'my country is the whole world' belies a radical internationalism, a concept of global citizenship that can be traced back to Paine himself. The use of similar terms during the late nineteenth century is a crucial indication that women's relationship to and role within the nation was being subjected to unprecedented scrutiny, and it was particularly in pacifist, internationalist and humanitarian strands of feminism that such ideas developed. However, it was not until the twentieth century that such ideas gained a truly popular appeal.

Notes

1 See for example Bolt, *The Women's Movements in the United States and Britain*, pp. 70–1, 81, 87; Rendall, *Origins of Modern Feminism*, p. 254; Walkowitz, *Prostitution and Victorian Society*, pp. 126–7.

2 Liddington, *Long Road to Greenham*, chs 1–4.

3 Cooper, *Patriotic Pacifism*; Sandi E. Cooper, 'The work of women in nineteenth century Continental European peace movements', *Peace and Change*, 9:4 (1984) pp. 11–28; Sandi E. Cooper, 'Women's participation in European peace movements: the struggle to prevent World War One', in Ruth Roach Pierson (ed.) *Women and Peace: Theoretical, Historical and Practical Perspectives* (London: Croom Helm, 1987), pp. 51–75.

4 Cooper, 'Women's participation in European peace movements', p. 68.

5 Rupp, *Worlds of Women*, pp. 111–29; Leila J. Rupp, 'Constructing internationalism: the case of transnational women's organizations, 1888–1945', *American Historical Review*, 99:5 (1994), pp. 1571–1600; Leila J. Rupp, 'Sexuality and politics in the early twentieth century: the case of the international women's movement', *Feminist Studies*, 23:3 (Autumn 1997), pp. 577–605.

6 Burton, *Burdens of History*, pp. 5–6.

7 *Ibid.*, p. 34; Antoinette Burton, 'Rules of thumb: British history and "imperial culture" in nineteenth- and twentieth-century Britain', *Women's History Review*, 3:4 (1994), pp. 483–500.

8 *Woman's Signal* (21 January 1897), p. 40; (14 July 1898), p. 441.

9 *WSJ* (1 October 1872), p. 137 and *Herald* (1 October 1872), p. 135.

10 *WSJ* (1 April 1884), p. 69.

11 Rupp, *Worlds of Women*, pp. 210–25.

12 *WSJ* (1 November 1876), p. 145.

13 *Journal* (31 July 1886), p. 76.

14 E. M. Southey to A. Gobat, 8 April 1911, Document 10, Box 109, IPB.

15 Aberdeen, *Report of Transactions*, p. 217.

16 Universal Peace Congress, *Report of the Thirteenth Universal Peace Congress*, p. 117.

17 Becker, 'Liberty, Equality, Fraternity', in Lewis (ed.), *Before the Vote was Won*, pp. 228–9.

18 Universal Peace Congress, *Report of the Thirteenth Universal Peace Congress*, p. 119.

19 Thomas Paine, *Rights of Man* (1791), in A. Norman Jeffares and Martin Gray (eds) *Collins Dictionary of Quotations* (Glasgow: HarperCollins, 1995), p. 502; William Lloyd Garrison, prospectus for *The Liberator* (1803), in *The International Thesaurus of Quotations*, complied by Rhoda Thomas Tripp (London: George Allen and Unwin, 1974), 98:6.

20 Virginia Woolf, *Three Guineas* (London: Hogarth Press, 1938; reprint, London: Penguin 1993), p. 234.

21 Catherine Sandbach-Dahlstrom, 'Virginia Woolf's *Three Guineas*: a theory of liberation for the modern world?', *Women's Studies International Forum*, 17:2–3 (1994), p. 231.

22 Woolf defended her position in *Three Guineas* against much opposition, for example in a letter in which she remarked 'Of course I'm "patriotic"'. Virginia Woolf to Ethel Smyth, 7 June 1938 in Hermione Lee, *Virginia Woolf* (London: Vintage 1997), p. 710.

Select bibliography

Manuscript collections

Fawcett, Millicent Garrett, Diary kept in South Africa during the Concentration Camps Commission, July to December 1901, GB/106/7/MGF/90/B/2, Fawcett Library, London.

Fawcett, Millicent Garrett, Letter Collection, Manchester Central Library, Manchester.

Fried-Suttner Papers, International Peace Movement Collection, League of Nations Archives, United Nations Library, Geneva, Switzerland.

Mill-Taylor Collection, London School of Economics and Political Science, London.

Wisbech Local Peace Association, Box 4, Miscellaneous Letters, Literature. Swarthmore College Peace Collection, microfilm copy in Wisbech Public Library, Wisbech, Cambridgeshire.

Minute books and papers of organisations

International Peace Bureau, International Peace Movement Collection, League of Nations Archives, United Nations Library, Geneva, Switzerland.

Moral Reform Union. Annual Reports, 1881 to 1897. Fawcett Library, London.

National Union of Women Workers, Minute Book, 1891–1900, National Council of Women of Great Britain, London Metropolitan Archives, London.

Peace Society, Letter Book, 1851–1889 and Executive Committee Minute Books, 1861–1902, Peace Society Archives, Fellowship House, London.

Miscellaneous material

Fawcett, Millicent Garrett. *Report on the concentration camps in South Africa, by the Committee of Ladies appointed by the Secretary of State for War; containing reports on the camps in Natal, the Orange River Colony, and the Transvaal.* London: HMSO, 1902, Cd 893, annotated copy, GB/106/7/MGF/90/B/1, Fawcett Library, London.

Newspapers and periodicals

British Friend
Concord: Journal of the International Arbitration and Peace Association
Correspondance bi-mensuelle
Englishwoman's Review of Social and Industrial Questions
États-Unis d'Europe

Friend
Friends' Quarterly Examiner
Herald of Peace and International Arbitration
Isle of Ely and Wisbech Advertiser
Journal of the International Arbitration and Peace Association
Labour Leader
Peace and Goodwill: A Sequel to the Olive Leaf
Pioneer of Social Purity: Being the organ of the Social Purity Alliance and the Moral Reform Union
Shield: The Anti-Contagious Diseases Acts Associations' weekly circular
Wisbech Advertiser (and Supplement)
Woman's Herald
Woman's Signal
Women's Penny Paper
Women's Suffrage Journal

Books

Aberdeen, Lady (ed.), *The International Congress of Women of 1899: Report of Transactions of the Second Quinquennial Meeting, held in London, July 1899* (London: T. Fisher Unwin, 1900).

Aberdeen, Lady, *The Canadian Journal of Lady Aberdeen, 1893–1898*, ed. John Saywell (Toronto: The Champlain Society, 1960).

Aberdeen, Lord and Lady, *We Twa: Reminiscences of Lord and Lady Aberdeen* (London: W. Collins and Co., 1925).

Actes du Congrès International des Œuvres et Institutions Féminines (Paris: Bibliothèque des *Annales Économiques*, 1890).

Bacon, Margaret Hope, *Mothers of Feminism: The Story of Quaker Women in America* (San Francisco: Harper and Row, 1986).

Bebbington, David, *Evangelicalism in Modern Britain: A History from the 1730s to the 1980s* (London: Unwin Hyman, 1989).

Bellamy, Richard, *Liberalism and Modern Society: An Historical Argument* (Cambridge: Polity Press, 1992).

Blackburn, Helen, *Women's Suffrage: A Record of the Women's Suffrage Movement in the British Isles, with Biographical Sketches of Miss Becker* (London: Williams and Norgate, 1902).

Blake, Catriona, *The Charge of the Parasols: Women's Entry to the Medical Profession* (London: The Women's Press, 1990).

Bland, Lucy, *Banishing the Beast: English Feminism and Sexual Morality, 1885–1914* (London: Penguin, 1995).

Bolt, Christine, *The Women's Movements in the United States and Britain from the 1790s to the 1920s* (Hemel Hempstead: Harvester Wheatsheaf, 1993).

Bridenthal, Renate, Claudia Koonz and Susan Stuard (eds), *Becoming Visible: Women in European History* (Boston: Houghton Mifflin Company, 1987).

Brock, Peter, *The Quaker Peace Testimony, 1660–1914* (York: Sessions Book Trust, 1990).

——, *Freedom from War: Nonsectarian Pacifism, 1814–1914* (London: University of Toronto Press, 1991).

Bruce, Mary L., *Anna Swanwick: A Memoir and Recollections, 1813–1899* (London: T. Fisher and Unwin, 1903).

Burton, Antoinette, *Burdens of History: British Feminists, Indian Women, and Imperial Culture, 1865–1915* (London: University of North Carolina Press, 1994).

Butler, Josephine, *Our Christianity Tested by the Irish Question* (London: T. Fisher Unwin, n.d. [1887]).

——, *The Native Races and the War* (London: Gay and Bird, 1900).

Caine, Barbara, *Victorian Feminists* (Oxford: Oxford University Press, 1993).

——, *English Feminism, 1780–1980* (Oxford: Oxford University Press, 1997).

Ceadel, Martin, *Semi-detached Idealists: The British Peace Movement and International Relations, 1854–1945* (Oxford: Oxford University Press, 2000).

Chatfield, Charles and Peter van den Dungen (eds), *Peace Movements and Political Cultures* (Knoxville: University of Tennessee Press, 1988).

Colaiaco, James A., *James Fitzjames Stephen and the Crisis of Victorian Thought* (London: Macmillan, 1983).

Colley, Linda, *Britons: Forging the Nation, 1707–1837* (London: Yale University Press, 1992).

Collini, Stefan, *Public Moralists: Political Thought and Intellectual Life in Britain, 1850–1930* (Oxford: Clarendon Press, 1991).

Cookson, J. E., *The Friends of Peace: Anti-war Liberalism in England, 1793–1815* (Cambridge: Cambridge University Press, 1982).

Cooper, Sandi E., *Patriotic Pacifism: Waging War on War in Europe, 1815–1914* (Oxford: Oxford University Press, 1991).

Cott, Nancy, *The Grounding of Modern Feminism* (New Haven, Conn.: Yale University Press, 1987).

Cullen, Mary and Maria Luddy (eds), *Women, Power and Consciousness in Nineteenth Century Ireland* (Dublin: Attic Press, 1995).

Daley, Caroline and Melanie Nolan (eds), *Suffrage and Beyond: International Feminist Perspectives* (Auckland: Auckland University Press, 1994).

Davidoff, Leonore and Catherine Hall, *Family Fortunes: Men and Women of the English Middle Class, 1780–1850* (London: Hutchinson, 1987).

Doughan, David and Denise Sanchez, *Feminist Periodicals, 1855–1984: An Annotated Critical Bibliography of British, Irish, Commonwealth and International Titles* (Brighton: Harvester, 1987).

DuBois, Ellen Carol, *Feminism and Suffrage: The Emergence of an Independent Women's Movement in America, 1848–1869* (Ithaca: Cornell University Press, 1978).

Fawcett, Millicent Garrett, *Mr Fitzjames Stephen on the Position of Women* (London: Macmillan and Co., 1873).

Fisher, John, *That Miss Hobhouse* (London: Secker and Warburg, 1971).

Fletcher, Ian Christopher, Laura E. Nym Mayhall and Philippa Levine (eds), *Women's Suffrage in the British Empire: Citizenship, Nation and Race* (London: Routledge, 2000).

French, Doris, *Ishbel and the Empire: A Biography of Lady Aberdeen* (Oxford: Dundurn Press, 1988).

Fry, A. Ruth, *Emily Hobhouse: A Memoir* (London: Jonathan Cape, 1929).

Gardiner, Frederic John, *History of Wisbech and Neighbourhood, 1848–1898* (Wisbech: Gardiner and Co., 1898).

Gilbert, Alan D., *Religion and Society in Industrial England: Church, Chapel and Social Change, 1740–1914* (London: Longman, 1976).

Gilley, Sheridan and W. J. Shiels (eds), *A History of Religion in Britain: Practice and Belief from Pre-Roman Times to the Present* (Oxford: Basil Blackwell, 1994).

Gilligan, Carol, *In a Different Voice* (Cambridge, Mass.: Harvard University Press, 1982).

Gleadle, Kathryn, *The Early Feminists: Radical Unitarians and the Emergence of the Women's Rights Movement, 1831–51* (New York: St Martin's Press, 1995).

Gordon, Maria Ogilvie, *The International Council of Women and the Meetings of the International Congress of Women in Berlin, 1904* (Aberdeen: Aberdeen Free Press, n.d. [1904]).

——, *Histories of Affiliated National Councils, 1888–1938* (privately published, ICW, 1938).

Hamann, Brigitte, *Bertha von Suttner: A Life for Peace*, trans. Ann Dubsky (Syracuse, New York: Syracuse University Press, 1996).

Hannam, June, *Isabella Ford* (Oxford: Blackwell, 1989).

Hannam, June and Karen Hunt, *Socialist Women: Britain, 1880s to 1920s* (London: Routledge, 2002).

Harrison, Brian, *Separate Spheres: the Opposition to Women's Suffrage in Britain* (London: Croom Helm, 1978).

Harvie, Christopher, *The Lights of Liberalism: University Liberals and the Challenge of Democracy, 1860–1886* (London: Allen Lane, 1976).

Hause, Stephen C. with Anne R. Kenney, *Women's Suffrage and Social Politics in the French Third Republic* (Princeton: Princeton University Press, 1984).

Helps, Arthur, *Conversations on War and General Culture* (London: Smith, Elder and Co., 1871).

Hewison, Hope Hay, *Hedge of Wild Almonds: South Africa, Pro-Boers and the Quaker Conscience, 1890–1910* (London: James Currey, 1989).

Hollis, Patricia, *Ladies Elect: Women in English Local Government, 1865–1914* (Oxford: Oxford University Press, 1987).

Holton, Sandra Stanley, *Suffrage Days: Stories from the Women's Suffrage Movement* (London: Routledge, 1996).

International Council of Women, *Women in a Changing World: the Dynamic Story of the International Council of Women since 1888* (London: Routledge and Kegan Paul, 1966).

Isichei, Elizabeth, *Victorian Quakers* (Oxford: Oxford University Press, 1970).

James, Edward T. (ed.), *Notable American Women, 1607–1950: A Biographical Dictionary* (Massachusetts: Harvard University Press, 1971).

Jeffreys, Sheila, *The Spinster and her Enemies: Feminism and Sexuality, 1880–1930* (London: Pandora Press, 1985).

Kempf, Beatrix, *Suffragette for Peace: the Life of Bertha von Suttner*, trans. R. W. Last (London: Oswald Wolff, 1972).

Kirkby, M. W., *Men of Business and Politics: The Rise and Fall of the Quaker Pease Dynasty of North-East England, 1700–1943* (London: George Allen and Unwin, 1984).

Koss, Stephen (ed.), *The Pro-Boers: The Anatomy of an Antiwar Movement* (London: University of Chicago Press, 1973).

Laity, Paul, *The British Peace Movement, 1870–1914* (Oxford: Oxford University Press, 2001).

Levine, Philippa, *Victorian Feminism 1850–1900* (London: Century Hutchinson, 1987).

——, *Feminist Lives in Victorian England: Private Roles and Public Commitment* (Oxford: Basil Blackwell, 1990).

Lewis, Jane (ed.), *Before the Vote was Won: Arguments for and against Women's Suffrage, 1864–1896* (London: Routledge and Kegan Paul, 1987).

Liddington, Jill, *The Long Road to Greenham: Feminism and Anti-Militarism in Britain since 1820* (London: Virago, 1989).

Linden, W. H. van der, *The International Peace Movement, 1815–1874* (Amsterdam: Tilleul Publications, 1987).

Malmgreen, Gail (ed.), *Religion in the Lives of English Women, 1760–1930* (London: Croom Helm, 1986).

Mendus, Susan and Jane Rendall (eds), *Sexuality and Subordination: Interdisciplinary Studies of Gender in the Nineteenth Century* (London: Routledge, 1989).

Mill, John Stuart, *The Subjection of Women* (London: Longman's, Green, Reader and Dyer, 1869; reprint, Oxford: Oxford University Press, 1991, as *On Liberty and Other Essays*, ed. John Gray).

Moses, Claire Goldberg, *French Feminism in the Nineteenth Century* (Albany: University of New York Press, 1984).

National Woman Suffrage Association, *Report of the International Council of Women assembled by the National Woman Suffrage Association, Washington, DC, US of America, March 25 to April 1, 1888* (Washington, DC: Rufus H. Darby, 1888).

Newton, Douglas J., *British Labour, European Socialism and the Struggle for Peace* (Oxford: Clarendon Press, 1985).

Peckover, P. H., *Incidents in the Rise and Progress of Wisbech Peace Association* (Wisbech: W. Poyser, 1906).

Pentland, Marjorie, *A Bonnie Fechter: The Life of Ishbel Marjoribanks, Marchioness of Aberdeen* (London: Batsford, 1952).

Phelps, Christina, *The Anglo-American Peace Movement in the Mid-Nineteenth Century (1835–1854)* (London: P. S. King and Son Ltd., 1930).

Pierson, Ruth Roach (ed.), *Women and Peace: Theoretical, Historical and Practical Perspectives* (London: Croom Helm, 1987).

Playne, Caroline E., *Bertha von Suttner and the Struggle to Avert the World War* (London: George Allen and Unwin, 1936).

Posthumus-van der Goot, W. H., *Vrouwen Vochten Voor de Vrede* (Arnhem: Van Loghum Slaterus, 1961).

Prochaska, F. K., *Women and Philanthropy in Nineteenth-Century England* (Oxford: Oxford University Press, 1980).

Pyle, Andrew (ed.), *The Subjection of Women: Contemporary Responses to John Stuart Mill* (Bristol: Thoemmes Press, 1995).

Ramelson, Marian, *Petticoat Rebellion: A Century of Struggle for Women's Rights* (London: Lawrence and Wishart, 1967).

Rendall, Jane, *The Origins of Modern Feminism: Women in Britain, France and the United States, 1780–1860* (Basingstoke: Macmillan, 1985).

—— (ed.), *Equal or Different: Women's Politics, 1800–1914* (Oxford: Basil Blackwell, 1987).

Richards, E. F. (ed.), *Mazzini's Letters: To an English Family 1844–1854*, vol. 1 (London: John Lane, The Bodley Head, 1920).

Riley, Denise, *Am I That Name? Feminism and the Category of 'Women' in History* (Basingstoke: Macmillan, 1988).

Roberts, Brian, *Those Bloody Women: Three Heroines of the Boer War* (London: John Murray, 1991).

Rubinstein, David, *A Different World for Women: The Life of Millicent Garrett Fawcett* (London: Harvester Wheatsheaf, 1991).

Rupp, Leila J., *Worlds of Women: The Making of an International Women's Movement* (Princeton: Princeton University Press, 1997).

Ruskin, John, *The Crown of Wild Olive: Four Lectures on Industry and War*, 3rd edn (Orpington, Kent: George Allen, 1889).

Sewall, May Wright (ed.), *The World's Congress of Representative Women: A Historical Resumé for Popular Circulation of the World's Congress of Representative Women* (Chicago and New York: Rand, McNally and Company, 1894).

—— (ed.), *The International Council of Women from 1899 to 1904: Report of Transactions, Berlin, June 1904* (Boston, USA: published by the author, 1909).

——, *Genesis of the ICW and the Story of its Growth, 1888–1893* (privately published, ICW, 1914).

Smith, K. J. M., *James Fitzjames Stephen: Portrait of a Victorian Rationalist* (Cambridge: Cambridge University Press, 1988).

Stephen, James Fitzjames, *Liberty, Equality, Fraternity* (London: Smith, Elder and Co., 1874; reprint, Cambridge: Cambridge University Press, 1967).

Strachey, Ray, *The Cause: A Short History of the Women's Movement in Great Britain* (London: G. Bell and Sons, 1928).

Summers, Anne, *Angels and Citizens: British Women as Military Nurses, 1854–1914* (London: Routledge and Kegan Paul, 1988).

Sykes, Alan, *The Rise and Fall of British Liberalism, 1776–1988* (London: Longman, 1997).

Universal Peace Congress, *Proceedings of the Tenth Universal Peace Congress, held in Glasgow, 1901* (Berne and London: International Peace Bureau, 1902).

——, *Official Report of the Thirteenth Universal Peace Congress, held at Boston, Massachusetts, USA, October 3rd to 8th, 1904* (Boston: the Peace Congress Committee, 1904).

Valenze, Deborah, *Prophetic Sons and Daughters: Female Preaching and Popular Religion in Industrial England* (Princeton, NJ: Princeton University Press, 1985).

Walkowitz, Judith R., *Prostitution and Victorian Society: Women, Class and the State* (Cambridge: Cambridge University Press, 1980).

——, *City of Dreadful Delight: Narratives of Sexual Danger in Late-Victorian London* (London: Virago, 1994).

Ward, Paul, *Red Flag and Union Jack: Englishness, Patriotism and the British Left, 1881–1924* (Suffolk: Boydell Press, 1998).

Ware, Vron, *Beyond the Pale: White Women, Racism and History* (London: Verso, 1992).

Wiltsher, Anne, *Most Dangerous Women: Feminist Peace Campaigners of the Great War* (London: Pandora Press, 1985).

Articles and chapters in books

Annas, Julia, 'Mill and the subjection of women', *Philosophy*, 52 (1977), pp. 179–94.

Bacon, Margaret Hope, 'The establishment of London Women's Yearly Meeting; a transatlantic concern', *Journal of the Friends' Historical Society*, 57:2 (1995), pp. 151–65.

Black, Naomi, 'The Mothers International: the Women's Co-operative Guild and feminist pacifism', *Women's Studies International Forum* 7:6 (1984), pp. 467–76.

Brown, Heloise, 'An alternative imperialism: Isabella Tod, internationalist and "Good Liberal Unionist"', *Gender and History* 10:3 (1998), pp. 358–80.

——, '"The gentle process of womanly sympathies"? The founding of the Manchester Women's Peace Association', *Women's History Notebooks*, 8:1 (Summer 2001), pp. 21–30.

Burton, Antoinette, 'Rules of thumb: British history and "imperial culture" in nineteenth- and twentieth-century Britain', *Women's History Review*, 3:4 (1994), pp. 483–500.

——, 'Colonial encounters in late-Victorian England: Pandita Ramabai at Cheltenham and Wantage, 1883–6', *Feminist Review*, 49 (Spring 1995), pp. 29–49.

Burton, Antoinette, '"States of injury": Josephine Butler on slavery, citizenship and the Boer War', in Ian Christopher Fletcher, Laura E. Nym Mayhall and Philippa Levine (eds), *Women's Suffrage in the British Empire: Citizenship, Nation and Race* (London: Routledge, 2000), pp. 18–32.

Carroll, Berenice, 'Feminism and pacifism: historical and theoretical connections' in Ruth Roach Pierson (ed.), *Women and Peace: Theoretical, Historical and Practical Perspectives* (London: Croom Helm, 1987), pp. 2–28.

Conway, Stephen, 'The politicization of the nineteenth-century Peace Society', *Historical Research: Bulletin of the Institute of Historical Research*, 66:161 (1993), pp. 267–83.

Cooper, Sandi E., 'The work of women in nineteenth century Continental European peace movements', *Peace and Change*, 9:4 (1984), pp. 11–28.

——, 'Women's participation in European peace movements: the struggle to prevent World War One', in Ruth Roach Pierson (ed.) *Women and Peace: Theoretical, Historical and Practical Perspectives* (London: Croom Helm, 1987), pp. 51–75.

Costin, Leila B., 'Feminism, pacifism, internationalism and the 1915 International Congress of Women', *Women's Studies International Forum*, 5:3/4 (1982), pp. 301–15.

Cunningham, Hugh, 'The language of patriotism, 1750–1914', *History Workshop Journal*, 12 (1981), pp. 8–33.

Dekar, Paul R., 'Baptist peace-makers in nineteenth-century peace societies', *Baptist Quarterly*, 34 (1991), pp. 3–13.

Finn, Margot, '"A vent which has conveyed our principles": English radical patriotism in the aftermath of 1848', *Journal of Modern History*, 64 (December 1992), pp. 637–59.

Hirshfield, Claire, 'Liberal women's organisations and the war against the Boers, 1899–1902', *Albion*, 14 (1982), pp. 27–49.

——, 'Blacks, Boers and Britons: the anti-war movement in England and the "Native Issue," 1899–1902', *Peace and Change*, 8 (1982), pp. 21–34.

Holton, Sandra Stanley, 'From anti-slavery to suffragette militancy: the Bright circle, Elizabeth Cady Stanton and the British women's movement', in Caroline Daley and Melanie Nolan (eds), *Suffrage and Beyond: International Feminist Perspectives* (Auckland: Auckland University Press, 1994), pp. 213–33.

——, 'To educate women into rebellion: Elizabeth Cady Stanton and the creation of a transatlantic network of radical suffragists', *American History Review*, 99 (1994), pp. 1112–36.

Holton, Sandra Stanley and Margaret Allen, 'Offices and services: women's pursuit of sexual equality within the Society of Friends, 1873–1907', *Quaker Studies*, 2 (1997), pp. 1–29.

Kennedy, Thomas C., 'Heresy-hunting among Victorian Quakers: the Manchester difficulty, 1861–73', *Victorian Studies*, 34:2 (Winter 1991), pp. 227–53.

——, 'An angry God or a reasonable faith: the British Society of Friends, 1873–1888', *Journal of the Friends' Historical Society*, 57:2 (1995), pp. 183–98.

Kinzer, Bruce L., 'J. S. Mill and Irish land: a reassessment', *Historical Journal*, 27:1 (1984), pp. 111–27.

Krebs, Paula M., '"The last of the gentleman's wars": Women in the Boer War concentration camp controversy', *History Workshop Journal*, 33 (1992), pp. 38–56.

Mayhall, Laura E. Nym, 'The South African War and the origins of suffrage militancy in Britain, 1899–1902', in Ian Christopher Fletcher, Laura E. Nym Mayhall and Philippa Levine (eds), *Women's Suffrage in the British Empire: Citizenship, Nation and Race* (London: Routledge, 2000), pp. 3–17.

Mendus, Susan, 'The marriage of true minds: the ideal of marriage in the philosophy of John Stuart Mill', in Susan Mendus and Jane Rendall (eds), *Sexuality and Subordination: Interdisciplinary Studies of Gender in the Nineteenth Century* (London: Routledge, 1989), pp. 171–91.

Milligan, Edward H., '"The ancient way": The conservative tradition in nineteenth century British Quakerism', *Journal of the Friends' Historical Society*, 57:1 (1994), pp. 74–101.

Nicholls, David, 'Richard Cobden and the International Peace Congress movement, 1848–1853', *Journal of British Studies*, 30 (October 1991), pp. 351–76.

Offen, Karen, 'Liberty, equality and justice for women: the theory and practice of feminism in nineteenth-century Europe', in Renate Bridenthal, Claudia Koonz and Susan Stuard (eds), *Becoming Visible: Women in European History* (Boston: Houghton Mifflin Company, 1987), pp. 335–73.

Rupp, Leila J., 'Constructing internationalism: the case of transnational women's organizations, 1888–1945', *American Historical Review*, 99:5 (1994), pp. 1571–1600.

——, 'Sexuality and politics in the early twentieth century: the case of the international women's movement', *Feminist Studies*, 23:3 (Autumn 1997), pp. 577–605.

Sager, Eric W., 'The working-class peace movement in Victorian England', *Social History*, 12 (1979), pp. 122–44.

——, 'The social origins of Victorian pacifism', *Victorian Studies*, 23:2 (Winter 1980), pp. 211–36.

Sandbach-Dahlstrom, Catherine, 'Virginia Woolf's *Three Guineas*: A theory of liberation for the modern world?', *Women's Studies International Forum*, 17:2–3 (1994), pp. 229–34.

Shiman, Lilian Lewis, '"Changes are dangerous": Women and temperance in Victorian England', in Gail Malmgreen (ed.), *Religion in the Lives of English Women, 1760–1930* (London: Croom Helm, 1986), pp. 193–215.

Steele, E. D., 'J. S. Mill and the Irish question: the principles of political economy, 1848–1865', *Historical Journal*, 13:2 (1970), pp. 216–36.

——, 'J. S. Mill and the Irish question: reform, and the integrity of the Empire, 1865–1870', *Historical Journal*, 13:3 (1970), pp. 419–50.

Tyrrell, Alex, '"Woman's mission" and pressure group politics in Britain (1825–1860)', *Bulletin of the John Rylands Library*, 63 (1980–81), pp. 194–230.

Uglow, Jenny, 'Josephine Butler: from sympathy to theory (1828–1906)', in Dale Spender (ed.), *Feminist Theorists: Three Centuries of Women's Intellectual Traditions* (London: Women's Press, 1983), pp. 146–64.

Vellacott, Jo, 'A place for pacifism and transnationalism in feminist theory: the early work of the Women's International League for Peace and Freedom', *Women's History Review*, 2:1 (1993), pp. 23–56.

Walker, Linda, 'Party political women: a comparative study of Liberal women and the Primrose League, 1890–1914', in Jane Rendall (ed.), *Equal or Different: Women's Politics 1800–1914* (Oxford: Basil Blackwell, 1987), pp. 165–91.

Walkowitz, Judith R., 'Male vice and feminist virtue: feminism and the politics of prostitution in nineteenth-century Britain', *History Workshop Journal*, 13 (1982), pp. 79–93.

Dictionaries

Baylen, Joseph O. and Norbert J. Gossman (eds), *Biographical Dictionary of Modern British Radicals*, vols. 2–3 (London: Harvester Wheatsheaf, 1988).

Josephson, Harold (ed.-in-chief), *Biographical Dictionary of Modern Peace Leaders* (London: Greenwood Press, 1985).

Kuehl, Warren F. (ed.), *Biographical Dictionary of Internationalists* (London: Greenwood Press, 1983).

Unpublished work

Dictionary of Quaker Biography, Library, Friends' House, London.

Parker, Joan E., 'Lydia Becker: her work for women', Ph.D. dissertation, University of Manchester, 1990.

VanArdsel, Rosemary T., 'Florence Fenwick Miller, feminism and the *Woman's Signal*, 1895–1899' (Tacoma, Wash.: University of Puget Sound, 1979), unpublished paper, Fawcett Library, London.

VanArdsel, Rosemary T., 'Victorian periodicals yield their secrets: Florence Fenwick Miller's three campaigns for the London School Board' (Tacoma, Wash.: University of Puget Sound, 1980–1985? [*sic*]), unpublished paper, Fawcett Library, London.

Index

Note: 'n.' after a page reference indicates the number of a note on that page.